Joe P
Pla

CW00730921

Some Voice:
Love and Unders

'*Some Voices* is a beautifully written piece focusing on Ray, a young schizophrenic trying to get back on the rails . . . It's dark material, but Penhall handles it with a light touch. He doesn't romanticise Ray, neither does he vilify his brother, and their relationship is riveting.' *Independent*

'The most thrilling playwriting debut in years . . . Penhall is talking about the dark undergrowth of modern life, where people are first allowed to lose their way and then prevented from finding it. The writing is razor-sharp, sensitive, quietly eloquent, full of the touchingly drab poetry of lost lives.' *Sunday Times*

Pale Horse: 'Compellingly and rivetingly well written . . . Penhall is writing about violence and loss . . . You are gripped by the moody dialogue and the pervasive sense of aimlessness and emotional deprivation.' *Sunday Times*
'A consolidation of Penhall's talents . . . Black comedy and bleak tragedy bleed into one another.' *Independent*

Love and Understanding: 'This is one of the best plays I've seen, ever, at this powerhouse of new writing. Joe Penhall is writing about love, loyalty, understanding and freedom, about the need to belong, the danger of marauding outsiders and the fatigues and panics of life . . . tough, eloquent, bruising.' *Sunday Times*
'An extremely fine play . . . Invigoratingly, Penhall champions the untrumpeted common man.' *Time Out*

The Bullet: 'A *Death of a Salesman* for Britain in the nineties, and it is typical of Penhall's grace as a writer that it consciously echoes Arthur Miller while also emerging as an entirely distinctive work . . . *The Bullet* is a play with the courage to be unflashy, yet there is depth in Penhall's writing, and a maturity.' *Daily Telegraph*
'An exquisite tragi-comedy of embarrassment and aggression . . . Penhall has made an individual and highly effective piece about masculinity in a changing world, and has done so with an impressive mixture of comedy and bleak revelation. His attention to language – the telling infelicities, the repeated notes – confirms him as a writer of great ability.' *Times Literary Supplement*

Joe Penhall lives in London. His first play, *Wild Turkey*, was performed at the Old Red Lion as part of the 1993 London New Play Festival. *Some Voices* (Royal Court Theatre Upstairs, 1994) won him a Thames Television Bursary and the John Whiting Award in 1995. *Pale Horse* (Royal Court Theatre Upstairs, 1995) won the Thames Television Best Play Award. *Blue/Orange* (Royal National Theatre, then Duchess Theatre, 2001) won several awards for Best Play. His most recent play is *Dumb Show* (Royal Court, 2004).

JOE PENHALL

Plays: 1

Some Voices
Pale Horse
Love and Understanding
The Bullet

introduced by the author

Methuen Drama

METHUEN DRAMA **CONTEMPORARY DRAMATISTS**

5 7 9 10 8 6 4

This collection first published in Great Britain 1998
by Methuen Publishing Ltd

A CIP catalogue record for this book
is available from the British Library

ISBN 978-0-413-73150-0

Caution

Contents

Joe Penhall
Chronology

1993   *Wild Turkey* (one-act play) premiered at the London
       New Play Festival, Old Red Lion, directed by
       Kath Mattock
1994   *Some Voices* premiered at the Royal Court Theatre,
       London, directed by Ian Rickson
1995   One year writer-in-residency at the Royal National
       Theatre
       Pale Horse premiered at the Royal Court, directed by
       Ian Rickson
       John Whiting Award for *Some Voices*
       Thames Television (Pearson's) Award for *Pale Horse*
1997   *Love and Understanding* premiered at the Bush Theatre,
       London, directed by Mike Bradwell
       Appointed Literary Associate at the Donmar
       Warehouse, London
1998   *Love and Understanding* first produced in the US at
       Long Wharf, Connecticut, directed by Mike
       Bradwell
       The Bullet premiered at the Donmar Warehouse,
       directed by Dominic Cooke
2001   *Blue/Orange* premiered at the Royal National
       Theatre, and later transferred to the Duchess
       Theatre in the West End. The play won Best Play
       at the Orange Awards, *Evening Standard* Awards, and
       the Critics Circle Awards.
2003   Wrote a four-part serial for the BBC, *The Long Firm*,
       based on the novel by Jake Arnott.
       Wrote a screenplay for Pathe/Film Four, based on
       Ian McEwan's novel, *Enduring Love*.
2004   *Dumb Show* premiered at the Royal Court, directed
       by Terry Johnson.

Introduction

I was a news reporter on the *South London Guardian* in 1994 when I got a call from Stephen Daldry, then the Royal Court's artistic director. He'd read my first full-length play *Some Voices* and wanted me to come in for a chat. I said No. I'd been for that type of 'chat' before and it had got me nowhere. I think I said, 'I'm not meeting anybody unless they make it worth my while.' Stephen was a little surprised and vaguely irritated. He sighed and gritted his teeth, 'Well we can't make it worth your while until we've met you.' So after about five more minutes of playing hard to get, I met him and director Ian Rickson and the deal was done. There were no cigars but I persuaded Stephen to persuade one of his minions to come up to his office with a light for my cigarette. That afternoon I handed in my notice at the paper, bought a bottle of scotch and celebrated with friends until unconscious.

Over the next few months Ian and I worked in a few cuts and he suggested one or two rewrites. I'd already done half a dozen rewrites under the inspired tutelage of my friend the actor Brian Croucher, who had successfully directed a reading of the play at the Battersea Arts Centre. It was Brian who'd encouraged me to finish the play and motivated me through several rewrites. In September the play was produced with the formidable Ray Winstone as Pete. It was a masterpiece of casting against type and a personal coup, as Ray had been one of my childhood heroes. I'd seen him in the TV serial *Fox* and the film by The Who, *Quadrophenia.* Now – for reasons known only to himself – he'd sprouted a pansy's perm and was practising a limp-wristed feyness especially for the part.

Some Voices was about the difficulties of assimilating in the metropolis. I'd been living in Shepherd's Bush and writing crime stories for the *Hammersmith Guardian* as well as the South London paper. The place was full of former mental patients and Irish and Kiwis and Croatians and drunks and drifters in amongst the media types. I'd learnt from a government white paper that the incidence of mental illness and suicide amongst the Irish in London was higher than for any other community in Britain. I wasn't surprised. Anybody who spends time in a city doing anything other than going to work and coming home understands the soullessness of city life. I'd had years on the dole and doing dead-end jobs and then a year writing journalism about people on the dole and in dead-end jobs. I felt strongly that newspaper articles weren't enough to convey the true misery and loneliness of schizophrenia, unemployment, redundancy, alcoholism, domestic violence and everything else that was going on around me.

The protagonist, Ray, was based on a gifted musician friend who I'd always imagined had gone mad under the weight of his own pure genius, drink, wild women and sense of failure. His Tourette's-like outbursts had struck me as an inspired and truly honest response to the world around us. He lived alone in a bedsit and had lost all his friends. His family had one by one turned against him. When I found out years later he actually had schizophrenia I was haunted and abashed. Suddenly the news stories I was writing concerning Virginia Bottomley's draconian Mental Health legislation had a personal resonance. The play was a critical and commercial hit, bagged the John Whiting award and was nominated for every prize going. The BBC wanted a film about schizophrenia which was duly written, shot and screened (*Go Back Out*, BBC 2). Suddenly I felt I had a legitimate voice.

In 1995 the National Theatre's literary manager, Jack Bradley, appointed me writer-in-residence. Ray Winstone was also more or less in residence there, playing poker, eating sushi and occasionally rehearsing *Dealer's Choice*. We ate sushi together and, with playwright Stephen Jeffries on hand to supply tea, sympathy and bad jokes, I wrote *Pale Horse*. The premise for *Pale Horse* came to me during a particularly dark and arduous night of the soul in my Shepherd's Bush studio, when it had occurred to me that it was only the truly religious who could deal with death. A bereaved atheist doesn't have the full picture when it comes to mourning. I had been brought up agnostic and felt that I'd never properly mourned the premature deaths of all my grandparents, a former girlfriend and an uncle. Years later, in my mid twenties, there was still melancholy and bafflement at odd moments.

Ray loved the play. As the bereaved Charles Strong he was given the opportunity to behave very badly indeed, steadfastly refusing to take his wife's death on the chin and succumbing instantly to the temptations of booze, brawling, scantily clad women and theology. Ray had a bemused warmth when he wasn't being menacing which made men want to buy him beers and women want to take him home. Something in his grasp of the part transcended the simple story-line. When he badgers his local vicar for spiritual insight, we know he's grasping for self-knowledge – indeed for insight into humanity.

To research the play thoroughly, Ian and I took the cast to see a morgue, a Church of England vicar, a gaggle of winos and hookers holding court in a desultory fashion on Tooting Common and a bunch of women dressed as schoolgirls in the West End – School Dinners Club. No stone was left unturned. The actors left the morgue utterly shaken up. They had glimpsed death and destiny. Everyone came away thinking about somebody close to them. When I see pictures of Ray staring into space as Charles Strong I know where it comes from – but then I remember many people in the audience feeling they knew too.

As a writer I was beginning to enjoy myself and draw upon favourite influences. The exasperated absolutism of Beckett struck a chord. Büchner's desolate Woyzeck had been a huge influence in the writing of *Some Voices* and again in *Pale Horse*. Raymond Carver's melancholy existential short stories were a major influence. I liked the characters' alienation, bemusement, occasional innocence and outbursts of pissed-off loquaciousness. I liked their hang-ups and their jumpy misfit psyches. They were the poor relations of Chekhov's Ivanov and Astrov and I felt at home with them.

Again the play was a success, was nominated for awards, bagged one and earned me more film work. Suddenly everybody wanted a 'big play' that spoke to the wider constituency. Something with lots of people in it, big ideas, perhaps a famine or two. Something for the Cottesloe or the Court downstairs. I couldn't think of a subject with Land

Rovers and boulders in it for the National and the Court weren't keen on the ideas I was espousing at the time, so I did the only decent thing. I wrote a three-hander about an agoraphobic doctor in Putney. This time Mike Bradwell wanted to do it at The Bush.

I intended *Love and Understanding* to be lighter and funnier than the others. Frivolous even. Preferably no baseball bats. I wanted articulate, witty characters for a change. I was tired of grand, easily identifiable drama about madness and death. That stuff seemed self-evidently dramatic. Any idiot knows that somebody dousing themselves in petrol or losing a loved one is intrinsically interesting. Perhaps I was being too self-conscious, but I became interested in small, niggly things. People's values. The codes they lived by. Their neuroses. Their self-awareness and lack of it. Our simultaneous lusts for freedom and stability. Petty battles in confined spaces between articulate, silver-tongued baddies and stammering, well-intentioned goodies. The complexity and paradox of the human experience.

I had learnt a little about the politics of PR and the PR of politics at the newspaper. It was a revelation to me that the nastiest, most reactionary, bigoted council members were always the most articulate and floridly quotable on the phone. They could write your front-page story for you minutes before deadline with one juicy quote. They were also invariably the Conservatives. (I remember one misguidedly telling me why the council shouldn't put up a homeless shelter over Christmas – 'They steal from shops and urinate in people's gardens.') Labour spokesmen five years ago always seemed vaguely well-intentioned, unassuming, honest – and quite reluctant to comment. No help to me . . .

In *Some Voices*, Ray is a product of legislation which was at best ill-advised and at worst an exercise in cruelty and greed unparalleled in post-war England. Ives says of the legislators, 'They profess to care. They pretend to be in the business of caring, which to me is no different to a butcher professing to know how to operate on the brain.' In *Love and Understanding* Richie spreads stories about Neal's apparently racy sexual peccadilloes because it beats being perceived as 'the mincing lefty goody-goody jobsworth you really are'. The play is about postures. Richie, like the slick, worded-up spokesmen of the Thatcher era – and latterly the Blair era – has a manipulative articulacy which can sell any line he chooses. He also happens to be very sexy – he has the X factor. Neal is horrified. He spends his life saving lives and Richie spends his self-destruct-ing and generally being a 'bad seed'. But as Richie says, 'If you don't care enough you're a bad doctor and if you care too much you'll go insane and be no use to anybody.'

Nick Tennant was already in place as Neal from a reading I had directed at the National studio where I had spent a week workshopping, rehearsing and rewriting. Mike Bradwell and I then auditioned the incendiary Paul Bettany, who left the audition with most of my fags and my new lighter – already practising to be the mendacious Richie. Celia Robertson and designer Es Devlin were suggested by Mike and a few weeks later the play was sold out. A year later the success was repeated in the US, with the same tight-knit cast. It remains my favourite, most gratifying theatre experience.

As *Love and Understanding* opened in the US, *The Bullet* was in rehearsal in London. *The Bullet* continued my love affair with neurotics and disgruntled misfits. Again I was concentrat-ing on personal politics, contradictions and paradoxes. Ideals for living. Charles is a chippy old leftie – but is that a product of his working-class roots and painful assimilation into the middle-class intelligentsia – or was he just born argumentative? Born to wage war on the world in general and undermine the status quo – whatever it may be. Robbie adores Carla's squeaky-clean positivity – he shows it off to his cynical family and she indulges Charles' outbursts – but when she fails to endorse Robbie's own cynical despair he turns on her. If *Love and Understanding* is about Neal becoming cynical, *The Bullet* is about Robbie's desperate attempts to reverse the process.

I grew up in a wonderful, joyful, affectionate seventies nuclear family. Very physical and demonstrative. When I was about four, my mum used to take me to work, to cookery classes, everywhere. She'd wear Pru Acton T-shirts and play the Beatles and cuddle me to her breasts, bundling me into an old Renault 4 and whisking me off to watch her perform physiotherapy or cook coq au vin. My dad coming home from work was the high point of my day. He bought me boxing gloves and we'd spar, kiddy fashion. They'd have dinner parties. Dad would play jazz – Teddy Wilson – and Mum would wear a kaftan and cook fondue. My brother and I played with Scalextrix and Meccano and re-enacted bits from James Bond films in the sandpit (I always insisted on playing the villain and always refused to die).

Years later, as the recession hit, I grew up a bit and realised that all my parents ever did was work and it was killing them. They have both worked every single weekday of their lives right up until recently and many nights too. When my dad was twice laid off – as were many of my friends' dads – I was infuriated by the pain and injustice – and the anger it had engendered in him. I was glad he was angry, but we were all conscious that the family was becoming a different family and that the innocent playful idyll would only ever return momentarily. I'd learnt about injustice and the way it impacts on you personally. The way injustice, not fear, eats the soul.

The Bullet is about the pathological need to go home and then – once you get there – the pathological need to leave again as quickly as possible. In common with *Love and Understanding* it's about the way our professional vicissitudes impact on our private lives. In common with all the plays it's about neurosis – the fear that in a godless world, when the going gets tough, nobody understands. The irresistible paranoia that your family or lover or boss or friends are turning against you because they've glimpsed the real you and think you're an idiot after all.

In *The Bullet* Charles grows exasperated with Billie's scorn for his conspiracy theories. 'Must I keep humiliating myself for one shred of understanding?' Robbie tells Carla 'I want you to agree with me'. In *Some Voices* Ray risks everything to be with Laura because, he tells her, 'You understand me'. In *Pale Horse*, Charles grabs his local vicar by the throat and bawls, 'Don't you understand?' In *Love and Understanding* . . . there's precious little love and understanding . . . More than acceptance, everybody in my plays wants understanding – the way a close family or lovers do – but it's as elusive as it is enchanting.

The last time I saw Ian Rickson and Stephen Jeffries was in the spring, over lunch. And Stephen said, 'This may sound idiotic, but we want to put you in jail.' They said it was a way of distracting me from the introspection and self-expression I'd been privileged to enjoy as a playwright and goad me into writing something more outward-looking. And I said, 'You're right. It does sound idiotic.' But it was nice to be asked – and I may yet do it. It seems strangely apposite to have me grope for stories in a dark and brutal place about which I've had nightmares since I was a child.

The themes of these four plays – death, madness, love, loss, families, failure, communication and the lack of it – may seem self-evident – not particularly original certainly – but they are deeply embedded in our collective unconscious. Stories from dark places. They are the stuff of dreams and nightmares. Just like flying saucers and sex, they're an irresistible source of curiosity. Anybody who hasn't experienced the sort of goings-on contained herein can rest assured that you may yet do. And anybody who has . . . I invite you to feel at home.

For their invaluable help and inspiration, I would like to thank warmly Ray Winstone, Ian Rickson, Mike Bradwell, Paul Bettany, Nick Tennant, Celia Robertson, Es Devlin, Debra Ayden, Stephen Jeffries, Jack Bradley, Graham Whybrow, Stephen Daldry, Sue Higginson, Alan Radcliffe, Brian Croucher, Jim Harnwell and Jane and Georgie Duits.

Joe Penhall
London, 1998

Some Voices

For Brian, Sue, Piet and Polly Penhall

Some Voices was first performed at the Royal Court Theatre Upstairs, London, in association with the Royal National Theatre Studio on 15 September 1994. The cast was as follows:

Dave	Lloyd Hutchinson
Laura	Anna Livia Ryan
Ray	Lee Ross
Ives	Tom Watson
Pete	Ray Winstone

Directed by Ian Rickson
Designed by Rae Smith
Lighting by Jim Simmons
Sound by Paul Arditti
Music by Stephen Warbeck

Characters

Ray, *in his early twenties*
Laura, *Irish, the same age*
Pete, *Ray's brother, in his early thirties*
Dave, *Irish, the same age*
Ives, *around fifty*

The action takes place over a period of about six weeks in west London.

Note
An oblique/stroke within a speech serves as the cue for the next speaker to overlap with the first.

Act One

Scene One

Mental hospital. **Ray** *is standing by a window, a suitcase at his feet.* **Ives** *is nearby.*

Ray You shat on my window sill again, didn't you, Ives?

Ives No.

Ray Yes you did. You were drunk again and you couldn't be bothered –

Ives No.

Ray Couldn't be bothered going to the toilet so you –

Ives Bring me your shit!

Ray So you went to the window and dropped a turd out of your window and it landed on my window/sill.

Ives Bring me your shit!

Ray You did. It's the only explanation. (*Sniffs.*) Jesus, it's disgusting.

Pause.

Ives Are you a betting man?

Ray Don't change the subject.

Ives Like the horses, do you?

Ray No I don't.

Ives I used to like following around behind the horses and scooping up their shit.

Ray Well, why don't you scoop/up your own?

Ives It gave me something to do. Would you like to scoop up my shit?

Ray No.

Ives   Because I would like somebody to scoop up my shit. I am tired of scooping up other people's shit. Somebody should scoop up mine. That's why I leave it there.

Ray   Where d'you get the booze from, Ives?

Ives   I ought to rub your nose in it.

Ray   *What?*

Ives   Then you'd learn.

Ray   But it's yours.

Ives *puts a hand on the back of* **Ray***'s neck.*

Ray   Hey, Ives, Ives –

Ives   Do you know what they do to me?

Ray   What?

Ives   Everything. Worm balls in my mouth, fur balls in my mouth, tape-recordings. They play the tape-recorded voices then they make me eat them.

Ray   Who does?

Ives   The loonies. They think that I'm loony too. They think that just because they like it, I like it. But I never liked it. Not in my food for God's sake – it's weird.

Ray (*beat*)   You could complain.

Ives   I *am* complaining. I am complaining to you and you're not even listening!

Ives *lets go of* **Ray**. *Pause. They look at each other.*

Ray   I have to get going.

Ives   Where?

Ray   I'm going home. They're letting me out today.

Ives   No they're not.

Ray   They are, Ives.

Ives   They're just 'letting you out'. Just like that. Listen to me, you'll never survive out there. They know it, you know it. They been promising to let me out for years – years – and they haven't. Why? I don't know why.

Ray   They don't want me any more, Ives. I'm not crazy enough.

Ives   I think you're crazy.

Ray   My time's up.

Ives   You're damn right your time's up.

Ray   My twenty-eight/days.

Ives   You're fucking right your time is up.

Ray   I'm/off.

Ives   Everybody's time is up. You only have to look at things out there. A world which drives people bananas.

They look at each other. **Ray** *takes out a piece of paper from his pocket and scrawls on it. Hands it to* **Ives** *who reads it and stuffs it in his mouth.*

Ray   This is my brother's address. When you get out, look me up.

Ives   Twenty years I been here and never once has anyone offered to let me out. They made me eat shit. Not horse shit, real shit. I try to kill myself all the time and they stop me. They don't even care.

Ray   I'm going now.

Ives   They pretend to care – they profess to know how to be in the business of caring, which to me, sonny Jim, is no different to a butcher professing to know how to operate on the brain. I like it here. D'you understand? I love it! They won't/get rid of me.

Ray   Ives –

Ives   I belong here.

Ray   I'll see you round.

Ives   Probably yes probably birds of a feather and all that.

Ray   What?

Ives   Stick together.

Ray   Yeh.

Ives *clutches* **Ray**'s *arm to stop him leaving.*

Ives   You are marked, my friend. Do you understand me?
Marked.

Ray *shakes his head, then nods it.*

Ives   For life.

Pause.

Ray   See you, Ives.

Ives   Yes.

Ray *exits.* **Ives** *spits out the chewed-up piece of paper and catches it
neatly in his hand.*

Scene Two

Pete's *flat. Morning.* **Pete** *is sitting at a kitchen table.* **Ray** *enters
carrying a four-pack of beer and wearing a long old coat. He looks
dishevelled, sleepless. They look at each other.*

Ray   All right, Pete?

Pete   Yeh, I'm all right, you all right?

Ray   Yeh.

Pete   Where you been?

Ray   Oh, here and there.

Pete   Well, where? What's the matter – couldn't you sleep?

Ray   It's the room you gave me. The walls keep moving. It's
shrinking.

Pete   What d'you mean shrinking? D'you have a nightmare?

Ray   I told you. It's getting smaller. It's a nice place, Pete, but
it's definitely getting smaller.

Pete   Don't be daft. Smaller?

Ray   Where's the railway line? It was out there a minute ago.

Pete (*indicating beers*)   What's this?

Ray   D'you know I always like to know where the railway line is. Increases my sense of mobility.

Pete   Where'd you get 'em?

Ray   When does the train come?

Pete   Never mind when the train comes. Where d'you get those?

Ray   I found 'em.

Pete   Where did you find 'em?

Ray   An old man gave 'em to me.

Pete   What old man?

Ray   This old fella down by the canal. I don't know his name. I was watching the sunrise and there were lots of 'em all asleep.

Pete   What have you done?

Ray   It's all different now. Most of it's wasteland but on some they planted trees, plant boxes, little pathways.

Pete   And this fella just gave you his beers, just like that.

Ray   I was thirsty.

Pete   You didn't do anything, did you?

Ray   No. You want one?

Pete *pulls out a little phial of capsules from his pocket, shakes it.*

Pete   Just hand 'em over. Have some breakfast and take one of these.

Ray   Is it just me or are things not the same colour any more?

Pete   What d'you mean?

Ray   Green things. Green things aren't the same any more, much more faded. Yellow's not the same any more neither. And then there's the sun which is more . . . white. Silver. It's either too bright or else not even there. And the sky.

Pete   Yeh, all right, Ray . . .

Ray   Look at the sky, Pete. It's not the same. It's not even a proper blue any more. Everything is different.

Pete   Ray.

Pete *pushes the phial towards* **Ray**.

Ray   No thanks.

Pete   You have to, Ray, you know you do.

Ray   I'm not taking any more of that stuff. It addles my brain. Affects my judgment.

Ray *swigs on a beer and grins at* **Pete** *who holds out his hand for the beer*.

Pete   Give it to me.

Ray   You know what those are, Pete?

Pete   I know what they are and I know you need 'em.

Ray   Horse tranquillisers. Major knockout drops.

Pete   Just take a couple.

Ray   Chlorpromazine. Like Lithium times ten. Or a smack on the head with a claw-hammer, if you know what that's like. Hardly the elixir of life.

Pete   Listen –

Ray   I'm not listening.

Pete   If this stuff is going to keep you out of that place and stop you doing stupid things then you have to take 'em.

Ray   I don't want to.

Pete   That's not the point.

Ray   Well, what is the point?

Pause.

Have a beer with me, Pete. Let's sit down and talk about old times together.

Pete We will, Ray, but first you have to do this. If this is going to work, you have show willing.

Ray Bollocks. Since when did willing get anyone anywhere? Eh? Eh, Pete?

Pause.

Thanks for picking me up yesterday.

Pete It was a pleasure.

Ray No, I mean it. When you came to the gate in the car and you got out and opened the boot for my bags it was . . . it was a good feeling. I mean I really had that, that leaving feeling. That feeling. That feeling of leaving . . . and arriving.

Pete Good.

Ray Remember all those times when you were either picking me up from somewhere or dropping me off? Taking me to the train. Meeting me off the coach. Remember the time I got lost in Scotland? Perth. Took myself off and got arseholed with the old men of Perth for three weeks.

Pete Yeh, it was very clever.

Ray And remember the time I got lost in Wales?

Pete It's difficult to forget, Ray.

Ray Tenby. Got myself arseholed with the young people of Tenby for three weeks. All rock shops and little pubs done up to look like barns and little barns done up to look like pubs.

Pete Give us the beers, will you.

Ray Leaving and arriving, Pete, that's what I was doing. Following a pattern established over years which –

Pete The beers, Ray.

Ray Because I'm a travelling man.

Pete Ray.

Ray Swap.

Pete (*confused*) No, no swaps. I mean yes, swap.

Pete *holds out the pills,* **Ray** *holds out the beers, withdrawing them as* **Pete** *tries to grab them. Eventually* **Pete** *takes the four-pack and* **Ray** *takes the phial of pills.* **Pete** *stands, puts the beers out of reach.*

Ray   Hey, Pete.

Pete   Yes, Ray.

Ray   I'm sorry I never made the wedding.

Pause.

Pete   Well, you were tied up, weren't you.

Ray   I was going to be best man, wasn't I?

Pete   That's right, yeh.

Ray   I had a special little book and everything, all about what you do when you're a best man. The 'etiquette' of being a best man.

Pete   And what do you do?

Ray   I dunno. Never read it.

Pause.

And, and I'm sorry I never made the divorce neither.

Pete   You didn't miss much.

Ray   Quick, wasn't it?

Pete   Like lightning.

Ray   I mean it, Pete. I am sorry. You been growing into an old fart without me.

Pete   Well, you disappeared. Things change when you disappear.

Ray   That's what I was saying, Pete. Everything's changed. Even the . . . even the smells have changed.

Pete   Ray, listen . . .

Ray   Except for one. One smell hasn't changed.

Pete   Ray, please . . .

Ray   Remember when we was kids and we used to play in that old stream that runs underneath the brewery?

Pete   No.

Ray   Yes you do. We'd play with sticks having races. And sometimes the horses from the brewery came down and drank there. And sometimes dad came down and drank there and all, when he was working at the brewery. You remember that smell? That *mysterious* smell which we could never figure out what it was.

Pete   Horse shit.

Ray   Nah, it was a nice smell.

Pete   Ray, I've got to go to work.

Ray   I've figured out what it was. You want to know what it was, Pete? It was hops.

Pause. They look at each other.

Pete   I'm expecting deliveries. You going to go and see that woman today?

Ray *opens the phial and tosses a capsule in the air, catches it in his mouth like a peanut.*

Ray   What woman's that then?

Pete   The one they fixed you up with to sort out the thingie for your whatsit.

Ray   What whatsit?

Pete   After-sales service.

Ray *throws another capsule in the air, catches it in his mouth.*

Ray   You want one?

Pete   No thanks.

Ray   It'll calm you down.

Pete   When are you going?

Ray .   I'm not going.

Pete   You're going, Ray.

Ray *shakes his head.*

Pete   Have a bath and get ready.

Ray   I didn't ask to be fixed up with any woman.

Pete   You gotta do it, Ray. The people said you gotta do it. She'll fix you up with that fella. He's supposed to be very good.

Ray   What fella?

Pete   The fella they recommended for the whatsit.

Ray (*exasperated*)   What whatsit?!

Pete (*beat*)   Observation. He's gonna help you now you're out.

Ray   Help me?

Pete   Watch you. See you don't get in any/trouble.

Ray   He's not gonna help me.

Pete   Yes he/is, Ray.

Ray   They're not here to help, these people.

Pete   They're here to –

Ray   They're here to investigate the mind.

Pete   Yes. *Your* mind.

Ray   For fun.

Pete   No, not for fun!

Ray   Because they find it interesting. They do.

Pete   Ray!

Pause. **Pete** *pulls out a ten-pound note from his pocket and hands it to* **Ray**.

Ray   What's this?

Pete   Money.

Ray   I thought we were going to talk.

Pete   Call me when you've finished. I'll give you directions, we'll talk.

Ray   I know where it is.

Pete   Corner of Askew and –

Ray   Yeh yeh yeh off you go.

Pete *hesitates, then puts on a jacket and exits. Pause.* **Ray** *tips his head back, spits the capsules one by one into the air and catches them in his hand. Puts them back in the bottle, stands, grabs the beers and exits.*

Scene Three

The street. **Dave** *is standing over* **Laura** *who has her back against a wall.*

Dave   I'm going to count to three, Laura.

Laura   I don't know where it is!

Dave   One.

Laura   I swear, Dave, I haven't/even seen it.

Dave   Two.

Laura   Let go of/me.

Dave   I'm warning you.

Laura   What're you going to do?

Dave   Three. I'm only going to ask you this once, Laura. Once. And then I swear I'm going to get angry.

Laura   Then you're going to *get*/angry?

Dave   Where is it?

Laura   You're going to get *more*/angry.

Dave   Now I'm losing my temper.

Laura   I told you I lost it.

Dave *shoves her into the wall.*

Dave   Don't lie to me, tell me.

Laura   I don't fuckin' know where it is.

Dave   And mind your language. You got a mouth like a fuckin' sewer so you have.

Laura   Leave me alone.

Dave   You're a dirty slut. I don't need to waste my time with dirty sluts.

Laura   Then leave me alone.

Dave   I'll leave. I'll leave all right just as soon as you tell me what you did with it.

Laura   Go on get.

Dave   I am. I will. I'm gone. Believe me, boy.

Pause.

Laura   Good. Goodbye then.

Dave   You probably sold it. Sold it to pay for a holiday with your fuckin' fancy man. Is that what you did?

Laura   What fancy man?

Dave   Your little fancy man. I know you got one. To pay for your hacienda abroad with yer man there.

Laura   What haci – I don't have a fancy man.

Dave   They know I took it, Laura. Five stone sapphire. In a cluster. Not a half hoop. A cluster!

Beat.

They know I been taking stuff to give it to you.

Laura   Who?

Dave   The boys, Laura.

Laura   What 'boys'? You live in a world of your own, so you do.

Dave   The people I work for.

Laura   But you don't work!

Dave   Every job we've done I took stuff to give to you.

Laura   I don't want it.

Dave   I am trying to make you happy.

Laura   By giving me a thick ear, I suppose.

Dave   I love you, you stupid ugly cow.

Laura   That's why you put my head through a third floor window last week.

Dave   I am under pressure.

Laura   That explains it then.

Dave   They're coming after me. I am desperate.

Laura   So next time you stick my head through a window and leave me to bleed to death I'll understand.

Dave   Laura!

Pause. He takes his hands off her, brushes her shoulder with his hand. Steps back.

Just tell me who's it is. Come on, I can take it, if you tell me who's it is I promise I won't do anything. Not to you.

Laura   It's yours, Dave.

Dave   Tell me who you been getting friendly with.

Laura   I haven't been getting friendly with anybody. I don't have any friends to be friendly with.

Dave   So what am I?

Laura   Don't be stupid.

Dave   Don't call me stupid! I hate that.

Laura   I haven't been outside that stinking flat in three months. I haven't even been out to sign on.

Dave   I don't ask you to sign on still.

Laura   I like to sign on. It makes me feel normal.

Dave   I look after you.

Laura   I don't want you looking after me.

Pause.

Dave   Give me the ring and we'll call it quits.

Laura   Are you deaf?

Dave   That's all I want. Or an arm or a leg or your guts!

He slams her against the wall.

Laura   I lost it!

Dave   Where did you lose it?

Laura   If I knew that it wouldn't be lost!

Ray *wanders on and watches, unseen.*

Laura   Down the sinkhole probably.

Dave   'Probably'?

Laura   I don't know.

Dave   Well, 'probably' I'll just smash your brains out with this brick, shall I?

He stoops and picks up a loose brick, **Laura** *screams.*

Eh? Maybe I'll finish it right here. How would you like that?

Laura   Christ, help me somebody please!

Dave   Shut up!

Laura   Please!

Dave   Oh, 'please please!' D'you think they care? D'you think anybody really cares about you, Laura? Eh?

He waves the brick about.

I'll tell you something. I care about you, you don't care about me, so you know what suddenly — I don't care about you.

Laura *weeps.*

Ray   Put the brick down.

Dave *looks around in wonder. Sees* **Ray**.

Dave   Fuck off.

Ray   No go on. You could take somebody's eye out with that thing.

Dave   What?

Ray   It's dangerous.

Dave   Is it now? And who the fuck are you?

Ray   Nobody.

Dave   That's right, pal. Mister Fucking Nobody. You wanna have a go?

Ray   Not really.

Dave *looks at* **Ray**, *then* **Laura**, *then* **Ray** *again, then* **Laura**.

Dave   Wait a minute, wait a minute. (*To* **Laura**.) Who's this?

Laura   I don't know.

Dave *heads for* **Ray** *with the brick*.

Laura   No, Dave, don't!

Dave   I'll murder the pair of you!

He flings the brick to the ground, marches up to **Ray** *and grabs him by the shirt*.

You wanna fuck with me? Eh? You wanna rescue a poor cunt in distress? Think that'll earn you brownie points?

Laura   Please, Dave, leave him alone.

Dave   Why?

Laura   I don't know why, I just think you should.

Ray   Yeh leave me alone.

Dave   Where's the ring?

Ray   I don't know what you're talking about.

Dave   Don't play games with me, cunt.

Laura   He doesn't know for Christsake! He's just some nutter. (*To* **Ray**.) Go away. Go on.

Dave   One word of advice, nutter.

He headbutts **Ray** *who instantly collapses.*

One little gem of wisdom.

He kicks **Ray** *in the guts.*

Don't ever, never fuck with another man's misery.

(*To* **Laura**.) And if I ever catch you with another man I will kill you. Both of you.

Dave *exits leaving* **Laura** *frozen in shock. She snaps out of it and goes to* **Ray**.

Laura   O Jesus. Oh shit. What did you think you were doing?

She helps him sit up. She touches his nose.

Hello? Can you hear me? It's just a nose bleed is all. Can you feel your nose?

Ray   Ow!

Laura   Sorry . . .

Ray *breathes hard, his breathing gets slower and slower, he cradles his ribs, his head hangs down, he seems to pass out.*

Laura   Jesus. I'll get you to a hospital.

Ray   No! No hospitals.

Laura   You should see a doctor.

Ray   I hate doctors.

Laura   (*at a loss*)   Come on then.

She gets him to his feet and they hobble off.

Scene Four

Laura's *bedsit*. **Ray** *is sitting on the bed*. **Laura** *is attending to his face*.

Ray   It's all closed up. I can't see. I'm going blind. Was that your old man then?

Laura   No.

Ray   Who is he then?

Laura   Just a fella.

Ray   Just a dangerous bloody nutter. It's funny how you never see it coming. One minute you've got your feet on the ground and the next you're five feet away staring at the stars.

Laura   You'll live.

Ray   He's not coming back, is he?

Laura   I doubt it.

Ray   Very reassuring.

Laura   You shouldn't have got involved.

Ray   He was going to kill you.

Laura   I'll be the judge of that.

Ray   He was. He said so.

Pause. **Laura** *works*.

What was he doing that for anyway?

Laura   That's my business.

Ray   He's lucky. He caught me when I wasn't looking.

Laura   You'll know to mind your own business next time.

Ray *looks at her*. *Pause*.

Ray   You're a bit of a hard nut, aren't you?

Laura   What d'you mean?

Ray   You don't say much. I just saved your life, you saved mine. That's not to be sneezed at. I'm only being friendly.

She works.

Laura   That's what I'm afraid of.

Ray   Why?

She sticks a sticking plaster over the bridge of his nose and steps back.

Laura   Done.

Ray   Is that it?

Laura   It'll do.

Ray   But my nose. I'm sure it's broken. Feels like his head's still up there.

Laura   D'you want to go to the hospital or not?

Ray   All right.

Laura   Can you stand?

Ray *stands shakily, pauses, then plonks back down clutching his ribs.*

Ray   No.

Laura   Try.

Ray   I just tried.

Laura   Try harder.

Ray *tries again but can't.*

Ray   It's sitting down that's done it. I shouldn't have sat down. It's like whatchmecallit, rigor mortis. I can't move my legs. I think I'm becoming a paraplegic maybe.

He rubs his ribs. She puts her hands on her hips and weighs it up.

Laura   Lift your shirt up.

Ray   What're you gonna do?

Laura   I'm gonna check your ribs. You probably cracked one.

He lifts up his T-shirt, she probes his ribs. He laughs involuntarily.

What?

Ray Cold.

She probes again. He laughs again.

Laura D'you want me to help you or not?

Ray Yeh.

Laura What's so friggin' funny then?

Ray Nothing.

Laura Does this hurt?

Ray No.

Laura This?

Ray No.

Laura This?

Ray N . . . yeh. That does.

Laura This?

Ray Up a bit . . . up a bit more. Just there. Nice.

Laura *stops instantly.*

Laura Look, if you're going to take the piss –

Ray I'm not taking the piss.

Laura You can clear off right/now.

Ray I'm not/I'm sorry.

Laura Friggin' cheek.

She packs away the Band-aids etc. in a small cabinet next to the bed, returns to **Ray.**

Laura What's the date today?

Ray I dunno, why?

Laura When were you born?

Ray August seventy-two. (*Beat.*) I'm a Leo.

Laura   I'm seeing if you're concussed or not. How's your head feel?

Ray   Are you a nurse then?

Laura   Don't be daft. I'm on the dole.

Ray   Well, for on the dole you make a great nurse. You know exactly what they do.

Laura   I think I'd rather be on the dole. Pay's better.

Ray   No, but you're an expert. How do you know all this?

Laura   Will you leave it.

Beat.

Ray   What about this place then, is it yours?

Laura   It's council, I rent it.

Ray   Does he live here too then, whatshisname?

Laura   No, he doesn't – now do you think you can stand up?

Ray   Does he often do this sort of thing?

Laura   Would you stop asking awkward questions.

Ray   Scrape you up against walls, fling bricks at people it's not/nice.

Laura   If you don't mind –

Ray   It's rude.

Laura   I think it's time you were on your/way.

Ray   I've met his sort before. Got nothing better to do than go round whacking people and scaring the shit out of them. You see them walking around wired, angry, wound up ready to ping. He probably practises. It's not the first time this has happened to me, you know. It's not the first time I've completely unwittingly provoked somebody. I just –

Laura   If it's all the same to you –

Ray Say the wrong thing or look at them the wrong way. People like this do not like to be looked at. It's instinctive. And it's like –

Laura If I could just get a word in/edgeways.

Ray Pardon me for being so bold as to exchange a look in the street while I'm going about my business, pardon me for daring to speak to you because we do not speak to each other.

Laura I'm trying.

Ray We just don't, not if we are complete strangers.

Laura Are you listening?

Ray And it's like/what –

Laura Jesus Mary and Joseph!

Ray Is your problem, pal? That's what I say.

Pause.

Laura I have to go out. I don't want to be rude but I have an important appointment and so I have to go out.

Ray Will I see you again?

Laura What kind of question's that?

Pause. **Ray** *gets up.*

Ray Makes sense to me.

Laura It would do, wouldn't it.

Ray I'm sorry.

Laura So am I.

Ray I'm going.

Laura Thank you.

Ray Out the door.

Laura Thank you.

Ray *goes to the door.*

Ray I'm going out the door now.

Laura   Thank you very much.

Ray   You're welcome. Are you going to be/all right?

Laura   What? Yeh fine.

Ray   Fine then.

Ray *nods and exits.*

Scene Five

The restaurant kitchen. Spanish guitar music plays. **Pete** *is preparing two plates of food on a prep table.* **Ray** *watches, his face bandaged and eye black.*

Pete   What the fuck happened?

Ray   Nothing happened.

Pete   What happened to your face?

Ray   Nothing happened to my face.

Pete   You shot your mouth off again, didn't you?

Ray   No.

Pete   Look at yourself, Ray. Christ.

He examines **Ray**'s *face.*

This is a serious fuck up. A serious one. I leave you alone five minutes and you're in trouble.

Ray   I'm not, Pete.

Pete   Yes, Ray, this is what I call trouble. What would you call it?

Ray   An accident.

Pete   You cannot afford to get into trouble. How can I impress this upon you? Because if you get into trouble I get into trouble. They'll come to me and they'll see this and they'll think what?

Ray   I dunno, what?

Pete   What do you think they'll think? They'll think you're in trouble that's what they'll think.

Ray   Maybe they'll think it was an/accident too.

Pete   Because the patient's brother, this person to whom we've entrusted him to, cannot be trusted. And nor can the patient. And so they put you away again.

Ray (*beat*)   It's quite a long/story.

Pete   I signed a form. I signed a bit of paper to get you out of that place. They said 'Let's let him out, let's send him back to his family – even though he doesn't have a family any more we'll find somebody' and they found me. I haven't seen you in years, I don't even know who you are any more but, fuck, yes I'm here for you, Ray, and I put that in writing we go through a whole procedure and you don't . . . appear to give a shit.

Ray   I do give a/shit, Pete.

Pete   Don't tell me you walked into a door. Always walking into doors, weren't you? You'd vanish off the face of the earth and walk into a door somewhere.

He speaks into an intercom on the wall.

Two curly sausages for table five.

He takes two plates to a serving hatch and puts them down.

Got yourself arrested. Did you get arrested again?

Ray   I didn't get arrested, honestly.

Pete   You been beaten up – how else do you explain it? Why don't you just move into Hammersmith nick? You used to practically live there. Either that or me or mum God rest her soul would be knocked up at all hours by the police cos they found you in some heap somewhere. You could be dead for all I know but all you think about is me me me . . . (*Into intercom.*) Two curly sausages for table five what the hell's going on?

Intercom   Sorry, guv.

Pete (*to* **Ray**)   Oh no, Pete, I'm all right, Jack-the-Lad I am. The wind changed and my face turned to pulp by itself.

Ray   Are you listening to me?

Pete   You can't live like that again, Ray, you're not up to it. You understand? (*Beat*.) It's what sent you screwy in the first place.

Ray   Nothing 'sent me screwy'.

Pete   Well, it hardly helped, did it?

Ray   Nothing 'sent' me screwy, Pete. Nothing sent me.

Pete   I just don't understand it that's all I just . . . don't understand.

Ray   Nobody understands it.

Pete   Why can't you just . . . pull yourself together?

Ray   Pull myself together.

Pete   Something like that, yeh. (*Into intercom*.) Two curly sausages for –

Intercom   Curly sausage.

Pete   What?

Intercom   Curly sausage, yeh?

Pete   Yes curly –

Intercom   Not Polish?

Pete   No, not Polish Spiced –

Intercom   They want pizza –

Pete   Well, they can't have pizza –

Intercom   They changed their minds –

Pete   Tell 'em to make up their bloody minds.

Ray   How do I pull myself together, Pete? Is there a string or something that people just pull on every time they're in the shit?

Pete   You know what I mean.

Ray   Yes I do and I don't fucking like it.

Pete (*into intercom*) The curly fucking sausages are getting curly fucking cold all right? (*To* **Ray**.) I employ imbeciles. It's cheaper but it has its drawbacks.

He starts preparing another two plates.

My kitchen hand is unwell, probably hung over. I'll sack him tomorrow.

Ray Are you listening, Pete?

They look at each other.

Pete I'm sorry. You'll have to be patient with me, OK? You have to be patient with me I have to be patient with you.

Long pause as **Pete** *works.*

Ray You want a hand?

Pete I'll be all right.

Ray I could wash up the plates.

Pete I've got an imbecile to do that.

Ray Remember when dad was here and I used to wash up? Chief dishwasher. It was his dream to have a place like this, wasn't it?

Pete I dunno, was it?

Ray It was. All that simple stuff he was doing, bacon, beans, omelette, he couldn't give it away, could he?

Pete I still do that during the day.

Ray And at night you do this. What is it? Italian? He liked Italian.

Pete Mediterranean. Pizzas and curly sausage. Gourmet pizzas like with smoked salmon and artichoke hearts. Sour cream. The yuppies love it. (*Into intercom.*) Ask table seven if they're ready to order and interest them in the fish soup.

Silence.

Intercom Why?

Pete   Because I made fish soup today and if I don't get rid of it those fish'll start swimming again. (*To* **Ray**.) Sorry, where were we?

Ray   I could persuade 'em to have the soup.

Pete   Did you go and see that woman today?

Ray   Which woman?

Pete   Did you?

Ray   Yeh.

Pete   Because it's important, you know that.

Ray   I know that.

Pete   What did she say?

Ray   Said keep up the good work and come back in two weeks.

Pete   Two weeks, why two weeks?

Ray   Why not two weeks?

Pete   Was your face like that when you went to see her?

Ray   No, why?

Pete   Because if it was then she wouldn't have said that, would she? It'd be a different kettle of fish altogether. (*Into intercom.*) Pesto pizza pie for table four.

Ray *takes a plate to the hatch, puts it down.*

Pete   What did happen to your face, Ray?

Ray   What's pesto pizza pie?

Pete   It's pesto and pizza . . . in a pie. Now just tell me/what –

Ray   In a pie?

Pete   Folded over like a pie, yeh, not many people do it . . .

Ray   I'm not surprised.

Pete   Ray, I haven't got all night.

Ray (*beat*)   I met this girl. Her old man was giving her a hard time – I mean a really hard time, Pete.

Pete   Oh, Ray, you didn't –

Ray   So I –

Pete   You stuck your nose in.

Ray   He was gonna brick her face. I told him to stop.

Pete   Oh, good plan, Ray, I'm sure that worked/a treat.

Ray   Quite freaked me at the/time.

Pete   Never get involved.

Ray   He was murdering her!

Pete   That's not your problem.

Ray   I didn't know what to do.

Pete   It's her problem. Every person has their own set of problems. Every person has a hand of cards they are dealt in this life. If somebody has a bad card you don't pick up their bad card.

Ray   Yeh, but murder, Pete –

Pete   You have your own bad cards.

Ray   Puts a different slant on things.

Pete   What are you doing tomorrow?

Ray   I dunno.

Pete   Yes you do know, Ray, because I just told you. Didn't I just tell you? You go and see the woman and you do what she tells you to do.

Ray   Yes, Pete.

Pete   And you do what I tell you to do.

Ray   Yes, Pete.

Pete   And you do what they told me to tell you to do. All right?

Ray   All right, Pete. But, Pete, I mean I just feel, Pete –

Pete   Ray Ray Ray – everybody feels. We all have feelings but we don't let them rule our lives. (*Beat.*) Are you hungry?

Ray   Starved.

Pete   Clear a space.

Ray *clears a space on the prep table.* **Pete** *goes to the service hatch.*

Ray   But what am I gonna do with my time besides all that?

Pete   We'll cross that bridge when we come to it.

Ray   We have come to it.

Pete   Give it one more try. Eh? (*Beat.*) Have you ever had curly sausage before?

Ray   No.

Pete   Well, today is your lucky day.

He plonks the plate down in front of **Ray**. **Ray** *looks at it.*

And tomorrow will be my lucky day if you do what you're supposed to. Is that a deal?

Ray   It's a deal.

Pete   Eat your grub.

Pete *gets back to work.* **Ray** *stares at his plate.*

Ray   Pete?

Pete   Yes?

Ray   What's curly sausage?

Pete   It's just sausage, Ray. It's just like straight sausage only it's curly.

Ray (*eating*)   Nice.

Pete   It's got spices in it, I dunno, herbs or something.

Ray   Tastes good.

Pete   Yeh?

Ray   Yeh.

Pete   Good.

Scene Six

The pub. A few days later. **Laura** *is sitting at a table drinking and smoking a cigarette. Music blasts out.* **Ray** *wanders over with drink in hand.*

Ray   Is . . . is anybody sitting there?

Laura   Only if they're very small.

Ray   Can I sit there?

Laura *shrugs.* **Ray** *sits.*

Ray   All right?

Pause.

It's nice here. (*Beat.*) All my friends come here. (*Beat.*) They're not here at the moment.

Laura   I like it.

Ray   It's a friendly place. I like the music they play. It's not old and it's not new. Very few pubs play this type of music nowadays. Are you Irish?

Laura   What?

Ray   This is an Irish pub.

Laura   I'm from Limerick.

Ray   Did you know that there is more drunkenness, suicide and madness amongst the Irish in London than any other race on earth?

Laura   Is that so?

Ray   Yes, well, that's what they say because mostly you see they're away from their family and they're lonely probably and sometimes there's prejudice against 'em because of who they are and they can't get jobs and things but also mainly it's just loneliness. Have you got any family here or are you just on your own?

Laura   I'm on my own.

Ray   Me too. I just got my brother. Me dad vanished some years ago but there's still my brother. My mother's dead. Cancer I believe.

Pause.

No cats, no dogs, no – what are they – little hairy things, in a cage . . . I don't have any sisters. Do you have any sisters?

Laura   Yeh, I've got a couple of sisters.

Ray   And do you like them?

Laura   They're all right.

Ray   That's good because you have to be able to like your family. You have to be able to trust them but mainly you have to like them. And sometimes you just don't. Sometimes you don't trust anybody. Then again sometimes you form a vague attachment/to –

Laura   I have no idea, no idea at all, what you are talking about. Can you see that?

Pause.

Ray   Would you like a drink?

Laura   Look, I'm sorry if it looked like I wanted you to sit down but in fact I really didn't. What I wanted was to be left alone. And I'm not just saying that, I mean it. I don't want to talk to anybody I don't want to see anybody I don't want to fight with anybody I don't want to drink with anybody smile at anybody play Let's Get To Know Each Other I just don't want to know. I'm in a bad mood.

Ray   Well, why'd you come here?

Laura   Because . . . I'm in a bad mood. Why did you come here?

Ray (*beat*)   I was bored.

Laura   You were bored so you thought you'd come and talk to me.

Ray *shrugs. Pause.*

Ray   It's nice here. I live round here. My brother he runs a restaurant it's very busy, sometimes I help out.

Laura   Really.

Ray   Yes, all the time. (*Beat.*) No, never. What happened to your face?

Laura   What?

Ray   You/all right?

Laura   Nothing happened.

Ray   That doesn't look like nothing to me. You got quite a shiner. And your lip's all cut. And your arm, look at your arm.

Laura   I fell out of bed.

Ray   Ah, I'm always falling out of bed. Falling out of bed and walking into doors. You want to get some carpet in that place that way you won't bruise so easy. So so so did you get to your appointment?

Laura *looks at him then glances around the pub uneasily.*

Laura   Yes, thank you.

Ray   You must be up the spout then. Am I right?

Laura   I beg your pardon?

Ray   Is it his then? That fella of yours?

Laura   Yes it's his all his handiwork just like your nose. Any other/questions?

Ray   I'm surprised people still want to have babies. I find it fascinating. I mean they say you get a special glow and everything when you have a baby. Like a special . . .

She gets up.

Laura   I have to go.

Ray   Please stay, sit down don't get all –

Ray *gets up and puts a hand on her arm, she bats it away.*

Laura   Don't touch me!

Ray   Sorry!

Laura   What is wrong with you?

Ray   I just want to get to know you a bit, what's wrong with that?

Laura   You don't get to know somebody by just walking up to them in a pub and talking absolute friggin' rubbish to them for half an hour.

Ray   What d'you want me to do?

Laura   Are you simple or wha'?

Ray   I offered you a drink.

Laura   That is not how it happens.

Ray   Well, how does it happen?

Laura   I don't know!

Ray   You don't believe me, do you? I like you. I'm not being funny. I thought you liked me seeing as I saved your life and all. I can't do that every day you know, my brother ain't half got the hump. He don't believe me neither.

Pause. **Laura** *sighs and sits.*

Ray   You got nice eyes.

Laura   I don't believe this.

Ray   Incredible blue like two swimming pools.

Laura   You don't give up, do you?

Ray   Not really/no.

Laura   I'm not going to sleep with you, you know.

Ray   What?

Laura   I said . . . (*Lowers her voice.*) I'm not going to sleep with you. If that's what you're getting at.

Ray   I don't want you to sleep with me.

Laura   It's out of the question.

Ray   I didn't ask you to sleep/with me.

Laura   Because, because –

Ray   I don't want you to sleep/with me.

Laura   I'm not sleeping with/anybody.

Ray   I don't want you/to.

Laura   Just at the moment. Sleeping with people is not the answer to/anything.

Ray   I don't want you to sleep with me.

Pause.

Laura   And I'm not doing anything else either.

Ray   I don't want you to.

Laura   Nothing, you understand? Nothing.

Ray   I don't want to.

Pause. They look around sheepishly.

Laura   Well, good. I'm glad we got that sorted/out.

Ray   Who said anything about sleeping with you?

Laura   I just thought that might have been where things were heading.

Ray   Course not. (*Beat.*) I don't like sleeping anyway, it's boring. I've been asleep for too long.

Laura   You know that's not what/I meant.

Ray   I can't sleep, at night my brother says, 'Go to sleep,' and I can't. I don't want to. I have nightmares.

Pause.

Laura   What d'you have nightmares about?

Ray   Strange things. Things are always the wrong colour or the wrong size. Things speaking to me. Like birds. I mean real birds that fly.

Laura   What's so scary about that? I'd love to have nightmares about birds.

Ray   I scare easily. Well, I can't speak to them, can I? I'm not Doctor fuckin' Doolittle. (*Beat. She laughs a little.*) What about yours?

Laura   Who said I get 'em?

Ray   You must do.

Laura   Yeh, well . . . I wake up before anything really bad happens.

Ray   I know that sort and all. Awful.

Laura   Yeh . . . awful.

Pause.

I'm/sorry I –

Ray   No, I'm/sorry.

Laura   I didn't/mean to –

Ray   I just barged/in –

Laura   No you –

Ray   I –

Laura   I –

Ray   I'll get the drinks in.

Laura   Get the drinks in good idea.

Ray   A pint is it?

Laura   Vodka. Double.

Ray *gets up hurriedly and goes to the bar.* **Laura** *smokes her cigarette. Pause. She fidgets.* **Ray** *returns and plonks a vodka orange and a beer down.*

Ray   You shouldn't smoke and drink you know.

Laura   There's a lot of things I shouldn't do.

Ray But you still do 'em. Me too. I personally like to live as if I'm gonna die tomorrow.

Laura You might do.

Ray Yeh, yes that's exactly it. That's exactly it.

Pause.

I'm Ray, by the way.

Laura Laura.

He puts his hand out, they shake. Beat.

Ray Can I have a feel?

Laura What?

Ray Of your . . . of the . . .

He indicates her belly.

Laura Of this?

Ray *nods.* **Ray** *puts his hand on her belly.* **Laura** *looks straight ahead.* **Ray** *puts his ear to her belly and listens.* **Laura** *looks around awkwardly.*

Scene Seven

Split scene. **Ray** *is in a telephone box at the seaside, the sound of gulls overhead and waves.* **Laura** *strolls about outside throwing chips from a bag at the gulls.* **Pete** *is in his kitchen talking on the wall phone.*

Ray Pete.

Pete Ray, is that you?

Ray Pete, it's me.

Pete Where are you?

Ray Can you hear me?

Pete I can hear you, Ray, where are you calling from?

Ray *turns to* **Laura**, *opens the door a crack.*

Ray   Where are we?

Laura   Southend.

Ray   Southend.

Pete   Southend? What are you doing in Southend?

Ray   I came to see the sea. Get away from it all.

Pete   Who are you with?

Ray   I met a girl.

Pete   What?

Ray   You know. A woman.

Pete   Don't fuck me about, Ray. I'm not kidding.

Ray   Nor am I. I met someone, a bird, a chick, a little tweetie-pie –

Pete   All right I get the message – who?

Ray   Her name's Laura.

Pete   Yeh and?

Ray   Lives up near the canal. Up Harlesden way. She's got her own place. It's a nice place, Pete.

Pete   How did you meet her?

Ray   You'd like her.

Pete   How did you meet this person, Ray?

Ray   Does it matter?

Pete   Yes it does matter.

Ray   I was just hanging around and she was hanging around and our paths just crossed.

Pete   You met her in the pub.

Ray   No/I swear.

Pete   You bloody fool, what on earth do you think you're doing?

Ray   Remember how I told you about the –

Pete No more stories, Ray, I'm not/listening.

Ray This bloke right –

Pete Just come home.

Ray And now he's –

Pete Now.

Pause.

Ray You don't believe me, do you?

Pete Oh, I believe you all right.

Ray Do you want to speak to her?

He leans out of the phone box.

He wants to speak to you.

Pete Ray, it's just fast work that's all.

Ray It's a fast world, Pete. Sometimes things happen even too fast for even you to understand.

Pete Oh, is that so? (*Beat.*) Listen, Ray, are you sure you didn't . . . blackout or something?

Ray Positive, Pete.

Pete Because it wouldn't be the first time, would it?

Ray No it wouldn't but I'm fine. I'm dandy in fact you could say I'm well chuffed. I like it here. It's like I'm in a movie, you know? All the people on the beach drink beers out of plastic cups and they play nineteen-fifties music.

Pete You haven't been taking your medication, have you?

Ray What's that?

Pete Your pills. You left 'em here, you hardly touched 'em.

Ray I forgot.

Pete Jesus!

Pause.

Ray You still there, Pete?

Pete   When are you coming home?

Ray   I dunno. I might stay a while, we been having a wicked/
time.

Pete   Get on a train and come home. I got enough to deal with
without you wandering off again. D'you want me to come and
get you?

Ray   We'll be all right.

Pete   No, I'm coming to get you. Where are you?

Ray   What's that?

Pete   What's the name of the street.

*Ray makes static noises with his mouth, pulls a crisp wrapper from his
pocket and ruffles it against the phone.*

Ray   I can't hear you, Pete . . . it's breaking up . . . bad line
. . . I . . . oh no.

Pete   Ray? Ray! Hello?

*Ray hangs up the phone. Pete listens for a moment then slams the phone
down. Ray gets out of the phone box, lights a fag and looks around
happily. Laura comes over, he gives her a fag and lights it up. Lights
down slowly on Pete as he paces.*

Laura   What did he say?

Ray   Said stay as long as we like.

Laura   Do you always have to ring him when you go
somewhere?

Ray   He gets bored. I just ring to cheer him up.

Laura   Are you sure he's OK about it? Sounds like you might
have some explaining to do.

Ray   Nah, he just worries too much. Worries I might
accidently enjoy myself. He's like an old woman sometimes.

Laura   Well, I think it must be nice to have somebody to
worry about you like that.

Ray   It's a drag. Let's go on the pier.

Laura   We been on the pier all day for goodness sake!

Ray   We'll go again. I like the pier.

He grabs her hand and tows her away.

Scene Eight

Tube station. **Ives** *stands with shopping bags of belongings, drinking from a beer can and examining the note* **Ray** *gave him.* **Dave** *walks towards the tube dressed in a black suit and white shirt, top button done up, clean-shaven. He stops, turns and stares in the direction he's just come from, puffing on a cigarette.*

Ives   Psst.

Dave *ignores him.*

Ives   Psst.

Dave   Get lost.

Dave *continues searching.*

Ives   The corner of Uxbridge and Askew.

Dave   What about it?

Ives   Where is it?

Dave   Have you seen a girl come out of that pub there?

Ives   Are you local?

Dave   Have you? Red hair. Skinny.

Ives   It's important.

Dave   Have you?

Ives   No.

Dave *checks his cuffs and collar and goes on staring.*

Ives   I'm lost.

Dave   Everybody's lost. Now leave me alone before I break your fuckin' legs off.

Beat.

Ives   That's a nice suit.

Beat.

Bespoke.

Dave   Yeh yeh.

Ives   Nice.

Dave   Yeh.

Ives   I had a suit once.

Dave *ignores him.*

Ives   Tailored. Five inch vents. Three buttons. All the rage.
You can respect a man in a suit and the ladies like it too.
Wear A Suit Today And Keep Heartache At Bay.
Once I Had A Secret Love and all because I wore a suit.

Dave   You're a bit old for that kind of talk, aren't you?

Ives   My old man swore by them.

Dave   I look all right then?

Ives   Beautiful, man, beautiful.

Dave   Yeh?

Ives   I had a friend and then he scarpered.

Dave *snatches the note off* **Ives**, *reads it and points.*

Dave   Straight ahead. Through the market.

Ives   Thank you.

Ives *moves to go,* **Dave** *stops him with a restraining arm.*

Dave   Then left.

Ives   Right.

Dave   Then straight on. Then left.

Ives *moves again.* **Dave** *stops him.*

Dave   There's a kind of a . . . kink in the road. Watch for the
kink. It'll be there for you somewhere.

Ives   Thank you.

Dave   Any time.

Ives   Have a Guinness.

Dave   G'way with yer.

Ives   You need it.

Dave   I said no, OK?

Pause.

I'll go stark staring if I don't find her, you know that, don't you?

Beat.

D'you believe me?

Beat. **Ives** *drinks.*

I'll wind up like you. Fuck me.

He digs into his pocket, pulls out a fiver, hands it to **Ives**.

Go on get out of my sight. Get lost.

Scene Nine

A field, **Ray** *and* **Laura** *are on a blanket holding each other, not speaking. There is food and a bottle of wine and a four-pack beside them.* **Ray** *strokes* **Laura**'s *cheek.*

Laura   You know we shouldn't be doing this. (*Beat.*) You could be some type of maniac. (*Beat.*) I could be some type of maniac. (*Beat.*) So why are we doing it?

Ray   We're just stupid I guess.

They kiss.

Wow.

Laura   Yes, wow.

Ray   You're a good kisser.

Laura   Yeh, well . . .

Ray   Has anybody ever told you that?

Laura   No. I mean yeh, so are you.

Ray   You got nice big lips.

He puckers his mouth experimentally.

Nice and firm. What shall we do now?

*She breaks away, folds her knees under her chin. **Ray** chews on a piece of straw.*

Laura   I didn't want this to happen, you know that, don't you?

Ray   Yeh.

Laura   I've only just escaped from the last man I was with.

Ray   You can't keep escaping forever otherwise you'll run out of places to escape to.

Laura   Depends on what you're escaping from. When I say escape I mean really escape. Like jump out of windows and dig tunnels type of escape that's what I'm talking about.

Ray   Mm.

Laura   I mean, I thought I had escaped. This is me escaping. I escape all right but he just keeps coming back.

Ray   Persistent.

Laura   Yes.

Ray   Why?

Laura   He has to be with me the whole time or something. He goes mad if he's not with me. I go mad if he is.

Ray   Is that why he hit you?

Laura   I don't know why he hit me.

Ray   Maybe he couldn't . . . couldn't express himself or something.

Laura   Maybe he just likes hitting people.

Ray   Maybe he was confused.

Laura   I was confused but it's no excuse to –

Ray   Maybe he loved you so much . . . that he just hit you.

Laura   What on *earth* are you talking about?

Pause.

Ray   No, maybe not. (*Beat.*) You must've liked him once.

Laura (*sighs*)   He could be quite charming when he wanted to be so. Well . . . not so much charming. Persuasive, I suppose.

Ray   What about when he hit you?

Laura   Oh, he could be very persuasive then.

Ray   But you stayed with him.

Laura   You get used to it after a while.

Ray   How can you get used to it?

Laura   You don't expect it to . . . keep happening, I suppose. (*Beat.*) He was always after calling me a slut or a whore and then the next minute I was frigid. He'd accuse me of going with other men, then he'd say I'd never find another man who'd have me. (*Beat.*) If someone says something like that often enough, you find yourself believing it. It's a miracle the things you find yourself believing.

Ray   I know what you mean.

Laura   I used to worry that I was going a bit mad because I still liked him. I'd get lonely without him and miss him because sometimes at night he could be something warm to get up against or something. When we'd been together his skin and his hands would always be warm . . . but when he came in after a night out he was cold, I mean his hands were cold his . . . knuckles. At first he could make things feel different. But then he couldn't.

Pause.

Ray   Couldn't you go somewhere? Go home?

Laura   They say I cause trouble.

Ray   I've heard that before and all.

Laura   I don't need anyone telling me how to redeem my mistakes.

Pause.

Ray What d'you think would happen if we stayed here and didn't go back?

Laura Stayed here in this field?

Ray Yeh.

Laura (*shrugs*) We'd die of starvation probably.

Pause.

Ray Kiss me.

They kiss chastely. Beat. They kiss passionately and fall back on the rug. He kisses her neck and chest wildly, peppering her with kisses. She giggles.

Laura Euch, stop! (*He does.*) No keep going. Here . . . on my mouth.

He kisses her on the mouth.

Now squash me. On top. I want to feel your weight.

He climbs on top.

Ray Like this?

Laura Harder. Squeeze the breath out of me.

He does so.

Harder!

He wriggles and laughs.

Ray Why?

Laura Makes me feel safe.

They lie like that for a moment. **Ray** *kisses her neck, starts unbuttoning her dress.*

Ray You've got beautiful breasts, Laura. I want to suck them.

They kiss, he puts his hand between her legs.

Laura Bit higher . . . down . . . just there.

Blackout.

Act Two

Scene One

Pete's *flat.* **Ray,** **Ives** *and* **Pete** *sit around the kitchen table.* **Ives** *and* **Ray** *drink beers.*

Ives (*singing loudly*)   'I wish I was in London or some other seaport town I'll set myself on a steam boat and I'll sail the ocean round,'

Ray (*simultaneously*)   De da de da de da . . .

Ives   'While sailing round the ocean while sailing round the sea I'd dream of handsome Molly wherever she might be,'

Ray   Join in Pete – 'Wherever she might be,'

Ives   'Her hair's as black as raven her eyes as black as coal her teeth are like the lilies,'

Ray (*simultaneously*)   Da da de da . . .

Ives   'That in the morning glow!'

Pete   I don't think I can take much more of this.

Ives   'And now you've gone and left me go on with who you please,'

Pete   Enough!

Ives   'My poor heart is aching . . .'

Ray   Ives, schtum.

Pause.

Pete   So . . . Ives, you were at Epsom with Ray?

Ives   Ah, yes, he's a good boy, lovely fella.

Pete   And . . . how long have you been back in London?

Ray   He got out just after me.

Ives   Escaped.

Ray   Escaped just after me.

Pete   And you're living round here?

Ives   That's right. Underneath the arches. (*Singing loudly.*) 'Underneath the arches . . .'

Ray   Under the bridge. The flyover, isn't that right, Ives?

Ives   I, I, I, I, I, I'm not from round here no. I come from far away. A distant and very beautiful planet, the Planet Vega as a matter of fact.

Pete   I see.

Pause.

So . . . where is this Planet Vega, then?

Ives   Don't patronise me. Do you think it's funny?

Pete   No.

Ives (*to* **Ray**)   Does he?

Ray   I don't think so.

Ives   Do you?

Ray   Of course not.

Ives   It's not my fault. They came and got me, I didn't go to them. They took me away, took me to their leader. He told me all about you. Described you perfectly. (*To* **Pete**.) Especially you.

Pete   Really?

Ives   I was in the gasworks before that. Sixteen years in the gasworks and the whole fucking lot goes sky high. Explosion. I was there, I saw the missiles go up. High into the sky they went and on the ground a great flaming fireball. No safety precautions on account of the fact they wanted it to happen, you understand? They sent the missiles up as a signal. Why? To let them know I was ready. Why? Because they wanted to get rid of me.

Pause.

Pete   Why would they want to get rid of you?

Ives   To save on early retirement. One month off early retirement I was. One month. Now look at me. There's not enough room any more. They want us all to go away!

Pete   I'm sure they don't.

Ives   What would you know about it? Look at you with your little baby-arsed face scrubbed clean and beautiful.

Pete   Ray –

Ives   I shall tell you what I think about the monied classes. They are the progenitors of beauty. The rich copulate with the beautiful and they breed. They breed more rich and beautiful. I do not like to be told that beauty is within because beauty is a commodity. I do not like to hear people say money is no obstacle because money is the obstacle. I don't need to be told as long as you have your health because you buy your health and so it is a question of as long as you can afford it. I'm not stupid. I can think. I can see the people that pass me by.

Pause.

Pete   Can I have a quiet word, Ray?

Ives   Hey you yes you! I'm talking to you.

Pete *and* **Ray** *get up and move a short distance away.* **Ives** *stands on his chair.*

Ives   THERE IS NO REVOLUTION! THERE NEVER WILL BE BECAUSE YOU ARE NOT THE REVOLUTIONARY TYPE!

Pete   Get him out of here.

Ives   NEVER IN THIS COUNTRY WILL THERE BE ANYTHING THAT SMACKS OF JUSTICE!

Pete   Enough is enough. This is my home.

Ray   Where's he gonna go?

Pete   Take him to a hostel or something. The Novotel – anywhere.

Pete pulls out a wad of notes from his pocket and hands Ray a couple.

Ives   You can't buy me.

Ray   It's not that easy, Pete.

Ives   You could make me an offer but I wouldn't think about it.

Pete   It is that easy. I want him out and I want you to deal with it. It's not too complicated even for you.

Ray   I said he could stay over. Stop here/for a while.

Pete   What?!

Beat. They look at each other. Ives climbs down.

Ives (*to* **Pete**)   I remember you.

Pete   Oh, Jesus . . .

Ives   You and this area and everybody here from when I was small . . .

Pete (*simultaneously, ignoring* **Ives**)   Are you insane? What are you trying to do to me?

Ives   My old mum she used to take us to the Bishop's Park as it was known then/when it was sunny . . .

Pete   I can't do it! I can't help! OK? Don't you understand?

Ives   The golden mile we trekked to the Bishop's Park where they had a lagoon with a little fake island/in the middle like a pot plant . . .

Ray   You'll get used to it, Pete.

Pete   It's blowing my circuits! He stinks, Ray. He won't shut up. It's like being in a . . . fuckin' lunatic asylum!

Silence. Ives stands, drains his beer, pats his pockets, gathers up two more empty cans, shakes them and moves to the door.

Ives   . . . I'm sorry.

Ray   Wait, Ives . . .

Ives exits. Pete sighs and sits at the table. Pause.

Pete   You know, Ray . . . if you wanna piss your life away then fine but don't piss mine away too. You . . . see what I'm saying?

Pause. **Ray** *sits at the table.* **Pete** *picks up a can from the table, crushes it and throws it back.*

Pete   This is just what dad used to do.

Ray   Is it now.

Pete   That's how he pissed his caff away, pissed it all away drinking.

Ray   He was a drunk. That's what drunks do.

Pete   You never went through with him what I went through. Is that how you wanna end up? Is it?

Pause. **Pete** *pulls out the phial of pills from his pocket and plonks them on the table.* **Ray** *grabs them.*

Ray   I been looking for those everywhere.

Pete   Do I have to stand over you morning and night every night for the rest of your life? (*Beat.*) For the rest of your life, Ray.

Ray *shrugs.*

Pete   And . . . for the rest of my life. I mean how weird are things gonna get? You been out two weeks and you haven't done any of the things you're supposed to do. I'm keeping my end of the deal what about yours?

Ray   Don't talk to me about deals – I'm not doing any more deals.

Pete   You want me to force you, is that it?

Ray   How you gonna force me?

Pete   I don't know, Ray. I'm sure I'll think of something.

Ray   Drugs are bad for you, Pete. Everybody knows that.

Pete   Not these ones! Jesus.

Ray   They lead to worser things.

Pete   Oh, like what? Like . . . him? Do you wanna end up under a bridge as well?

Ray   I'm weaning myself off 'em.

Pete   What?

Ray   Going for a more natural approach. I need a whatisit . . . stable environment. Need to be around people I know and can trust and all that.

Pete   But you never are around, Ray, I never know where you are! Where do you go? Where have you . . . Where have you been?

Ray   With Laura. I told you.

Pete   Oh, don't start that again.

Ray   'Don't start'? Don't start what again?

Beat.

You still don't believe me, do you?

Beat.

I'm tired of living here.

Pete   Why?

Ray   You got noisy neighbours. Every damn night I hear them revving up their fancy cars and popping champagne corks. What's the matter, Pete, you grown out of the Bush? You in a different bracket now so you don't notice things any more?

Pete   What am I supposed to notice?

Ray   These . . . *arseholes*. I've seen them trotting about in their tennis outfits with their dolly birds with the sunbed tans. I've seen them go where the sunbeds are and come back orange. They're probably all your customers. It's disgusting. What I need is a gun, a Sten gun, that'd put a few holes in their party frocks.

Pause.

Pete   Jesus, Ray, they're only –

Ray   Fuckers.

Pete   They're my neighbours.

Ray   It's doing my head in.

Pete   They're just people.

Pete   People do my head in.

Pause.

Pete   You mean . . . 'doing your head in' or actually doing your head in?

Ray   I mean it gets on my tits.

Pete   Well, Ray, you don't have to live here. You don't have to do any of this. Nor do I. I mean . . . (*Beat.*) Maybe you could get your own place. Bedsit or something. That's the idea, isn't it? Get you on your own two feet. (*Beat.*) I mean they can't expect you to stay here forever. Can they?

Ray   I'm going to Laura's.

Pete   Are you now.

Ray   Yeh.

Pete   Oh well, Jesus, why the hell not – you been going out with her for a whole two weeks. Good idea.

Beat.

You're serious, aren't you? There really is a Laura?

Ray   Yeh.

Pete   And that's where you been staying?

Ray   What's wrong with that?

Pete (*beat*)   OK, well then, maybe we should do something. (*Beat.*) Talk to them about it. (*Beat.*) We'll go in there and tell 'em there's a change in plan. Fuck their plan, it isn't working, there's a new one. Why not?

Ray   I already have.

Pete   What?

Ray   She said it's a good idea too.

Pete (*laughs*)   Just like that. Just like that she said, 'Go ahead, shack up with this bird enjoy yourself.'

Ray   That's right, more or less exactly what she said.

Pete   You actually went to see her?

Ray   Yeh, she had a . . . mole on her lip.

Pete (*sotto voce*)   I don't believe it . . .

Pause.

Ray   It's going to be all right, Pete.

Pete   Come on, Ray, this is stupid. It's stupid!

Ray   Don't worry about it.

Pete   I can't help worrying about it.

Ray   You have a business to run.

Pete   I know, yes I know that –

Ray   And there's nothing you can do anyway.

They look at each other.

Scene Two

Laura's *flat. Morning. The telephone is ringing.* **Ray** *and* **Laura** *are sitting up in bed.* **Ray** *is smoking a cigarette. After a while he leans over, picks up the receiver and hangs it up. Pause.* **Laura** *takes* **Ray**'s *hand and places it on her belly.*

Laura   Feel.

She plonks **Ray**'s *hand on her belly.*

He'll be wanting to come out soon enough. He'll be walking about and talking and expecting to learn things. What am I going to teach him?

Pause.

Ray   I never thought of it like that.

Laura   I dreamt that I'd already had it. It was tiny. About the size of my thumb and it was blue. Blue and white and red and made of plastic. With . . . some kind of light on it and the light said whether it was still alive. I carried it round on the bus with me waiting to tell somebody but I was too afraid. I worked out that the light meant how warm it was and I was afraid I didn't have enough warmth. I went into a pub and had a drink and when I came out . . . the light had gone out. And it was dead. I felt so ashamed.

Pause.

Ray   Which pub?

Laura   Ray!

Ray   What?

She hits him with a pillow.

Laura   You're supposed to listen to me!

Ray (*laughing*)   Am I?

Laura   Yes! Look at you – far away in your own little world, dreaming your dreams.

Ray   I know, I –

Laura   The lights are on but there's nobody within miles!

Ray (*delighted laughter*)   That's right. Not even, not even squatters.

Laura   I'm serious.

Ray   Me too. Because . . . you are more screwy than me. Sometimes. You are. You're off your head. You've flipped your lid. You've popped your hatch . . .

She hits him with the pillow.

Laura   Shut up.

Ray   You've popped your cork, you're off your stick, you've lost your conkers, marbles . . .

She hits him with the pillow.

Laura   Shut up, you fool!

Ray (*laughing*)   You've burnt the soup. You've shredded the screw. You've lost the soap. You, you . . .

Laura   Come here.

He puckers his lips and moves his face closer. **Laura** *smacks him in the face.*

Ray (*delighted*)   Beautiful. Do it again.

She grabs him by the ears, makes to kiss him and blows a raspberry into his lips.

I like it. I really do, Laura. It blows me away.

Pause.

I just . . . I just want to put my body against your body. That's all I want. I like your body. I like the curves. I like the bumps and the . . . mounds. And what's inside. Whatever it is that . . . powers you, Laura, I like it. So warm. So warm.

Laura   Are you trying to tell me something?

Ray   I just did.

They look at each other. The phone rings.

Ray   Don't answer it. (*Beat.*) You don't like answering the phone, do you? Why not?

Ray *picks up the phone.* **Laura** *snatches it.*

Laura   Hello . . . hello?

Pause.

No thanks.

Pause.

Because I don't want to that's why. No . . . Because I don't. And I don't want to go to the pub . . . I don't want to play pool . . . I don't want to play darts either.

Pause.

No!

Ray   Hang up.

Laura   Don't you call me that.

Ray   Hang up the phone.

Laura   What? That's not a man's voice, I just coughed . . . So when I cough I sound like a man.

Ray *grabs at the phone.* **Laura** *hangs on and speaks into the phone.*

Laura   Bastard.

She slams the phone down. Pause.

He wants me to meet him. (*Beat.*) He says I have to meet him. (*Beat.*) He says if I don't meet him he's gonna break my legs.

Ray   What're you gonna do?

Laura   What do you think?

Pause. **Laura** *gets out of bed and pulls on jeans and a jumper.* **Ray** *gets up and searches for his clothes.*

Ray   He'll break your legs anyway. It doesn't make any difference to him. He's a/psychopath.

Laura   If I don't go and he comes round here he'll break your legs too!

Ray (*beat*)   You think so?

Laura   I know so.

He hesitates, then pulls on a pair of pants and pulls a jumper over his head and hops about with the pants half up and the jumper half on.

Ray   You need looking after. He needs dealing with. That's where I come into it.

Laura   Ray, no.

Ray   What if something happens?

Laura *goes to the bed, pulls from under the pillow a hammer. She picks up her bag, puts the hammer in the bag.*

Laura   Nothing is going to happen.

Ray   What the fuck's that?

Laura   What? This 'hammer'?

Ray   Yeh.

Laura   It's a hammer.

Ray   You sleep with a hammer?

Laura   I lost my baseball bat.

Ray   I don't think that's wise, Laura. Nine times out of ten if you pull a hammer on somebody they'll use it on you. (*Beat.*) What if he tries to make friends with you or something? Tries to . . . worm his way back into your affections.

Laura   Then it'd be a miracle.

They look at each other. **Laura** *exits.*

Scene Three

The river. **Dave** *and* **Laura** *sit on a bench by the water.* **Dave** *is wearing his suit, which is a little shabbier now, top button undone etc. He drinks from a bottle in a brown paper bag and is drunk.*

Dave   I looked at myself in the mirror and I said to myself, I said, 'I am a man. A man who can look after his self but not a happy man. Not a complete man.' And then I asked myself, 'What is a man without a woman? What is he.' No job, no money, no faith will ever lead him to anything by his self. But with a woman . . .

Laura   Isn't the sight of the empty bridge the most beautiful thing you ever seen?

Pause. **Dave** *drinks.*

Dave   I was a miserable man, Laura. I saw the darkness stare me in the face. Sometimes I'd come over cloudy. All strangely cloudy and I'd ask myself, 'Why?' Why is the question. And then I'd put it to myself *hypothetically* what would we have done if we were married? And . . . and then I tell myself, 'We would've worked at it.'

Laura   But we weren't married.

Dave   Yes, but what if we were? And we did this to ourselves what we're doing now? Divorce? (*Singing vaguely.*) D.I.V.O.R.C.E. King Henry the Eighth – he was not a happy man. Why? Because he didn't work at it. And why? Because . . . he had no son.

Laura   But we *weren't married.*

Dave   And why that? Because . . . because . . . I don't know why. I'm no philosopher, Laura, but thinking aside, you light my wick. Eh? You do it for me.

Long pause. He looks at her.

I don't want to be with another woman in the whole of Shepherd's Bush. I love you, Laura.

Laura   But that's what you say every time.

Dave   I mean it this time.

Laura   That's what you say every time too.

Dave   And I mean it every time.

Laura   Well, maybe you don't mean it enough.

Pause.

Dave   You know you say no to me, Laura, you say no to me every time but I know and you know, you mean *Yes.*

Laura .   I have to go.

She makes a move to go, he puts a hand on her shoulder.

Dave   I'm trying to say I'm sorry.

Laura   You can't say you're sorry. There are things you can't apologise for, Dave. There are things you must not do and if you do 'em . . . then you can't apologise.

Dave   I never meant to hurt you.

Laura   Why did you?

Dave   I was under pressure . . .

Laura   *I* was under pressure!

Dave   There's a . . . force inside of me and I can't control it. I don't know what it is.

Laura   Thirteen pints of Guinness is most of it.

Dave   I'd do anything for you, Laura. I'd go on my knees for you. I'd do a ten stretch in the Scrubs, knock off Willy Hill's, blow up the Houses of fuckin' Parliament. I'm serious.

Pause.

I want to be a daddy.

Silence.

I said –

Laura   I heard.

Dave   But you –

Laura   I heard and I don't –

Dave   Can't comprehend.

Laura   No, I –

Dave   You're a bit surprised.

Laura   No, Dave –

Dave   You –

Laura   I don't believe my fuckin' ears is all.

Pause.

Dave   Think about it, Laura, eh? Will you do that?

Laura   He'll be born from the bottle but he won't be brought up by it.

Dave   I'll stop tomorrow.

Laura   You can't stop tomorrow.

Dave   I'm trying to do what's right.

Laura   You don't know what's right.

Dave   And bringing a helpless kiddie into the world to live off slops and benefits is?

Laura   We'll survive.

Dave   What are you going to tell him when he wants his da'? When he wants a father's hand to hold in the night?

Laura   It's not about that.

Dave   It's about blood, Laura. Our blood and his blood. You know that's all that matters.

He produces a ring from his pocket, holds it up.

I found this. You didn't lose it, Laura . . . I did.

Pause. **Laura** *regards him. He holds it out to her insistently but she refuses to touch it.*

Laura   You mean you lied.

Dave   We could be a real family, Laura.

Laura   Just leave me alone. I curse the day I met you.

Laura *gets up and walks away.*

Dave   And the day I met you was the day the Angel of Joy came down from the heavens, so it was.

Dave *drinks.*

Scene Four

Pete's *flat.* **Pete, Ray** *and* **Laura** *are at the table, the remains of lunch, a few cans and a couple of bottles of wine spread in front of* **Ray**.

Ray   Just lying around. Sleeping, eating, shopping. All the simple/things.

Laura   Shopping? Don't talk to me about shopping. I've never seen anybody so afraid of a supermarket in my/life.

Ray   Drinking, shagging –

Laura   He's allergic to it, I think.

Ray   It's not the supermarket, Laura, it's the people. All those people bickering over which brand to buy, whether to buy meat or fish, is it cheaper in the market?

Laura   Everybody has to eat – tell him he has to eat, Pete.

Pete   You have to eat, Ray.

Ray   Haven't they got anything better to do except drag their fat arses around with their fat husbands and their screeching kids? If I was a mother I'd leave 'em there – let 'em gorge themselves to death on fucking Mars Bars.

Laura   He's banned shopping entirely.

Ray   There's a lot of things I've banned entirely.

Laura   Won't be seen dead on a bus.

Ray   I hate buses. People on buses are fools.

Laura   Tubes . . .

Ray   Why there's not more homicides on the tube I can't understand.

Laura   Completely anti-social. I thought/I was.

Ray   I just mind my own business, Laura.

Laura   You do not mind your own business. You don't.

Ray   I need a drink.

Ray *reaches for a bottle and refills his glass. Drinks.*

Pete   I think you've had enough.

Ray   Enough? No, that's just where you're wrong, Pete old boy – I haven't had nearly enough.

Pete   Come on, Ray. You've had your fun.

Pete *pulls the phial of pills from his pocket. Puts it on the table.* **Ray** *looks at it. Pause.*

Ray   I haven't even started yet.

Pete   I won't take no for an answer.

Ray   That's the only reason you invited me, isn't it? You didn't want to meet her at all. You just got me round here to take me fuckin' dose.

Pete   Now don't make a scene.

Ray   'Don't make a' . . . a what? Listen to his Lordship. I am sorry, Peter old fruit –

Pete   Ray, come on.

Ray   For getting in . . . for getting on your nerves and ruining your special . . . lunch time thingie. (*He laughs.*)

Pause.

Laura   What are they?

Ray   I have heart trouble.

Pete   They're just pills he's taking.

Laura   What're they for?

Pete   They're just –

Ray   They're to stop me getting upset when my big fucking/ bastard brother –

Pete   Didn't he –

Ray   Get's on my big . . . fucking . . . on my tits that's what they're for.

Pause.

Pete   Didn't you . . . tell her about . . .

Ray   About what, Pete?

Pete   About . . .

Ray   Oh, about '. . .'

Pete   Yeh.

Ray   No.

Pause.

Pete   Ray has to take this medication this special medication because sometimes he gets depressed.

Ray   I get depressed.

Pete   Doesn't sleep too well sometimes.

Ray   Can't sleep that's true.

Pete   Sometimes he *only* sleeps.

Ray   I do stupid things.

Pete   Yes he, stupid things, he –

Ray   I –

Pete   He –

Ray   I mean really stupid. Schizo.

Pete   Yeh he . . . schizo. (*Beat.*) That's what he does.

Pause.

Laura   Oh.

Ray   I mean I don't eat babies or anything like that.

Pete   No no no no no. No, he doesn't do that.

Silence.

(*To* **Laura**.) So when's it due?

Laura   What?

Pete   The . . .

Laura   Oh, the . . . December. Yeh December.

Pete   December.

Laura   December, yes.

Pete   Just in time for Christmas.

Ray   Now we're talking about babies.

Pete   Is it kicking yet?

Laura   No –

Ray   Now we're – if he kicks you –

Pete   Ray, that's/enough.

Ray   Kick him back. Give yourself a . . . do it yourself abortion. Save yourself the agony.

Pause.

Pete   Oh, Jesus.

Ray   I mean it. You should see the father.

Laura   I beg your pardon?

Ray   Christ knows what's gonna hatch.

Laura *smacks him in the face and stands.*

Pete   No, Laura, please.

Laura   That's the most horrible thing you could say to me. That's the most . . . that . . .

Ray   What?

Pete   Jesus, Ray, can't you –

Laura   Don't you get it? Don't you understand anything? I want this baby, Ray. I want it. I'm worried about it and I know I probably can't look after it properly but I want it. More than, more than anything . . .

She sits down. Pause.

Ray   I don't know why.

Pete   Ray –

Laura   Because it would be mine . . . mine forever and it wouldn't hurt me and it wouldn't upset me and it would love me and it would trust me and I would . . . I would trust . . . it . . .

Ray   But babies are horrible, Laura. They stink and cry and piss and poo everywhere. Everybody knows that.

Pete   Ray, for Christsake!

Laura *gets up and starts clearing plates.*

Pete   It's all right I'll do that.

Laura *ignores him.*

Pete   Talk sense, Ray, if you can.

Ray   I'm trying, Pete, I'm honestly trying to.

Pete   Shh . . . just don't say another word. You push people too far.

Laura   It's all right, Pete, I'm sorry.

Ray   No, Pete, no I don't because you push me too far. You two . . . you don't even know each other. What the fuck do you care about each other? You pretend that's all . . . you pretend to care that she . . . you pretend to have this concern that I . . . you're just . . . You know what you are? You're . . . selfish. And . . . responsible. Incredibly responsible.

Pause. To **Laura**.

Not you, him.

Laura   I think we should be going.

Ray   I'm going to piss.

Ray *gets up,* **Laura** *stops him.*

Laura   Come now if you're coming. You can piss at my place. (*To* **Pete**.) Thanks for the –

Pete   Any time –

Ray   Why would I wanna piss at your place? Sit around at your place waiting for Joe Bugner to come home and –

Laura   That's enough!

Ray   Give us both another beating?

Laura   I'll give you a beating if you/don't –

Ray   Cos that's what's gonna happen. Oh yes, I can tell, he's gonna come around and he's gonna kill us both dead in our bed. And then I am going to kill him and then they'll put me away for good. They'll never let me go cos I'll be in Broadmoor or something with Jack The Fucking Yorkshire Ripper do you want that do you think that's reasonable? Eh? Well, do you?

Laura *just looks at him, can't speak. She grabs her bag and exits. Long pause.*

Ray   She's got a hammer in that bag. She has. She's more barmy than me.

Pete   Are you gonna tell me what that was about?

Ray   No.

Pause.

Pete   Why did you do that? Why do you have to . . . (*He breaks off. Pause.*)

Ray   I'm drunk, Pete.

Pete   Well, why do you have to drink like that?

Ray   I get depressed.

Pete   But, Ray, you drink when you're depressed, you drink when you're happy, when you're bored, it doesn't help.

Ray   It does.

Pete   She's having a baby, man. There's some fella out there who's having a baby *with* her. I mean a married woman's one thing but up the spout's a whole new kettle of fish, Ray.

Ray   She's not married.

Pete   Does she want to be?

Ray   She just –

Pete   How well do you know her? How well does she know you? Have you even considered –

Ray   No I haven't considered.

Pete   The implications? (*Beat.*) I mean I'm coming to the end of my rope here. I'm right at the end. This is just . . . you're just . . . this is just hanging on a hair here. I can't fucking do it any more.

Ray (*beat*)   Well, that's life, isn't it?

Pete   I mean . . . 'Selfish'? 'Responsible'?

Pause.

Maybe you're right. Maybe that's where I've gone wrong . . .
Maybe my wife left me because I was this selfish cunt who wore
a pinny and tossed salads all day for other people. Maybe I
should never have tried to save dad or his greasy old caff or his
doomed fuckin' life cos that would have just been responsible, I
dunno . . .

Ray You bought him out, Pete. It was the one thing he loved
and you took it off of him for a handful of notes.

Pete Jesus, Ray – I just . . . had this weird idea that the thing
to do was to go to work and do an honest day and pay a few bills
and look after your family and . . . I mean . . . he couldn't do it.
I mean sooner or later somebody's gotta . . . make a stand. I
don't see what's wrong with that.

Pause.

Ray Well, it's a bit boring, innit, Pete . . .

Pete You're not the only one going out of your mind. You
know I'd jack this in tomorrow if I had half a chance. Get on the
old rock'n'roll and piss off to the seaside with some little bird I
met in the pub . . . I'd love to.

Ray Why don't you?

Pete Because I am obliged, Ray . . . to do this thing for you.
It is what I have to do. You understand? The measure of a man
(no, listen to me) in this life is whether he can do . . . what he
thinks he has to do.

Pause.

I mean . . . why do you say these things to people?

Ray I don't know.

Pete Is it you or is it the . . . sooner or later you're gonna have
to make up your mind. (*Beat.*) Tell me. (*Beat.*) Please.

Ray (*suddenly laughing*)   You're breaking my heart.

Pete *What?*

Ray Who fucking cares?

Ray *continues to laugh and swigs on a bottle.*

Pete   Get out.

Ray   What?

Pete   It's none of my business. It isn't and I cannot make it my business no matter who says I should. I have my own business.

Ray *gets up and starts to go.*

Pete   I mean it I've had enough. You just –

Ray   OK.

Pete   Get.

Ray *exits.*

Scene Five

Wasteland. **Ives** *stands alone.* **Ray** *is huddled under old blankets, paper and his coat at the foot of a nearby wall.*

Ives   There will be a zone for the lost and the loveless and the Godless and the demented and the dead and the half dead and the damned and all of those who no longer live in the light, who only live in the dark. And that zone will be a terrifying place, and that zone will be the only place, and that zone will be all around you. You will not be able to walk in the streets that you walked in tonight. You will not be able to go where you are going without seeing the zone, or some small part of it, or one of the beasts that live in the zone, or the beast that made the zone. Believe me. There is nowhere. Nowhere you can go to hide from it. Nothing you can do to eradicate it. You will never be able to clean it. You will never sweep it under the rug. The city will become that zone. You will all be of that zone. The zone that is the turd that you can never polish. You are all flies. Flies on the fleck of shit that is this world.

Ray   Ives . . .

Ives   Your world. The new world. Your new home. It will be built by contractors and its management put out to tender.

There will be no crèche, no fire escape, no stairs and it will stink of piss and disease just like every other place before it.

Ray   I'm trying to sleep.

Ives   Don't deny it. You can't argue with me. You can't tell me, you don't believe me, when I tell you, that you are going to burn in hell. I am going to burn in hell, the blossoms on the trees are going to burn in hell.

Ray   Have you made any money yet?

Ives   I know what I am talking about. I am the authority on this kind of thing. I am the only authority you want to listen to and if you don't believe me you can jam it up your arses and whistle because I have had enough. I am disgusted with you, with me, with everything and I am tired of telling you.

Ray *gets to his feet and puts his hands over his ears.*

Ray   Shut up, I'm not listening.

Ives   I am disgusted with the sky. With the water. The trees bore the daylights out of me . . .

Ray   No, stop!

Ives *staggers and collapses.*

Ives   I know you don't like it. I don't like it. But I told you this would happen. I warned you. I'm trying to be reasonable about it . . .

Silence.

Ray   Ives . . . Ives old boy. Don't die on me now.

Ives   Nightmares . . . nightmares happen . . .

Ray   Come on, Ives . . . we'll go somewhere warm. I'll take you to a launderette.

Ives   I brought home the bacon once . . . I did . . . to my wife.

Pause.

From the Isle of Skye, she was.

He's dead. **Ray** *just stares at him, unable to shift his gaze. He looks around suddenly, distracted by a noise.*

Ray   What d'you mean?

Pause.

What's wrong with the launderette? He was cold.

Pause.

No, because there's nothing wrong with me.

Ray *stares straight ahead, listening.*

Scene Six

Laura's *bedsit. Early morning.* **Laura**, *dressed in leggings and a sweater, is sitting on the end of the bed, staring into space. There is a knock at the door.* **Laura** *doesn't move. Another knock and she goes to it.*

Laura   Who is it?

Ray (*offstage*)   It's me.

Laura *hesitates then goes to the door, thinks better of it and backs up, nervous.*

Ray   Laura?

Pause. Another knock.

Are you all right?

Laura   What do you want?

Ray   I want to come in.

Laura   It's seven o'clock in the morning.

Ray   I have to talk to you. I have something to tell you.

Laura   What is it, Ray?

Ray   Let me in and I'll tell you.

She opens the door a crack.

I missed you.

Laura   Ray, you have to go.

Ray   Did you miss me?

Laura   Not really, no.

Ray   I was worried about you.

Laura   Were you now.

Ray   Yes. I can't stop thinking about you. I keep thinking about when we were in the field in the countryside. The grass was like hay and the yellow sun shone and shone . . . we were making hay while the sun shone, weren't we, Laura?

Laura   Yeh, that's right —

He brushes past into the room.

Ray   We were making hay while the sun shone, weren't we?

Laura   What do you want?

Ray   But it was more than that, wasn't it?

Laura   Ray, I'm begging you —

Ray   It was more than that.

Laura   I'm not well.

Ray   What's wrong with you? Are you sick?

Laura   I'm just tired.

Ray   How sick?

Laura   It's too late.

Ray   You looked so beautiful . . .

Laura   Keep away.

Ray   We kissed and you smelt of blossom.

Dave *enters in trousers but no shirt, a towel slung over his shoulder. Stands at the door unseen by* **Ray**.

Ray   You understand me, Laura.

Laura   No I don't! Shut up!

Ray   Yes you do and I understand you and there is nothing else. There is nothing else is there Laura? Nothing that matters . . . I know I'm in trouble now. I can tell things are going wrong – but I just . . . I, I, I, I love you, Laura.

Dave *laughs.* **Ray** *glances over his shoulder and sees* **Dave**. *Turns around to face him. Pause.*

Dave (*mimicking*)   'I, I, l-l-love you Laura.' (*Beat.*) You gonna introduce us?

Pause.

Laura (*to* **Ray**)   I'll be seeing you.

Dave   Fine way to speak to a lady. Is everything all right then, Laura?

Laura   It's fine.

Dave   Who's yer man then?

Laura   Nobody.

Dave   I'll tell you what, he looks familiar.

Laura   He's going.

Dave *scrutinises* **Ray**.

Dave   Maybe it's the pub. You drink in the Adelaide there? I seen a few fellows like you in the Adelaide. Queer fellows. D'you think that's where our paths crossed? Doesn't say much, does he?

Laura   Ray . . .

Dave   He's got a name then. Nice name. Are you gonna tell me what's going on?

Laura   He's going, Dave.

Dave   Are you gonna tell me what's going on or not?

Ray   Leave, leave her alone please.

Dave (*mimicking*)   'L-leave her alone please. L-leave her a-l-one p-please.' (*Laughs.*) He can talk then yer man? Not very well but it's a start.

Laura   Ray, go.

Ray   What . . . what have you done?

Laura   Nothing, just –

Ray   What have you done!

Laura   I don't know I can't tell you!

Ray just stares at her then tries to leave, **Dave** *bars his way.*

Dave   No no no no no no no. No no no no no no no. Oh no. I don't think you should do that. I mean you can if you want – if you're the type of man who does something just because his lady friend gets her keks in a twist –

Laura   Don't start, Dave.

Ray   Get, get out my way please.

Dave   I beg your pardon?

Ray   Get out my way thank you. Please I would like you to get out my –

Dave   *SHE* LOVES *ME* – YOU UNDERSTAND? SHE. LOVES ME.

Laura   I don't, I don't!

Dave   Cunt. Shut up!

Laura   Please!

Dave   ON YOUR KNEES! (*To* **Ray**.) What are you looking at?

He grabs **Ray** *by the shirt, backs him up a few paces very fast against the bed and flings him across it,* **Ray** *lands on the floor beside the bed.*

Dave (*to* **Laura**)   Knees!

Laura, *panicked, gets on her knees.*

Dave (*to* **Ray**)   Watch.

Laura   No . . . no . . . no . . .

Dave undoes his belt, gets behind **Laura** *and ties her hands behind her back.* **Ray** *watches horrified. He wrestles with the belt, pushes* **Laura***'s head down roughly,* **Laura** *struggles.*

Dave   Why him, Laura? Eh?

Laura (*struggling*)   Why not him?

Dave *pulls* **Laura***'s leggings down, tying up her legs.*

Dave   Cos he's a fucking eejit that's why. I've seen him, mincing about like a fairy with his brother, talking to his self, I've seen him, everybody has. Mad as a fucking whippet. (*To* **Ray***.*) I know you. I know who you are. Did you think I didn't recognise you?

Laura   Please –

Dave   I warned you. Did I not say I'd kill you?

Laura *struggles and they move a semicircle. He pulls the belt tight with several jerks. Concentrating, his back to* **Ray***.* **Ray** *reaches under the pillow, withdraws the hammer, walks over to* **Dave** *and hits him twice with the hammer.* **Dave** *instantly collapses and* **Laura** *struggles out from under.*

Laura   No! Christ no!

Ray   Evil fucker. You're *evil*!

Ray *hovers,* **Laura** *wrestles the hammer away.*

Laura   Ray!

Ray   Burn in hell. Yes, you. *Hell.*

Pause. **Ray** *looks at* **Laura** *then runs out.* **Laura** *stands there in shock.*

Laura   Oh, Jesus . . . Jesus Mary and Joseph.

She catches her breath then kneels down beside **Dave***, tries to turn him over but can't. Suddenly he stirs, she jumps to her feet.*

I'll . . . call an ambulance.

Dave *struggles to get up,* **Laura** *picks up the hammer and fidgets with it watching* **Dave** *and dialling the telephone. He collapses again and tries to heave himself up.* **Laura** *drops the phone and watches* **Dave.**

Laura   Stay where you are, Dave . . . I'm warning you . . .

Scene Seven

Hospital. **Laura** *and* **Pete** *sit on chairs in casualty.* **Pete** *smokes a cigarette.*

Pete   I went in there. I went and saw this woman he's been seeing. Turns out he hasn't been seeing her – what am I talking about – I knew he hadn't been seeing her. They never even heard of him. I say, 'How come you never heard of him?' They say, 'Because he didn't fill out the form.' 'What are you talking about?' I say. 'I filled out the form.' 'No, you filled out *your* form,' they say. 'He's supposed to fill out his form and take it to a different building.' 'I filled out the fucking form,' I say. 'I did everything to the letter.' 'No,' they say, 'you filled out the form to say he filled out his form. If he didn't fill out his form then it's null and void.' (*Beat.*) Then they gave me more forms. Emergency forms or something. Review forms. They say it isn't too late for him to fill it in now, if he fills it in now and brings it back Monday they could help. If I can find him and be so good as to get a pen in his hand. What am I, a fucking magician? Where are these people who make the rules? Where are they hiding – can't they see what's happening? (*Beat.*) The man's lying in there with his brain stoved in. What are we gonna say? He . . . beat himself to death? Just for the hell of it? He could've died . . . We should tell somebody. Maybe we could explain.

Laura   Explaining never got anyone anywhere. We'll explain he fell out of bed.

Pete   Laura –

Laura   And down a flight of stairs. You'd be surprised what can happen to a person falling out of bed.

Pete   He'll tell them!

Laura He's a fucking vegetable – how's he going to tell 'em?

Pete If he comes round –

Laura He won't.

Pause.

Pete How do you know? He got a few whacks in the head a cracked skull they'll do this emergency operation and bob's your uncle.

Laura He got more than a few.

Pete What d'you mean?

Pause.

Laura He was trying to get up.

Pete When?

Laura Later, later he tried to get up so I . . . gave him a couple more is all. Just a tap. Here and there.

Pause.

Pete What are you telling me, Laura?

Laura I –

Pete That between the two of you you just hammered this man half to death? That you and him just took it in turns . . . hammering your boyfriend to . . .

Laura He just tried to kill me. What's he gonna tell them?

Pete I feel sick.

Laura Don't be such a baby.

Pete No I do, I really . . . I'm surrounded by maniacs.

Long pause.

I should go and . . .

Laura Yes you go and . . .

Pete If I know Ray he's probably in the pub. What d'you think? That wouldn't surprise me.

Laura   He won't be in the pub.

Pete   How do you know?

Laura   Face it, Pete!

Pause. **Pete** *gets up.*

Pete   Will you be all right . . . I mean . . . on your own?

Pause.

Laura   I want to be on my own.

Pete *exits. Lights down slowly on* **Laura**.

Scene Eight

Restaurant kitchen. **Ray** *is wearing* **Pete***'s whites and chef's hat. He holds a rusty old petrol can and walks in a circle around the kitchen, carefully pouring. He finishes and sets the can down. Pats his pockets.* **Pete** *appears at the door silently, looking haggard and wearing* **Ray***'s old long coat.* **Ray** *doesn't notice him for a moment and* **Pete** *hasn't yet noticed the petrol.*

Ray   You got a light?

Pete   What do you want a light for?

Ray   I got a few things here I want to set fire to.

Pete   What things?

Ray   Everything.

Pete *comes into the kitchen, sniffs with growing alarm, looks at* **Ray** *who produces a lighter and holds it up.* **Pete** *stops.*

Pete   JESUS WHAT ARE YOU DOING?

Ray   This is where it all happens, isn't it, Pete?

Pete   This . . . yes is where I work, Ray, you can't —

Ray   Yes and where dad worked before you and I worked with him.

Pete   That's right, Ray —

Ray   In this kitchen here.

Pete   Yes.

Ray   Which is in this restaurant.

Pete   Yes, my restaurant! Everything/I own.

Ray   Which is in this family.

Pete   Yes, it's in the family!

Ray   I don't like families.

Pete   Well, they're all different/aren't they?

Ray   I wasn't good enough at doing the dishes so they sent me away.

Pete   No, Ray –

Ray   And I got sick because I wasn't strong enough.

Pete   You were sick because you were sick/there's no –

Ray   And then dad killed mum.

Pete (*beat*)   *What?*

Ray   It's true. He left her and then she died.

Pete   It was breast cancer.

Ray   She died because she wasn't strong enough.

Pete   She was very ill, sometimes that happens . . .

Ray   Dad wasn't strong enough either, was he?

Pete (*desperate*)   I don't know what you're talking about!

Ray   None of us was strong enough.

Pete   Ray, please!

Ray   None of us! This fuckin' family . . . it's cursed . . . marked!

Pete   Give me the lighter!

Ray   Damned.

Ray catches his breath and hands **Pete** *the lighter, as* **Pete** *takes it* **Ray** *whips another from his pocket and holds it up.*

Pete   Jesus!

Ray   But you can cook, can't you, Pete?

Pete   Yes.

Ray   So let's cook! Uh?

He upends the petrol can over his head, **Pete** *covers his eyes in anguish.*

Pete   NO!

Ray   Cook everything and make it worthwhile! Make it something that people want.

Pete   . . . You can't . . .

Ray   And need.

Pete   Please, I'm . . . begging you.

Ray hands him the lighter quickly, **Pete** *takes it and* **Ray** *withdraws another from his pocket.*

Ray   You know what I think, Pete?

Pete   I have no idea.

Ray   I think I wasted my life. What are the chances of me getting a job in this gaff?

Pete   Well, Ray . . . this is a very small operation. I don't employ that many/people.

Ray   Yes but you could employ me! I'm your brother.

Pete   It doesn't work like that any more. It wouldn't help. What would help is me running this place/successfully.

Ray   It would help me, you cunt!

Pete   I am helping you this is how I'm helping you!

Ray tries to light the lighter. **Pete** *makes a lunge at* **Ray** *and* **Ray** *dodges.*

Pete   Christ, no, no!

Ray   I can't stand it, Pete! I just can't stand it any more!

Pete *keeps his distance as* **Ray** *attempts to ignite the lighter, it won't light.*

Pete   Leave it alone!

He grabs hold of **Ray***. They wrestle over the lighter and* **Pete** *gets it.*

STOP!

Ray   I can't stop – get off of me!

He breaks away, suddenly changing.

What?! Shut up! Shut . . . I'm not listening. Jesus, no!

Pete   You . . . you . . . talk to me for fuck's sake. Tell me what it is.

Ray *has his hands clamped over his ears and is watching* **Pete***. Silence. They catch their breath.*

Pete   It's the . . . it's the voices, isn't it?

Ray *trembling, finally nods.*

Pete   They've come back. (**Ray** *nods.*) What are they saying?

Ray   They say . . . all different things.

Pete   Like what?

Pause.

Come on, Ray, you can tell me.

Pause. **Ray** *produces another lighter from his pocket.*

Please . . .

Ray   They say to me that I should . . . go somewhere and . . .

Pete   Go somewhere. Go where?

Ray   Go everywhere . . .

Pete   Everywhere OK . . .

Ray   And and find . . . something although I don't know what it is.

Pete   Well, like what?

Pause. **Pete** *reaches out for the lighter slowly,* **Ray** *draws away slowly.*

Ray Find a way of stopping things happening.

Pete What things?

Ray Things like this obviously.

Pete And?

Ray Find a way of . . . living with . . . memory.

Pete Memory yes . . .

Ray Cos that's what triggers it I'm sure. Or else . . . signals from somewhere . . . possibly the saucepans and the metal objects transmit signals but I can't be sure.

Pete I doubt it.

Ray Yes, but if we set fire to everything then if there were any transmitters they'd be ruined wouldn't they?

Pete Let's just concentrate on the memories.

Ray OK . . .

Pete What memories?

Ray (*beat*) Like the time remember when we were kids . . . when things first started happening . . . and dad comes home and : . . it's hot, a hot summer and we're walking down Fulham Palace Road on the big wide pavement and we're talking and I turn to look at him . . . I just get a glimpse of him and . . . I just notice how filthy he is and unshaven and how he stinks and he wears . . . like an old blue safari suit . . . and there are little specs of blood round the collar where he cuts himself shaving . . . and his teeth, his eyes . . . his eyes are brown, all of it brown even the white bits are brown. And I think . . . I think . . . I'll be like that one day.

Pause.

(*Dazed. Listening.*) They scare the shit out of me. They say very fucking weird things I can tell you. Things even too weird for you to figure out, Pete. I try to get real people to talk to me so I can compare the difference but it's not easy.

Pause.

What do they say to you?

Pete   I don't get them, Ray.

Ray   Oh.

Silence.

Pete   But I know . . . I know dad had . . . a bit of difficulty with things. He had a sort of . . . faith . . . in things which ruined him.

Ray   I don't have any faith, Pete. (*Beat.*) Some people just don't.

Long pause. **Pete** *takes the lighter from* **Ray** *gently.*

What's going to happen to me?

Pete   Nothing.

Ray   Nothing? Ever?

Pete (*gently*)   What do you want to happen?

Ray   I don't want the injections.

Pete   Nobody's giving you injections.

Ray   My four-weekly injections. They'll give me them after four weeks, they're like that.

Pete *puts an arm round* **Ray** *to comfort him.*

Pete   Come on, it's OK.

Ray   I know it's OK but it doesn't seem OK and . . . have you got a fag?

Pete *shakes his head.*

Ray   I just thought I'd ask but I understand if you don't.

Pete *pats him on the shoulder, drapes a couple of dishcloths around him and carefully mops him dry as they speak.*

Ray   Because you don't smoke, do you, Pete?

Pete   Not normally no, no.

Ray   I got the lighters in King Street. I know that fellow who sells them, you know. I know that fellow. Six for a pound.

Pete   Bargain.

Ray   In Shepherd's Bush Market there's a fellow who sells real guns. Imagine that.

Pete   Real guns, really?

Ray   Yes for twelve pounds ninety-nine which is a bit steep.

Pete   For a real gun yes.

Ray   And monkeys. Real monkeys or at least very big bags of peanuts.

Pete   Well, that's wonderful.

Ray   Yes. Real monkeys.

Pete *takes his coat off and helps* **Ray** *into it.*

Scene Nine

A kitchen in a hostel. **Ray** *and* **Pete** *are cooking on a portable hot plate.* **Pete** *chops and stirs etc. while* **Ray** *looks on vaguely, sedated.*

Pete   I got it in the market. It's quite neat. It's compact, see, and it doesn't use much power so if you – if you do accidently set fire to anything you fling a blanket over it and the flames are contained. It's not much cop for fry-ups but if you want a plate of beans or a nice cup of warm milk to help you sleep it takes two minutes.

Ray   I thought gas was better.

Pete   It is better, but this is your own. Your own little cooker, you keep it in your room and you don't have to come out for anything.

Ray   They got gas here. I've seen it. Big – big hob.

Pete   Will they let you use it?

Ray   Dunno.

He considers it and makes a face.

You think of everything, Pete –

Pete   Yes I do.

Ray   You're a clever man.

Pete   You're a clever man too.

He stirs a pan on the hot plate.

Now. Onions.

Ray   Onions.

Pete   Always fry 'em in butter.

Ray   Yes.

Pete   Tastes better, gives it a better consistency. You come down and the pan's all dirty (cos all this stuff's dirty) and you use margarine it'll go black and thin. Butter stays thick.

Ray   Got it.

Pete   Especially for soup.

Ray   Soup, right.

Pete   They get the tinned soups in here every week but if you wanna make your own or you wanna make a sauce, a nice pasta dish, you use butter or oil and the fats from the thing. From what you're cooking. Have a whiff.

Ray *sniffs at the pan.*

Ray   Nice. What about eggs?

Pete   Fried eggs?

Ray   No, omelette.

Pete   In this instance yes we use butter.

Ray   Because it's better.

Pete   In this instance yes but just for an egg normally that can be expensive. (*Beat.*) Eggs aren't important. Eggs are eggs.

Ray   Everybody here likes fried eggs.

Pete   I don't often cook eggs. If I do, I don't fry 'em anyway. If I did, I wouldn't use butter. Just my preference.

Ray   Cos you're a businessman.

Pete   I'm a businessman, that's right.

Pause.

Ray   Laura used to use butter.

Pete   Laura's not a businessman.

Ray   No and she's not a business woman either. She just used to cook sometimes.

Pete   That's different. If you cook for a friend then you go that extra mile. If you ever have any friends over to this place I'll bring you some butter.

Ray   Thank you.

Pete   My pleasure.

He cooks.

Now. Always put your onions in long before any garlic. Garlic burns too quick and you can fuck it up.

Ray   Onions beforehand.

Pete   That's right.

Ray   Long long before.

Pete   That's right.

Ray   How long before?

Pete   Till they go translucent.

Ray   It's . . . an art, isn't it?

Pete   It's a very creative thing and it keeps your mind occupied. Feeding people is a serious business. Never use tinned tomatoes. Too watery and acidic. Use 'em fresh and always put 'em in last, very last so they don't disintegrate.

Ray   Disintegrate, yeh.

Pause.

Laura used to use tinned.

Pete   Well, it's not advisable.

Ray   It's cheaper. One time I saw them for twenty-three pee a tin. Tesco's.

Pete   Money isn't everything.

Ray   But twenty-three pee a tin, Pete . . .

Pete   What d'you wanna put in now?

Pause.

Ray   Did . . . did you speak to her then?

Pete   Yes I did. What do you want – mushroom?

Ray   Eggs.

Pete   We're not ready for eggs yet. Eggs come last.

Ray   Mushroom then.

Pete   Mushroom. Now we are talking.

Pete *puts the mushrooms in.*

Ray   What did she say? More mushrooms – what did she say?

Pete (*beat*)   Well . . . it's not really very good news, Ray.

Ray   Mm-hm.

Pete   She's had a lot to cope with.

Ray   Mm-hm.

Pete   She says she wants to try and . . . get herself together for a while. Get her life back together, for the kid maybe.

Ray   Can we put the eggs in now?

Pete   Not yet. (*Beat.*) She said she's actually quite happy on her own. She doesn't really want to . . . threaten that.

Ray *nods. Pause.*

Pete   She . . . she doesn't really want to see you again. For a while.

Pause.

Ray   Not till she's feeling better.

Pete   No.

Ray   And . . . and not till I'm feeling a bit better perhaps.

Pete   Not for a while.

Ray   Not for a long while no. How long?

Pete   She didn't say. I mean you can't really say, can you?

Pause.

Ray   Roughly.

Pete   She said she didn't know.

Ray   What, she didn't have any idea at all?

Pete   I think maybe she might try and go home or something.

Ray   She won't go home.

Pete   She said maybe she might write to you . . . in a few months.

Ray   How many months, six?

Pete   Six, maybe six, yes.

Ray   Six, OK. Six.

Pause.

Six months exactly or less?

Pete   It's just a guess, Ray. It could be less, could be a bit more . . . When she's had the kid maybe.

Ray   Right.

Pause.

Pete   I mean she's a nice girl Laura, but you . . . you gotta remember she's got her own life to lead. And she did before you came on the scene and before the other guy and she'll do what she can to keep that life on track. It's the way people are.

Ray   Because . . . we had a good time together. We understood each other.

Pete   I know but also you have your own life to lead too. You gotta think about yourself now. What you're gonna do with yourself.

Ray   I don't really want to think about that.

Pete   Well, it happens to the best of us. Sooner or later we're all on our own for a while. And then we're with someone again. And then we're alone again maybe. Swings and roundabouts.

Pause.

Ray   She's very very beautiful, Pete. Did you notice that? I don't think I've ever met anybody as beautiful as that. I mean . . . seriously, she's the type of girl you'd die for. People say they'd die for this person or for that person but I mean this time round I found out . . . what they meant. She's the type you could hold in your arms and gaze at without even . . . getting squeamish or anything. You could . . . you could say you loved her and have absolutely no regrets about it that's for sure. (*Beat.*) You'd love her all over, everything about her. Her face, her legs, her arms, her shoulders, her feet, her toes, breasts, hair, hands. (*Beat.*) Knees. Neck. Her laugh, she had a blindin' laugh, Pete, which was because of her eyes, she had very dark blue twinkling eyes. (*Beat.*) Her mouth. Her lips, lips like a duck's which – like this – which shows she's thoughtful, doesn't it, Pete?

Pete   Well . . . I'm sure she's thinking about you, Ray. I'm sure you'll never stop thinking about each other.

Ray   No.

Pete   No.

Long pause. **Pete** *picks up a clump of basil and sniffs it, then hands it to* **Ray** *who also sniffs it.*

When you chop the basil, always use more than you think you'll need. It grows on trees so use it like it grows on trees. Be generous with it. (*Beat.* **Ray** *nods.*) You have a go.

Ray *takes the knife and chops the basil carefully.* **Pete** *watches as he sprinkles it into the pan. Lights down slowly.*

Blackout.

Pale Horse

For Sarah Ward

'I looked, and behold a pale horse: and his name that sat on him was Death, and Hell followed with him.' (Revelation: 6,8)

Pale Horse was first performed at the Royal Court Theatre Upstairs, London, on 12 October 1995. The cast was as follows:

Charles	Ray Winstone
Lucy	Kacey Ainsworth
Undertaker	Terence Beesley
Vicar	Howard Ward
GP	Lynne Verrall
Maître d'	Howard Ward
Woman in Cemetery	Lynne Verrall
Woman Drinker	Lynne Verrall
Drinker One	Terence Beesley
Drinker Two	Howard Ward
Police Constable	Terence Beesley
Woman Police Constable	Lynne Verrall

Directed by Ian Rickson
Designed by Kandis Cook
Lighting by Johanna Town
Sound by Paul Arditti

The action takes place over a period of about four weeks at various locations around south London.

Act One

Scene One

Bar.

Charles *is speaking on a wall phone and holding an unopened bottle of rum.*

Charles   I know. I know. I know. I know.

Pause.

I didn't know that.

Pause.

I didn't know that either.

Pause.

Because I believe in giving people a chance.

Pause.

No. I sacked him.

Pause.

Because he was a wanker. The point is I've now got six cases of Navy rum on my doorstep and no staff.

Pause.

Six bottles I asked for.

Pause.

Captain Morgan.

Pause.

I'm not selling it on – it's not a chain letter.

Pause.

Who's going to buy six cases of Navy rum? It's evil-looking.

Pause.

She's OK. The very oxygen I breathe.

Pause.

No, she can't stand the place. Thinks it's a 'den of iniquity'.

Pause.

How can it be a den of iniquity? Nobody comes here.

Pause.

I gotta go. Ta ta. Yeah, ta ta.

He hangs up and it rings immediately. He lifts the receiver and hangs up. It rings again. He answers.

Hello.

Pause.

That's me.

Pause.

What about her?

Pause.

When? Where? No, I didn't know . . .

Pause.

I'll come down.

He hangs up and stares straight ahead.

Scene Two

Funeral parlour.

Charles *and an* **Undertaker** *stand either side of a body in a bag on a slab.*

Charles   You've done a good job.

Slight pause.

It's very lifelike.

Undertaker I haven't done it yet.

Charles Oh.

Pause.

Undertaker I've done the preliminaries but embalming is a laborious, very specialised process.

Charles Why's that?

Undertaker Eh?

Charles What makes it so specialised?

Slight pause.

Undertaker I don't discuss the embalming process with relatives.

Charles No, go on. What happens first?

Undertaker I can't discuss it.

Charles I'm curious. I might find it . . . therapeutic.

Undertaker I drain all the blood out and I replace it with formaldehyde to preserve the flesh. I suck the blood out with this piece of apparatus here and pump in the embalming fluid with this one here.

He holds up a piece of apparatus.

The blood goes in a big white bucket and when I've finished it goes down the drain.

Charles You can't reuse it? For a transfusion or something?

Undertaker Can't reuse it, more's the pity.

Charles Not even if she left herself to science?

Slight pause. The **Undertaker** *checks a clipboard.*

Undertaker How do you mean?

Charles Would you have to save it?

Undertaker Did she or didn't she?

Charles   No. But hypothetically, if that happened, would you have to hang on to the blood?

Undertaker   They keep it at the hospital.

Charles   Oh.

The **Undertaker** *looks at him.*

Pause.

Charles   I'm making conversation. At times like this it's recommended you make conversation.

Slight pause.

Because it's science, isn't it? And science isn't . . . emotional.

Slight pause.

It's unemotional.

Slight pause.

Like the weather. What's the worse job you've ever done?

Undertaker   I don't talk about that stuff.

Charles   No, you're all right, I'm interested.

Pause.

Undertaker   Suicides.

Charles   Suicides, really?

Undertaker   Found a young woman last week by the tracks at Southfields. Head completely severed. Body remained undiscovered for weeks. Picked her up, entrails gushed out in a puddle at my feet.

Charles   No.

Undertaker   Little children larking about, bringing their dogs along. I ask myself, Why? Week in, week out, dealing with the mutilated and the rotted and the dead. It's very sad.

Pause.

You want to know which type of people kill themselves the most?

Charles Which?

Undertaker People with families.

Charles Right.

Undertaker And people without families. Lonely people. Single people.

Charles Single people?

Undertaker Sometimes one goes and another follows. Sometimes it's like dominoes and the whole lot go. It's what life does to us. It kills us.

Silence.

Charles Any money in it?

Undertaker You reap what you sow.

Silence.

Any thoughts on a coffin?

Charles I don't want anything flash. Bit skint at the moment.

Undertaker Well, there's a nice teak just come in that's a bit special. Brass handles, silk lining and a kind of domed top with an arched support. It's nice.

Charles *gazes at the corpse.*

Undertaker It's very discreet. I'll show you a catalogue. When do you fancy the funeral?

Slight pause.

Mr Strong?

Charles As soon as possible. A weekday.

Undertaker Weekdays are booked out until the weekend I'm afraid. Less traffic on the roads. I could do a Monday, only not this Monday.

Charles Whenever.

Undertaker I can do a weekend only, again, you've left it a bit late for this weekend.

Charles Just do what you have to do.

He gently reaches into the bag and strokes the face of the corpse.

Could I say goodbye?

Undertaker Be my guest.

Charles *leans down to kiss the corpse.*

Undertaker Hey, don't kiss it.

Charles Why not?

Undertaker It's unhygienic. More than my job's worth.

Charles Oh ... sorry.

The **Undertaker** *goes.*

Scene Three

Cemetery.

A **Vicar** *and* **Charles** *stand by a grave. The* **Vicar** *scatters dust into the grave.*

Vicar '... Then shalt the dust return to the earth as it was: and the spirit shall return unto God who gave it.' Amen. Now let us turn our attention to Charles, to whom I give this counsel in his loss: 'Have ye not read in the Book of Moses, how in the bush God spake unto him, saying I am the God of Abraham, and the God of Isaac, and the God of Jacob?

Slight pause.

He is not the God of the dead, but the God of the living.'

Charles No. I haven't read that.

Slight pause.

So. What now?

Vicar The grave is filled in and you go home.

Charles I meant, what should I do now?

Vicar You don't do anything. The gravediggers do all that.

Charles Should I say some more prayers or something?

Vicar Would you like to?

Charles Which ones?

Vicar Any ones you like.

Charles I don't know any.

Vicar Perhaps you have a prayer of your own.

Charles Make one up, you mean?

Vicar Yes.

Charles Something about her. Personal.

Vicar Absolutely.

Charles About, you know, how lovely she was, stuff like that?

Vicar 'Whatsoever things are true, whatsoever things are just, whatsoever things are pure, whatsoever things are lovely ... if there be any virtue, if there be any praise, think on these things.' Philippians, chapter four, verse eight.

Charles Right.

Vicar Have you read the Bible?

Charles No, as it happens. Never had cause to.

Vicar Was it not read to you as a child?

Charles Family of agnostics.

Vicar Ah. 'The appropriate title of Agnostic.'

Charles Well, it's just C of E for atheist, innit?

Pause.

My grandad was a God-fearing man but my mother said she let go the hand of the Lord during the war. Because of the rationing and the evacuations. She didn't see a banana until she was eleven.

Slight pause.

Said it was 'taking the piss'.

Slight pause.

Sorry.

Vicar   'I gave my heart to know wisdom and to know madness and folly: I perceived that this also is vexation of spirit. For in much wisdom is much grief: and he that increaseth knowledge increaseth sorrow.'

Charles   What does that mean?

Vicar   You are of a generation which searched for self knowledge and identity through science. And it's no surprise when something happens, a fundamental sorrow alights, you find it perplexing.

Charles   So what do I do?

Vicar   Everybody deals with the passing on of a loved one differently.

Charles   On average, what do they do? Any little titbits will do.

Vicar   I can't advise you.

Charles   No, but you could –

Vicar   I listen. Such is the dilemma of faith that there is no advice, only the words of the scriptures. I am not an 'intermediary'. If you wish to petition the Lord, with supplication, you do so directly. You pray.

Charles   So you just –

Vicar   I listen.

Charles   You –

Vicar   I listen and perhaps guide you in –

Charles   Well, why don't you then?

Pause.

Vicar   Perhaps you'd like to come to a congregation. Share your grief.

Charles   Share my grief?

Vicar   Yes.

Charles   Share it with who?

Vicar   The community. Have you not heard 'how good and how pleasant it is for brethren to dwell together in unity'?

Charles   I keep myself to myself.

Vicar   Only the brethren we deserve are manifest.

Charles   How d'you mean?

Vicar   I mean, the people we come to love in this life are only the people we deserve to love.

Charles   'The brethren we deserve are manifest'?

Vicar   Thieves, for example, are thick as thieves because the only people they know are thieves.

Slight pause.

Charles   I like that. Well put, Father . . .

Vicar   Reverend . . .

Charles   Eh?

Vicar   You just converted me. Or promoted me.

Charles   How d'you mean?

Vicar   In an Anglican parish you don't have priests. I'm a vicar.

Charles   Oh.

Pause.

It's quite complicated, innit.

Pause.

D'you think she might be up there watching me?

Vicar   Of course.

Charles   D'you think she's smiling?

Vicar   Yes.

Charles   I bet everybody smiles in the kingdom of Heaven, don't you think, Reverend?

Vicar   Perhaps you'd like something to read.

*He hands **Charles** his Bible.*

Charles   I'll have a bash. Thanks.

*The **Vicar** goes, **Charles** examines the Bible.*

Scene Four

Doctor's.

Charles *sits opposite a **GP** who makes notes when appropriate.*

Charles   ... Bus drivers ... I find myself losing my temper with perfectly normal bus drivers and it's not just because of what happened.

Pause.

Always stopping too late or stopping too early, slamming the brakes on, they drive like they got a club-foot some of them. It just makes me want to hit somebody.

GP   I do understand, Mr Strong.

Charles   They're so careless.

GP   But we all have these trials to contend with. We'd all love to lash out and get things off our chest but we live in a society governed by rules and it's these rules which are holding it together.

Charles   It's doing my head in.

GP   Personally, there's people I'd love to hit. Then I think to myself, 'I'm a doctor ... My God!' You see?

Pause.

Has anything else been troubling you?

Charles   I'm having nightmares. I dream of finding my mother and father lying murdered in a pool of blood, or I get shot, or the till gets robbed, my car gets stolen . . . I mean, what next?

GP   It's all part of the grieving process. Your mind is probably very restless at the moment.

Charles   You think they're telling me something?

GP   I'm not a psychiatrist.

Charles   Have a stab.

GP   It's more than my job's worth to attempt the work of a specialist.

Pause.

Charles   I've had other dreams. I dream about sex all the time.

GP   Yes.

Charles   Sex with some imaginary woman who I've never met before.

GP   That's perfectly normal.

Charles   I fall in love with her.

GP   Absolutely.

Charles   And she loves me . . .

GP   Of course . . .

Charles   Then I lose her.

GP   Everybody has those dreams. Man has dreamt of the elusive perfect partner since time began. It's a very healthy sign for someone in your position. If you were suffering from depression you might not dream at all.

Pause.

Charles   Then this woman turns into a cat.

GP   I see . . .

Charles   Next thing I know I'm rogering the cat. And it's only afterwards that I realise that this is no ordinary cat but . . . it's my cat.
From when I was a little boy. A tom-cat.

Pause.

I felt so guilty.

Silence.

GP   Obviously you're still quite depressed.
And this gives rise to morbid thoughts.
Questions about the past and guilt about trivial things . . .

Charles   Trivial things . . . how trivial?

GP   It could be anything, things which ordinarily wouldn't trouble you at all.

Pause.

Were you happily married?

Charles   We had the occasional ruck. Who doesn't?

GP   Nothing serious?

Charles   She'd always wanted children.

GP   Did you?

Slight pause.

Charles   Even if we could have had a family . . .

GP   'Even if . . . '?

Pause.

Charles   See, I bought the bar when everybody was buying a place. A year later they're all going into middle management – but I stay put. Her body clock is ticking away and she wants kids and pets and a front lawn and a mortgage and holidays in Orlando . . . and I think that she thought I didn't care about that. But I did care. I cared about her with every drop of life in my body. I cared about her and I adored her more than life itself.

Pause.

But I had a business to run.

Pause.

I told her, 'It beats working for some bastard in a Merc.'

Pause.

That's when I started drinking. On the sauce every other night.

GP   I see.

Charles   Piss-arsed legless every night. Stinking. Senseless.

GP   Mm.

Charles   Shitless. Bombed. Maudlin.

GP   Yes.

Charles   Then I stopped. Just in time.

Pause.

GP   You stopped. Altogether?

Charles   She stopped me.

GP   So you no longer drink.

Charles   I have a glass of wine every now and then.

GP   Shall we say a glass a night?

Charles   More or less.

GP   So, that's seven glasses a week.

The **GP** *scribbles calculations.*

Charles   I have the odd bottle, every now and then.

GP   Maybe a beer after work?

Charles   Couple of beers, yeah.

GP   Spirits?

Charles   Bottle a week maybe.

GP   A week?

Charles *adds up on his fingers. He switches hands and adds up more.*

Charles   Sometimes.

GP   That's more than thirty units a week.

Charles   Yeah, scrub the beer.

GP   Mm, twenty's really the limit.

Charles   I'm good at it. I have a 'strong' constitution.

Laughs. Pause.

GP   Perhaps you need a holiday.

Charles   I don't have time for a holiday.

GP   Have an away day. How often do you exercise?

Charles   Never.

GP   You should try to exercise. It really does help to take your mind off things.

Charles   Does it?

GP   You'd be surprised.

Charles   I am surprised.

GP   Or I could arrange some counselling.

Charles   What about drugs?

GP   Drugs?

Slight pause.

Charles   Pills. I mean proper drugs, I mean, I've heard good reports about, you know, drugs.

GP   I'd give you counselling before I gave you medication.

Charles   Which is better?

GP   That's really up to you to decide.

Charles   Which is quicker?

GP   Ah, the blind faith of man in modern medicine.

Charles   Well, what else is there?

GP   Other than counselling?

Charles   Yeah.

GP   That's up to you as well.

Silence.

Charles   This is fucking nonsense.

GP   Sorry?

Charles   This is rubbish. You're paid to help me.
'Have an away day.'
You're a doctor.

He goes.

Scene Five

Club.

Charles *and the* **Maître d'** *sprawl at a table, drinking coffee and smoking cigarettes.*

Charles   Blah blah blah. Blah blah blah. Blah blah blah blah blah.

Pause.

Eh? Innit?

Pause.

Eh? All talk. (*Snorts.*) They're all cunts. 'Have an away day'? (*Snorts.*)

Maître d'   Where?

Charles   Absolutely. 'Where would you recommend, doc?'

Maître d'   No, I'm asking you. Where would you go?

Charles   Well, I wouldn't, would I?

Maître d'   Why not? Take the doctor's advice.

Pause.

Charles   My dream is to have an away day. What I would give to have an away day. I'd go tomorrow if I had someone to go with.

Maître d'   Go by yourself.

Charles   And someone to hold the fort.

Maître d'   Close for the day.

Charles   No. It wouldn't be the same.

Pause.

*A waitress, **Lucy**, comes over wearing a short skirt, black stockings, suspenders, white blouse and heels. She is carrying a bottle of wine. She shows the **Maître d'** the label, he nods, she pours, he tastes, she pours a full glass and he places his hand on her arse.*

Lucy   Oi. I won't tell you again.

Maître d'   What are you going to do?

She exits.

Maître d'   Bugger off to Malaga for the week.

Charles   Turn it in. Malaga?

Maître d'   What's wrong with Malaga?

Charles   Oh, stop. The Costa?

Maître d'   Malaga's not the Costa.

Charles   It's near the Costa.

Maître d'   Well, where do you want to go?

Charles   Somewhere hot.

Maître d'   Florida.

Charles   Camber Sands.

Maître d'   Don't be a cunt. Nobody goes to Camber Sands.

Charles   I used to go to Camber Sands with the missus. She loved it.

Maître d'   Oh, used to . . . certainly. Everybody used to.

Pause.

Charles You know I can still smell the salt, the odour of salt and sun cream on her skin. Sometimes I smell her perfume. Straight up. I can walk past a bird, a complete stranger, and suddenly bosh. I'm gone. What is that?

Maître d' Memories.

Charles Yeah.

Maître d' I'm so sorry, Charles. If I knew what to say, I'd say it.

Lucy *returns with a bowl of water and puts it on the table. The* **Maître d'** *runs a hand up her leg and she steps back quickly.*

Lucy Cheeky bugger.

Maître d' No.

Lucy That is rude.

Maître d' Is it?

Lucy Yeah.

Maître d' What are you going to do about it?

Lucy God.

She exits. **Charles** *sniffs the air.*

Charles Eh?

Maître d' Oh, stop.

Charles Eh?

Maître d' Turn it in.

Charles Why? I'm single.

Maître d' Charles, come on. It's undignified.

Lucy *returns wearing a black gown and mortar-board like a public school teacher and carrying a pepper-mill. She puts her foot on the chair and grinds pepper into the bowl. He puts a hand on her knee. He runs his hand up her leg to her crotch. She slaps him and takes her foot off the chair abruptly.*

Maître d'   Ow.

Lucy   That's naughty.

Maître d'   What did you do that for?

Lucy   I should send you to detention.

Maître d'   That hurt.

Lucy   I should –

Maître d'   Use the cane, the cane.

Lucy   Oh yeah. Whoops.

She extracts a cane from her waistline. **Maître d'** *stands and bends over.* **Lucy** *hesitates, then smacks his arse.*

Maître d'   Harder.

She smacks harder.

Lucy   Like that?

Maître d'   Spaghetti.

Lucy   'Please may I have ...'

Maître d'   'Please may I have my main course now.'

Lucy   Certainly, sir.

She exits. He rubs his cheek, sighs, sits. Pause.

Charles   How long you been in this lark then?

Maître d'   It's the new thing, Charlie.

Charles   Really?

Pause.

How long have we known each other?

Maître d'   Years.

Charles   Well, I'm glad you're around. Because I'm telling you, we live in a world of jobsworths. A world of people with no guts. No soul. But I can come here, any time of the day or night and you always listen.

Lucy *returns with a plate heaped with elastic bands.*

Maître d'   What's this?

Lucy   Your spaghetti.

Maître d'   Elastic bands. I said spaghetti.

Lucy   Spaghetti is elastic bands.

Maître d'   Spaghetti is shoe-laces. Elastic bands is green salad. What's dessert?

Lucy   Summer pudding.

Maître d'   No, what represents dessert? What's summer pudding?

Lucy   Sponges?

Maître d'   Sponge scourers.

Lucy   You want me to fetch dessert?

Maître d'   No just . . . put that down.

She puts down the plate.

What are you wearing underneath your gown?

Slight pause.

Lucy   Wouldn't you like to know?

Maître d'   I do know, for Christ's sake. You're wearing your fucking blouse, aren't you? Remove your blouse when you don the gown in future.
Do you want to learn this or not?

Lucy   Yeah.

Maître d'   How many times have we been through this? You've been at it a week and you can't carry out the simplest instructions.

She doesn't respond.

Do you know how many girls would give their eye teeth to work here?

She starts to go.

Take my plate.

As she takes it he grabs her around the waist and puts a hand down her cleavage.

Maître d' (*growls*).

She struggles, he holds tight, she slaps him and breaks away.

Ow! Stop doing that!

Lucy   You're supposed to like it.

Maître d'   Use the cane for fuck's sake!

Lucy   It was only a slap.

He stands clutching his cheek.

Maître d'   Never hit people in the head! OK? You'll knock somebody out.

He sits. She leans over to get the plate, he pinches her bottom, she steps back and pulls out the cane.

Maître d'   OK, fine. Now what do you say?

Lucy   'Would you like to go to detention?'

Maître d'   OK. 'No, thank you.'

He holds out a fifty-pound note. She doesn't take it.

Lucy   What's this?

Maître d' (*sighs*)   It's your 'tip'.

She reaches out to take it and he drops it on the floor, sweeps it under the table with his foot.

Well, do you want it or not?

Lucy   No, thank you very much.

Maître d'   You don't need an extra nifty?

Charles   My God, is that the time?

Lucy   No.

Maître d'   On your wages? Must be joking.

Charles   I best be off, eh?

Maître d'   No, you're all right.

Lucy   I think I'd prefer it behind the bar.

Maître d'   Pick it up.

Charles   Places to go, people to see.

Maître d'   Get under the table and pick it up, you bitch!

Charles   Uh, listen, old son . . .

Maître d' (*to* **Charles**)   In a minute.

Lucy gets under the table on hands and knees. **Charles** *stands and paces, embarrassed. The* **Maître d'** *rolls his eyes, and gestures with his hand.*

And so on and so forth. That's fine. Any questions?

Lucy   I've had enough of this.

She starts to go.

Maître d'   Now what?

Lucy   I'm not that type of woman.

He laughs slightly.

Maître d'   What type are you?
Come on.

Pause.

Lucy   I'm shy.

Maître d'   'Shy'? Men like shy women.

Lucy   I don't know what I'm doing.

Maître d'   Men like women who don't know what they're doing.

Lucy   It's driving me mad.

Maître d'   Men like mad women.

Charles   Mad women are great . . .

Maître d'   The point is, you're not really mad. You're not really shy.

Lucy   I'm not a prostitute.

Maître d'   Hey Hey Hey!

*Pause. They all look at each other. **Charles** goes and waits by the door.*

I can't afford to keep losing people. It makes the clientele
jumpy.

Lucy   The clientele are already jumpy.

Maître d'   You belong here. Take a day off and you'll come
back refreshed.

Lucy   (*tuts*).

She goes.

Maître d'   Lucy, you come back here.

She reaches the door.

If you walk out that door you'll regret it.

She exits.

If you're not back in twenty-four hours you'll regret it.

Charles *fidgets. Snorts. 'Growls.'*

Silence.

Charles *starts to go.*

Maître d'   Nice to see you again, Charles. Stay in touch.

Charles   We'll have a bevvie.

Maître d'   When I'm not so busy, perhaps.

Charles *exits.*

Scene Six

Bar.

Charles *stands behind the bar.* **Lucy** *sits on a stool on the other side of
the bar.*

Lucy   . . . So when the clientele misbehaved you had to smack 'em. Thing was, the more you smacked 'em the more they misbehaved, the dirty old sods.

Charles (*snorts*)   Ridiculous.

Lucy   Nah, that was the fun bit.

Charles   How d'you mean?

Lucy   Makes a change to be dishing it out for once. (*Laughs.*)

Charles   How d'you mean?

Lucy   Nothing.

Pause.

I wasn't very good at it.

Pause.

D'you have music?

Charles   No.

Lucy   Why not?

Charles   It's a boozer. People come here to booze.

Lucy   Oh.

Pause.

Charles   What was he paying you?

Lucy   Tenner an hour plus tips.

Charles   More than you'll get here.

Lucy   It's the principle, isn't it?

Charles   Where d'you live?

Lucy   Tooting Bec. Next door to the Lido.

Charles   Classy.

Lucy   Nah, it's just a bedsit.

Charles   It's quite a walk away.

Lucy   I don't mind.

Slight pause.

Charles   You're not a student, are you?

Lucy   Do I look like a student?

Charles   I can't have you pissing off to become a geologist all of a sudden.

Lucy   Nah, been in catering since school, haven't I?

Charles   Get your thingies, did you?

Lucy   How d'you mean?

Charles   Qualifications. A levels.

Lucy   All that. Yeah.

Charles   You've got A levels?

Lucy   Absolutely . . . lots.

Charles   And you wanna work in a pub?

Pause.

Lucy   Actually . . . I packed it in when I was fifteen.

Charles   How come?

Lucy   I was expelled.

Charles   What for?

Lucy   Oh . . . I don't know . . . something trivial. (*Laughs.*) Stealing. Arson.

Charles   Oh, stop.

Lucy   Alcoholism. Drugs.

Charles   I'll get the giggles.

They laugh.

Pause.

Lucy   No, I was just being difficult, I expect. You know, 'immature'.

Charles   As long as you can pull a pint.

Lucy   Absolutely.

Charles   When can you start?

Lucy   When d'you want me to start?

Charles   Tomorrow.

Lucy   I can start today.

Charles   Tomorrow's better. I've got a bit of business to sort out. I'll show you out.

Lucy   What sort of business?

Charles   It's personal. Don't worry, I'm not going under.

He comes around from behind the bar.

My wife just died. I'm tending the grave today.

Lucy   Oh. I'm sorry.

Charles   No, you're all right.

Lucy   Just making sure.

Charles   It's six quid an hour. You keep your tips, you don't have to spank nobody, no dope fiends, coke-heads, suits or lunatics. D'you want the job or not?

Lucy   'Course.

She joins him at the door.

Charlie   Tomorrow then?

Lucy   Yeah. See you.

She goes.

Charles   Hey.

She comes back.

D'you like rum?

He picks up a bottle from a crate by the door.

Lucy   Not really.

Charles   It's booze, isn't it?

Lucy   I don't drink.

Charles   Why not?

Lucy   I just don't.

Charles   Very wise.

She goes. **Charles** *puts the bottle back.*

Scene Seven

Cemetery.

Charles *places flowers on his wife's grave and stares at it. Nearby a* **Woman** *places flowers on another grave. She sees* **Charles**.

Woman   Hullo. I didn't see you there.

Charles   Hullo. All right?

Woman   Don't I know you?

Charles   Boozer in Garratt Lane.

Woman   I thought you looked familiar.
Who brings you here, if you don't mind me asking?

Charles   My wife. The funeral was on the weekend.

Woman   Oh, shame. Hot or cold?

Charles   How d'you mean?

Woman   Cremated or embalmed?

Charles   Embalmed.

Pause.

Woman   I read where they were supposed to cremate Albert Einstein. Then somebody came along and pinched his brain. Sliced the top of his head clean off like a lid and whipped it out. It's in three pieces now, pickled, somewhere in America.

Charles   Really?

Woman   Yes.

Pause. **Charles** *stares at his wife's grave.*

They took his eyes as well. Yes. Sucked them out with a . . . a sucker and kept them in a jam jar. Like the pope's relics, you know. It's bonkers.

Charles *looks at the* **Woman**.

Charles   Bonkers, yeah.

Woman   I'm up the pub after this. Fancy a stiff drink. You're welcome to join me.

Pause.

If you needed some company, that's all I meant.

Pause.

Because you're a very attractive man.

Pause.

It's probably a bit early, I suppose.

Charles   How'd you mean?

Woman   They say it takes three months before you finish mourning properly.

Charles   Three months?

Woman   Well, it all depends on your character, really.

Charles   Character, yeah.

Woman   Your nature.

Charles   Yeah.

Woman   And sometimes it's just not . . . not in your nature. Mind you, if you can bring yourself to be positive about it, the world's your oyster.

Charles   Absolutely.

Pause.

What if you can't?

Woman   Oh, I don't know.

Charles   Dear-oh-dear.

They laugh slightly.

Woman   'Dear-oh-dear', precisely.

She goes.

Scene Eight

Bar.

Closing time. **Charles** *is standing behind the bar, holding a baseball bat and examining it.* **Lucy** *walks in carrying a stack of glasses and whistling. She puts the glasses on the bar.*

Charles   Everybody gone?

Lucy   Yeah.

Charles   That was quick.

Lucy   I've got the touch.

Charles   Cop hold of this.

He hands her the baseball bat.

Lucy   What's this for?

Charles   Guess.

Lucy   I hate to think.

Charles   From time to time people misbehave.

Lucy   I'm not doing any funny stuff.

Charles   You don't have to use it, just look like you know how to.

He brandishes it threateningly.

Lucy   What if it doesn't work?

Charles   Then you have to use it.

Lucy   I wouldn't know where to start.

Charles   I'll show you.

Lucy   Why can't you get a bouncer or something?

Charles   I am the bouncer, love.
And when I'm not here, you're the bouncer.

Lucy   You're making me nervous.

Charles   There's a lot of funny people out there.

He has a few practice swings.

Lucy   You're bloody joking. Anything could happen.

Charles   Like what?

Lucy   I could miss.

Charles   Not if you learn properly. Now, you keep it under the bar resting in this crate so you can grab it quick. The minute anybody starts anything you grab it like so . . . and so . . . rest it on the bar and 'bang'. You slide it across the bar into his guts. Watch.

He demonstrates the manoeuvre.

Lift . . . and slide. And you want to get him in the solar plexus, just below the rib cage because you want to wind him, double him up. Then you come round and you get him on the ground.

He comes around from behind the bar.

Work on his body with clean, crisp smacks. Concentrate on the pressure points. Backs of the knees, elbows, ankles. Because you want to immobilise him. Yeah?

Lucy   Yeah . . .

Charles   Surprise him. You have a go.

She goes behind the bar and tries the manoeuvre.

Lucy   Lift . . . and slide. Lift and . . . slide.

Charles   Faster. See, it's all in the wrist. In your technique.

Lucy *practises,* **Charles** *watches.*

Charles   'Cause you want to break his ribs. Get to his vital organs. Teach the fucker a lesson! Go on . . . !

Charles *suddenly stares into space.* **Lucy** *stops.*

Lucy   Are you all right?

Charles   What am I saying?

Pause.

What am I like? Eh?

Pause. They look at each other.

Lucy   You look tired.

Charles   It's been a long day.

Pause.

Lucy   You miss her, don't you?

Charles   She was the sweetest, loveliest little girl I ever knew.

Pause.

Not a nasty bone in her body.

Pause.

You know the one thing she loved more than anything else in the world?

Lucy   What's that?

Charles   Her garden.
Clumping about the garden with her little boots on, her hair all over the gaff, growing things. She was magic with courgettes. She had a gift for courgettes. And her flowers. Not ordinary flowers. Special flowers. Rare, odd, funny coloured things. She had style. Yellow crocus. Clematis. Blue irises. Purple irises.

Pause. He puts the bat away.

You hungry?

Lucy   Starved.

Charles   Fancy a Chinese?

Scene Nine

Chinese restaurant.

Charles *and* **Lucy** *raise their glasses, smile and so on.* **Charles** *watches* **Lucy** *eat.*

Charles You remind me of her.

Lucy Who?

Charles My wife.

Lucy I've heard that before.

She stops eating.

Sorry.

Charles When she was young.

Lucy Ah.

They eat.

I want to get married one day. I think it must be nice to, you know, always, you know, have somebody there.

Charles Absolutely.

Lucy Somebody to keep you warm at night and all that.

Charles Yes.

Lucy Somebody to listen to all your silly ideas. Tell you you done the right thing when you done the wrong thing. That's romance, that is. That's what love is.

Pause.

Charles You don't have a fella then?

Lucy He's a fucking animal. I mean it. If he walked through that door right now I'd murder him.

Charles Ah.

Lucy Sadistic bastard. I hate him.

Pause.

Actually he's your mate from the club. It was just a fling, really. You must think I'm such a slapper.

Pause.

I know he does.

Charles I don't.

Lucy He does.

Charles I'm sure he doesn't.

Lucy He does.

Charles *stops eating and pats* **Lucy**'s *hand across the table. They look at each other. He takes his hand away.*

Charles Sorry.

Lucy I'm not, you know.

Charles I didn't say you were.

Lucy Your fucking wife just died.

Charles I was only . . .

Lucy What are you like, eh? Mad?

She prods **Charles**'s *food with chopsticks, lifts a mouthful to her mouth and eats.*

Call this chicken chow mein? Chicken shavings more like. I bet you they've got one chicken chained up out the back and they just shave bits off of it and mix 'em in with a noodle or two, fucking skinflints. Aren't you hungry?

Charles No.

Lucy Oh.

She stops eating. Wipes her mouth with a napkin.

Pause.

Charles I'll get the bill.

Lucy Bill, bill good idea.

Charles (*to* **Waiter**) Waiter . . .

Lucy (*to* **Waiter**)   Yoo-hoo, waiter . . .

Silence.

Charles   So. You all right to open up tomorrow?

Lucy   Absolutely.

Charles   Smashing.

Scene Ten

Bar.

The **Maître d'** *lies on the floor in a pool of blood.* **Lucy** *is still clutching the baseball bat in horror.* **Charles** *is squatting down feeling for a pulse.*

Charles   Jesus.

Lucy   Where were you?

Charles   I had things to do.

Lucy   I was waiting for you all day.

Charles   What did you let him in for?

Lucy   He wouldn't go away. He was hammering the door down.

Charles   Fuck.

Charles *goes and locks the door.*

Lucy   Then he started going on about how much he missed me and how sorry he was and how nice I was and how sensible I was. Then he got frisky.

Charles   Frisky?

Lucy   He started threatening me.

Charles   So you let him in?

Lucy   Yeah.

Charles   After he started threatening you?

Lucy   Yeah . . .

Pause.

Charles   You got a mirror?

Lucy   I've got a compact.

Charles   That'll do.

She exits and returns with a handbag from which she extracts the compact. She gives it to **Charles** *who blows on it and rubs it on his shirt.*

Charles   Covered in shit.

He breathes on it. Taps it.

Covered in powder.

He holds it to the **Maître d'***s mouth.*

Hang about.

He polishes it. Tries again. He hands it back to **Lucy** *and stands.*

Long pause.

Lucy   I was scared.

Charles   I'm scared now. What were you thinking?

Lucy   He had a knife. I panicked.

Charles   What sort of knife?

Lucy   A little one. With a . . . a pearl handle.

Charles   So he attacked you with a knife?

Lucy   He was about to.

Charles   Did he or didn't he?

Lucy   He really lost his temper. He had that look about him. He had that look in his eyes. He was about to snap . . .

Charles (*pause*)   Has he . . . has he done anything like this before?

Lucy   No. It was a complete surprise.

Charles *fetches a cloth and wipes up the blood.*

Lucy   You don't believe me, do you? You think I'm just being neurotic. Well, don't you?

Pause.

It was an accident. I didn't mean to hurt him.

Charles   You hit him in the head.

Lucy   I was trying to stun him.

Charles (*scrubbing*)   What did I tell you about that, Lucy? You weren't listening, were you? I told you precisely what to do, if there's a problem, we went through the whole procedure, but no, you had a better idea.

He goes behind the bar, wipes his hands and finds a bottle of rum. Opens it and drinks.

I leave you alone for five minutes . . .

Lucy   Oh, don't go on about it!

Charles *goes to the phone on the wall and dials.*

Lucy   What are you doing?

Charles   Phoning the police.

She goes to him and they briefly struggle over the phone.

Lucy   They won't believe me.

Charles   This isn't a game.

Lucy   . . . And it was your idea anyway. You told me to do it. I wouldn't do a thing like that in a million years.

Pause. He puts the phone down.

We could say you did it. Because you were depressed.

Pause.

Charles   Why?

Pause.

People will miss him. His family. His friends.

Lucy   He doesn't have any friends. We're his friends.

Charles   People will come looking for him. People . . . in the community.

Lucy   Who?

Silence.

Charles   Well, what are we going to do with him?

Lucy   We could throw him in the river.

Charles   No.

He picks up the phone and dials.

Lucy   We could bury him on Balham Common. It's a bit more appropriate.

Pause.

And, and easier ...

Charles   Oh, shut up. Just shut up.

Lucy   It's all winos and hookers. Nobody'll find him.

Charles   We're not doing it.

Lucy   Why not?

Charles   Because it's wrong!

Pause.

And we could get caught.

And then I'll go to prison because it's my bar and my baseball bat and I'm the oldest.

Pause.

How far is Balham Common?

Lucy   Ten minutes in the car.

Pause.

Have you got a car?

He just looks at her, still holding the phone.

Scene Eleven

Balham Common.

Evening. **Charles** *and* **Lucy** *lower the corpse, wrapped in a blanket, into the grave.*

Lucy   He was a vicious, pitiless bastard. He deserved it.

Charles   Much as I liked him, he was a pimp.

Lucy   Yeah.

Charles   I'm glad he's dead.

Lucy   Me too.

Charles   If a man can't play by the rules then he deserves every dark fucking day that befalls him.

Pause.

He wants to come into my place, with a knife, start throwing his weight around, he's got no manners, then it's not my problem.

Pause.

The good Lord giveth and He taketh and we, God bless us, made in His image, do the same and so fuck it.

Pause.

It makes me so angry, Lucy.

Lucy   D'you think we should say a prayer or something?

Charles   What sort of prayer?

Lucy   I don't know.

He looks at her, then pulls his Bible out of his coat pocket and flips through it. After a moment, he shuts it and hands it to **Lucy**.

Charles   Go on.

Lucy *looks through the Bible, shuts it and hands it back.* **Charles** *puts it in his pocket, takes out a flask of rum and drinks. He puts the flask away and fills in the grave.* **Lucy** *gazes at the corpse.*

Lucy   He doesn't look dead.

Pause.

Lucy What if he isn't? I mean, you're not a doctor.

Charles *stops work.*

Lucy What if I tell someone? You know what I'm like.

Charles *gets back to work. Pause.*

Lucy I've seen a few dead bodies in my time.

Charles Really.

Lucy My aunty died when I was thirteen. I saw her in her casket. She was yellow. And sort of waxy. Her skin looked like wax.

Charles Sometimes they use wax if there's any wounds.

Lucy There wasn't any wounds.

Charles They drain the blood out which is what makes the skin go yellow.

Lucy She gassed herself. Stuck her head in the oven. It was sad. She was always so cheerful and positive about things.

Pause.

I've known a lot of people who've died suddenly.

Charles I haven't.

Lucy Well, you're older. It's different for you.

Charles Is it?

Lucy Different generation. People do more now, don't they? Experience more.
Take more risks. Then there's suicides.
Everybody I know knows somebody who's either thought about it or tried it or actually done it.

Charles Yes, all right.

Lucy Live life while you can, when you can, as fast you can. Within reason. That's my motto.

He stops work.

Charles   What is the matter with you?

Lucy   D'you think there is something the matter with me?

Charles   Yes.

Lucy   What?

Charles   I don't know.

Charles *works.*

Lucy   Nearly finished?

Charles *flings the shovel down.*

Charlie   Are you thick or something?

Lucy   No.

Charles   Well, what is it?

Lucy   I don't know.

Charles *tramps down the dirt.*

Lucy   I expect this means I'm out of a job.

Pause.

I didn't have to stay you know, I could have fucked off home
hours ago.

Charles   Why didn't you?

Lucy   I don't know. I'd be bored.

Charles   We should open up. It'll look suspicious.

Pause.

Get in the car.

Lucy   Are you sure?

Charles   Get in the car before I change my mind. In the . . . in
the front.

Lucy   How d'you mean?

Charles   In the front where I can keep my eye on you.

Lucy   I'm not a child.

Charles   I know that.

Pause.

Lucy   Why are you doing this?

Charles   Stop asking questions.

Lucy   I want to know why.

Charles   Because I want to.

Lucy   Just tell me why.

Charles *picks up the blanket and folds it carefully.*

Charles   I don't know why.

She goes. He looks at the grave, picks up the shovel and goes.
Blackout.

Act Two

Scene One

Charles's *flat.*

Charles *is sitting on a bed, holding a phone and drinking from a tumbler. A bottle sits nearby.*

Charles   Mum?

Slight pause.

Dad, it's me. Charles.

Pause.

I'm all right. Yeah.

Pause.

It was all right. It was nice.

Pause.

Dozens. Yes. She was a popular girl.
Yes, she was lovely. I know that.

Pause.

Very pretty.

Pause.

It was a lovely day, yes.

Pause.

Lovely. Nice and hot.

Slight pause.

Smashing. All week. Beautiful. Listen, Dad . . . No, don't get
mum just yet. I want to talk to you.

Pause.

I just want to talk. See how you are.

Pause.

Who? Which side?

Pause.

He packs a chiv, I know. He's a cunt.

Slight pause.

His son's a cunt as well.

Slight pause.

They're a pair of cunts. The uncle's a cunt with glasses. Which makes him a glunt, yeah, very funny, Dad . . . I know they drink here but I never make them welcome. No, he's in Parkhurst – oh, really . . . ? Look, apart from that – you're well in yourself, yeah? Cutting down on the fags?

Pause.

And mum? No, don't go and get her. I want to talk to you. I just want to . . . all right put her on.

Pause.

Hullo, Mum. How are you?

Long pause.

I know he is, Mum . . . Friday . . . got a keg of spillage especially for him. Parkhurst.

Pause.

The funeral was lovely. Lovely day, yes . . . how are you, you, Mum? Never mind me.

Pause.

Marvellous. That's all I wanted to hear. I have to go now.

Slight pause.

Nothing's wrong. I'm just tired.

Slight pause.

You're absolutely right, Mum. Housework?
No. Can't say that I have been.

Pause.

I don't want a new girlfriend. You're absolutely ... but ... oh, good plan, Mum.

Pause.

No, I'm just a bit ... 'sad', yeah.

Pause.

No ... no ... no ... something happened in the bar and what with one thing and another ...

Slight pause.

Three square meals a day, Mum. You're absolutely right. Yes, Mum. I have to go now, Mum. Y – all right. Ta ta. Ta ta. Love to dad. Ta ta.

He hangs up and drinks.

Scene Two

Bar.

A lock-in is in progress. Music plays. **Lucy** *and fellow* **Drinkers** *sing along drunkenly.* **Charles** *wipes the bar and clears up.*

Drinkers   When no one else can understand me
When everything I do is wrong
You give me hope and consolation
You give me strength to carry on

Lucy *(simultaneously)*   Join in, Charlie.

He doesn't.

Drinkers   And you're always there to lend a hand
In everything I do
That's the wonder, the wonder of you
Da de da, da de da, da de da ...

Charles *turns the music off. He opens a bottle of rum and drinks from the bottle.*

Silence.

Woman   Charlie Charlie Charlie Charlie Charlie . . . This man . . . is a . . . where did my glass go?

Drinker One   Hello, cheeky chops . . .

Lucy   I don't remember your name.

Drinker Two   I planted my wife a week after my fortieth birthday. I stood around the grave with the in-laws discussing the weather . . .

Drinker One   Forgotten already?

Woman   Leave her alone, she's only little.

Drinker Two   Her mother had a smile like a thin streak of piss . . .

Drinker One   I think you are a dangerous woman.

Drinker Two   The old man had regressed into a sort of childlike hysteria somewhere around the third day of his honeymoon and hadn't spoken since . . .

Woman   Ignore him, pet, he's been in Parkhurst the past five years . . .

Lucy   No! What did you do?

Silence.

Sorry.

Pause.

I wasn't being funny.

Drinker One *laughs suddenly.*

Drinker One   What a character!

Lucy   I wasn't saying anything or anything . . .

Drinker One   Isn't she a character, Charles?

Woman   You leave her alone, you big hairy bastard, she don't know.

Drinker Two   The heavens pissed buckets and I stared into the hole and reflected on the banality that had gone before ...

Lucy   I was just interested.

Drinker One   Never ask me that again.

Lucy   I won't.

Drinker Two   .... And the banality that was to come.

Drinker One   Have I met you before? You remind me of someone.

Pause.

Lucy   I've heard that before.

Woman   Don't take any notice of him, love, he's a pervert.

Drinker One   Listen to me, no listen – you are a devastatingly handsome young woman. Devastatingly ...

Lucy   Oh, stop ...

Woman   Should pick on somebody his own age ...

Lucy   'A devastatingly handsome young ... '?

Woman   Live your life, girl, that's what you should do.

Lucy   He's asking for it, isn't he? Eh?

Charles   Lucy ...

Lucy   Come on, then. Let's have you.

Charles   Please ...

Drinker Two   'I'm a Captain of fucking Industry,' I thought. 'But I still shit in a toilet and like everybody else I'm going to die.'

Drinker One   I'm not being funny, I'm attracted to you.

Drinker Two   And the funeral bells tolled and a Mockingbird sang as if to ...

Lucy   I'll bury you.

Drinker One (*laughing*)   Priceless!

Woman   Don't say that, girl, it's bad luck!

Lucy   I killed somebody, I did.

Woman   Don't say that, girl, someone might believe you!

Lucy   Charles dug a hole and buried the body for me.

Drinker One (*laughing*)   Oh, my sainted aunty.

Drinker Two   'I looked, and behold a pale horse and his name that sat on him was Death, and Hell followed with him . . .'

Woman   No, you are joking!

Lucy   Yes – no!

Drinker Two   Which is to say, 'The shit is really going to hit the fan now.'

Lucy   He died right there, right where you're all standing.

Drinker One   Is this true, Charlie? Little girl says you and her stiffed a geezer.

Silence.

Woman   Not the wife, you mean?

Lucy   No, somebody else.

Drinker One   Oh, stop! I'll have a bloody heart attack in a minute.

Pause.

Woman   You're pulling our legs.

Lucy   It's true.

Drinker Two   This is unbelievable.

Woman   How did you kill him?

Drinker One   This is my type of lady.

Lucy   I hit him.

Drinker One   Chinned him? That's the stuff.

Lucy   I beat the shit out of him.

Drinker Two Outrageous.

Woman What, a drunk?

Lucy Actually . . .

Drinker One 'Actually, *actually*.' Go on.

Pause.

Lucy You won't believe me.

Drinker One You're all right . . . say it.

Lucy No.

Drinker One Say it.

Woman What, what say what?

Lucy Don't laugh.

Slight pause.

He was my lover.

Woman No . . .

Lucy Yes.

Woman Fuck off . . .

Lucy Fucking done him in because . . .

Woman Is this true, Charlie?

Drinker One Classic . . .

Lucy Because he was hurting me . . .

Drinker One (*laughing*) Absolutely.

Drinker Two And you got away with it?

Lucy It's not funny.

Drinker One This is hysterical!

Lucy Tell 'em, Charlie. Charles . . .

Charles *stares into space.*

Pause.

Lucy   Are you going to vomit?

Woman   Get a bucket, someone . . .

Lucy   Charles, what's wrong?

Woman   Quick, Charlie's gonna vomit.

*The **Woman** goes behind the bar and comes back with a bucket. She waits with the bucket.*

Lucy   I feel awful.

Charles (*to* **Lucy**)   You're drunk.

Drinker One   Aha! I thought so. I could tell.

Woman   What did he say? What was that?

Charles   Don't fuck about.

Lucy   The poor man.

Charles   Don't say another word.

Woman   Did she or didn't she?

Lucy   I am such a bitch.

Charles   Do you hear me? Do You Understand?

Woman   I won't tell anyone, I promise. Come on, Charlie . . .
Charles . . . ?

Pause.

Charles   Believe what you want to believe.

Pause.

Woman   What are you like, eh? Did he try and touch you up?

Drinker Two   I do not believe this. She admits to
slaughtering a living person on this exact spot . . .

Drinker One   Watch it . . .

Drinker Two   What was his name?

Woman   Oh, you can't ask that . . .

Drinker Two   No, we have a right to know . . .

Drinker One   Oh, do we? How jolly.

Charles   SHUT UP!

Pause.

Who are you people? What do you know about anything? You come here every night and drink and piss and moan and laugh and line up like so many pigs at a fucking trough. You're ignorant.

Silence.

Woman   You've upset him now.

Charles   What's it like to be so fancy-free, eh? Nothing whatsoever occupying your minds. Come on, I'm interested.

A long pause. **Lucy** *goes to* **Charles**.

Woman   So. How long have you two known each other?

Charles   Get out. Go on. Piss off, the lot of you.

Pause.

Charles *stands and 'fronts'* **Drinker One**. *Pause.*

Drinker One   Don't do anything you'll regret, Charlie-boy.

Pause. The **Drinkers** *slowly file out.* **Charles** *sits.* **Lucy** *sits too and holds his hand.*

Lucy   Shh. It's all right. I'll look after you.

Scene Three

Seaside.

Lucy *and* **Charles** *sit in deck-chairs side by side on the sea front. The sound of gulls overhead.*

Lucy   Cup of tea?

Charles   Lovely.

She pours a cup from a flask and hands it to him. Pours her own cup and they sip.

Lucy   Digestive?

Charles   Ta.

She hands him a biscuit.

Lucy   Holiday.

Charles   Lovely. Thank you.

Lucy   It's a pleasure.

Charles   Yeah.

Pause.

My old man says if you've got one friend in this life you're a lucky man. One person who you can still trust, when you're eighty years old, then you're a lucky man.

Pause.

You know, the one person he listens to? And the one person who listens to him? My dear old mum.

Lucy   Bless 'em.

Charles   Bless 'em. 'As long as you have your health,' she'd say, 'as long as you're still alive and still half-sane, what more can you expect? Eh? Keep things simple. Because the human race, son, is not worth a flying fucking bag of nuts.'

Pause.

Lucy   My parents divorced when I was ten. Spent most of the time 'round my aunty's.

Charles   Oh, I'm sorry.

Lucy   I never liked them. Too quiet.

Charles   Yeah.

Lucy   Not very affectionate.

Charles   No.

Lucy   Not much fun at all really.

Pause.

Still, I don't suppose parents are meant to be fun, are they?

Slight pause.

They're meant to be dignified.

Pause.
They link arms.
They look at each other.
They kiss.

Charles   Bloody hell.

Lucy   Whoops.

Charles   Sorry –

Lucy   No –

Charles   I –

Lucy   I –

Charles   You . . .

Pause.

Lucy   Isn't it a lovely . . . windy day?

Charles   Lovely.

Pause.

Lucy   You must think I'm such a slapper.

Charles   Don't say that.

Lucy   I'm not.

Charles   Why do you say these things?

Lucy   I don't know.

Charles   No, why? I really want to know.

Long pause.

Lucy   They say people do this after a trauma.

Pause.

You become closer to people. Out of relief. It's like you realise how lucky you are.

Charles   It was . . . it was inevitable.

Scene Four

Hotel.

Charles *is lying in bed.* **Lucy** *comes into the room wearing only knickers and bra. She has a towel around her head. She takes the towel off her head and shakes her wet hair loose. Sits on the end of the bed and brushes her hair. She applies talcum powder to her body.* **Charles** *watches.*

Charles   You know what I'm turning into? An unprincipled man.

Pause.

I find it easier to take a long hard look at myself after a good shag.

Lucy (*tuts*)   You're in a jolly mood all of a sudden.

Charles   I was just thinking how lovely it is to watch a woman dress. I'm not being funny. I used to watch my wife getting dressed in the mornings. Doing her hair, rubbing in the talcum powder. Makes being alive worthwhile.

Pause.

She was extremely clean. Always filling the bathroom with special little soaps and all sorts of new scents and smells. Always grooming herself. I got quite a kick out of watching her shave her legs. Legs, armpits, marvellous.

Lucy *puts on a sweater.*

Lucy   Really?

Charles   Yes.

Lucy *picks up a skirt and goes to the window. She opens the curtains and window and stands looking out, holding the skirt.*

Charles   I remember our honeymoon. I remember her sitting
on the bed in the hotel, with the sun and the sea-air streaming in
and her skin and her wet hair all golden in the light, gulls
cawing in the distance, and I thought to myself, What does this
mean? Eh? This is the only thing that matters.
Fuck work. I'm a cunt.

Pause.

We were in love. Love's great. Love wears a white hat.

Lucy   Are you going to get up or are you going to just stare at
my arse all morning?

Charles   Come here, babe.

Lucy   Oh, stop. You're not going to get all soppy on me, are
you?

Charles   I already have, girl.

Lucy   Because you know that was just a fuck, don't you?

Slight pause.

Charles   How d'you mean?

Lucy   A quick fuck to keep our spirits up.

Charles   It worked.

Lucy   It doesn't mean anything.

Charles   Really?

Lucy   Because you know this is what ruins friendships, isn't it?

Charles   I know.

Lucy   And we don't want that to happen, do we?

Charles   No . . . of course.

Lucy   I don't want anybody getting the wrong end of the
stick.

Charles   Who?

Lucy   You. I couldn't cope with another fiasco.

Pause.

Charles   Well, they certainly broke the mould when they made you.

Pause.

I nev . . . I never know whether to laugh or cry.

She goes to him.

Lucy   Look at you.
Big fat belly, hairy arse, toe-nails need cutting, you stink, boozer's breath, hungover again, big hairy bollocks like a gorilla, big ugly cock, look at it, look at all those veins. You haven't got a pot to piss in, no future, you're moody, ugly, bad tempered, old . . .

She kisses him.

What do you want for breakfast?

She puts her skirt on.

Charles   Toast?

Lucy *picks up the phone by the bed, dials, and clears her throat.*

Lucy   Toast for room nine.

She hangs up.

Scene Five

Bar.

Lucy *is working behind the bar.* **Drinker One** *is sitting at the bar with a drink, drunk.*

Drinker   Drink?

Pause.

I'm having one. You're not busy.

Lucy   You're drunk.

Drinker   Eh?

Lucy   No more drinks.

Drinker   Eh?

Lucy   You're drunk. No more.

Drinker   What is it? Rum and Coke?

Lucy   I won't tell you again.

Drinker   Just a tipple.

Lucy (*tuts*).

Drinker   You know what I like about this stuff? When you drink, the world's still out there, it just doesn't have you by the balls.

Lucy   Oh, absolutely.

Pause.

Drinker   I always wanted to own a fancy wine emporium. A fancy one in the Fulham Road perhaps, or New Malden. As a matter of fact, I was once mooted for a job with Balls Brothers. Only they said I was an alcoholic. Wound up running the Cash 'n' Carry in Wandsworth. Briefly. Before my incarceration.

Lucy   Really?

Drinker   Mm.

Lucy   I *say*.

She yawns. Pause.

Drinker   You know what I like about you? You're always here. I like that. Makes you feel that there are things that are at least a little constant in this world, you know what I'm saying?

Lucy   I would be, wouldn't I?

Drinker   Of course.

Lucy   I'm the barmaid.

Drinker   True.

Lucy   It's my job.

Drinker *nods and stares into his drink.*

Pause.

Drinker   Sad about the guvnor's wife.

Pause.

Well, he wasn't to know, was he?

Pause.

That's what married life is about. The good times and the bad. So long as you have your health and you don't hate each other's guts by the end then you're on top, in my book.

Lucy   What you on about?

Drinker (*tuts*)   The things they used to say about each other. My goodness. Always squabbling and carrying on like a pair of kids. Always rucking, like Tom and Jerry they was. I saw them in Northcote Road market one day, strolling about, hand in hand, bold as brass, and her with a pair of black eyes like a fucking racoon.

Pause.

That's what she was like, see. Spirited. Very emotionally strong and very lively before the separation . . .

Lucy   I beg your pardon?

Drinker   I was just saying . . .

Lucy   I think you've said enough.

Drinker   Funny bloke, Charles. He's a lovely man. One of the best. But you know the only trouble is he's a nutter. Still, I can see why he's drawn to you.

Lucy   Why?

Drinker   F.U.N.

Pause.

Fun.

Lucy   Oh, go away.

Drinker   Just look at this place. It's on its last legs. It looks . . . clapped. Enjoyed . . . Enjoyed by the men of Wandsworth. Is it still a going concern? Is it still a . . . sound business proposition, do you think? I'll tell you what; this place needs you.

Pause.

As a matter of fact, I get the feeling that if I was to proposition you right now, not in a grubby way, but in a genuine way, you'd say, 'Yes'.

Lucy   Sod off!

Drinker   Do me a favour. You're gagging for it.

She throws her drink in his face.

Lucy   Who do you think you are?

Drinker   You'd love it if I took your knickers down and stuck it right up you.

She smacks him in the face. He grabs her wrist and produces a knife. She slips the bat from under the bar and there's a stand-off.

Come on. Have a pop.

Scene Six

Bar.

Charles *enters carrying boxes of alcohol.* **Lucy** *is behind the bar, staring into space.*

Charles   Gordon's and Smirnoff thirteen to the dozen. Cunt only tried to stitch me up with more rum. Says he's got a case of Lamb's Navy written in his book. 'And I've got *cunt* written here,' I said. Lamb's Navy? What am I, a fucking sailor? I got him in the corner and I got hold of him and I said, 'Right, you cunt, right . . . Because you people do not give me the respect that I am due. Right,' I said. 'Fuck this, I'll take my business elsewhere. Fuck that,' I said. 'Because I won't take that from no one no more. Lack of respect.'

Pause.

I should have given him a slap.

Pause.

And you know me, Lucy. I'm not a violent man. What's up?

He goes through a door behind the bar to put the boxes down. He comes out.

What happened?

Lucy   He, he had a knife.

Charles   You did it again, I don't believe it.

Lucy   It happened again.

Charles   It's ridiculous!

Lucy   He attacked me.

Charles   Are you mad? My God!

Lucy *goes to him, he backs away.*

Charles   You stay away from me.

Lucy   He said I was a tart.

Charles   Well, are you?

Lucy   Don't you dare say that, what has got into you?

Charles   I'll go berserk in a minute.

Lucy   No wonder your marriage went for a Burton.

Pause.

Charles   What?

Lucy   Nothing.

Charles   What did you say?

Lucy   I'm sorry.

Charles   Who told you this?

Lucy   He did.

The **Drinker** *emerges from the back room looking stunned.*

Charles   And you believed him? Well, do you?

Lucy   No.

Charles   Well, why'd you say it?

Lucy   I don't know.

Charles   After everything I told you.

Pause.

He's a fucking boozer. Why do you talk to these people?

Lucy   He wouldn't go.

Charles   I'll make him go.

*The **Drinker** heads for the door. **Charles** follows and grabs his arm.*

Charles   Right, you cunt.

Lucy   Charles, don't.

Charles (*to **Drinker***)   What have you been saying? Eh? What did you say about me? Come on.

Drinker   What are you gonna do? Give me a slap?

Lucy   It's a wind-up. He's just trying to get a reaction.

Drinker   She told me all about you.

Charles   You should watch your fucking mouth.

Drinker   Came to me one night with such a face on her ...

Lucy   I'm not listening.

Charles (*to **Lucy***)   No, you're all right, it's all right ...

Charles *takes out his hankie, hands it to **Lucy**, who sniffles and blows her nose, then without looking, he turns to the **Drinker** and beats him to the floor, punching him repeatedly.*

Lucy   Stop!

Charles   You've got a reaction now!
You've got a reaction now! You've got a reaction now! Eh? Slag!

Lucy   You'll kill him!

Charles   Shut up!

*He raises his hand to slap **Lucy**.*

Lucy   No!

Charles   Get out.

Lucy   Don't you dare.

Charles   I mean it.

Lucy   I know you do, Charles.

Pause. He backs off.

Charles   It's none of your business.

Pause.

Don't look at me.

Pause.

What are you looking at?

He goes behind the bar, gets the bat. He smashes up the bar.

This? This?!

Charles *puts the bat down. Goes to the* **Drinker***. Kneels beside him and mops blood from the* **Drinker***'s head with his shirt.*

He'll wake up in a minute. He's just drunk.
Have you got a fag?

Lucy *fetches her bag from behind the bar, rummages in it and hands him a cigarette.*

Charles   Thank you.

He puts it in his mouth and she lights it.

Thank you.

Lucy *puts a cigarette in her own mouth and lights it. The* **Drinker** *comes to and groans vaguely.*

Lucy   I never did anything, you know. Just kept them company really. Everybody's entitled to that. I don't know how I got into this mess.

Pause.

Charles   I ask myself sometimes did she step in front of the bus on purpose?

Pause.

And I tell myself that's ridiculous. I loved her. I married her.

Lucy   I couldn't do it.

Charles   I haven't got the guts.

Lucy   I've considered it.

Charles   I have too.

Lucy   Tried to think of the best way and so on.

Charles   Me too.

The **Drinker** *eyes them warily and gets up.*

Lucy   I always think of the people I'd leave behind.

Charles   Me too. That's the only thing that worries me.

Drinker   You . . . you people are mad.

Charles *pulls out his wallet and offers the* **Drinker** *fifty pounds.*

Charles   Go on. You're all right.

Pause.

I'm apologising.

Pause.

You don't need an extra nifty?

He adds another fifty.

A monkey?

The **Drinker** *takes the money, screws it up and tosses it in* **Charles's** *face and exits.*

Charles (*snorts*)   Now I'm bribing people.

Scene Seven

Charles's flat.

Lucy and Charles sit on the bed. Charles drinks from a bottle of vodka and smokes.

Lucy   Have you ever thought about seeing a shrink?

Pause.

I mean, you were provoked, but you've been under a lot of strain. What if there's something wrong with you? I'm not saying he will press charges, but if he did . . .

Charles   'If, if, if . . . '

Lucy   Who knows what they'll find out?

Charles   If my aunty had balls she'd be my uncle.

Lucy   He'll tell them everything.

Pause.

Charles   We could go abroad. Get away from England.

Lucy   Go abroad?

Charles   Hide.

Lucy   Hide?

Charles   It's a terrible country.

Lucy   With you?

Charles   Nobody works, nobody smiles.

Lucy   I'm going home. I'm going home to watch telly and clean the cooker and do what normal people do.

Charles   I mean, I've got a conscience but I'm not going to torture myself for ever.

He picks up the Bible from by the bed, flips through it.

'The fruit of the Spirit is love, joy, peace, longsuffering, gentleness, goodness, faith, meekness and temperance.' Says who?

Pause. He drops the Bible.

Lucy   Do you believe in Heaven and Hell?

Charles   I don't know.

Lucy   I used to believe in Heaven.

Charles   I believe in Hell.

Lucy   Obviously there's a Hell.

Charles   I don't know. I don't care.

Lucy   Me neither.

Charles   Not any more.

Pause.

Lucy   I was watching telly, right, and they interviewed a man who said the anti-Christ had come and he knew who it was. He said the anti-Christ is living in south London with a woman half his age. Supposing that's true.

Pause.

Charles (*snorts*)   'The anti-Christ . . . '

Lucy   Don't laugh. I saw it on the telly.

Charles *laughs.*

Stop laughing. It makes sense to me.

Silence.

He drinks.

When my wife died, everything went with it. I didn't see the point in being good. I couldn't stop boozing, pay the bills, go to work, come home. Day after day we wade through shit.

Lucy   Oh, stop.

Charles   We grow old waiting for the big reward, something bigger than a good-night kiss, a slap on the back, a sun-tan . . .

Lucy   Now you're being silly.

Charles   The Easter Bunny, birthdays, anniversaries, 'Merry Christmas, Charles ... Merry Christmas, everybody ... ' I'd rather murder myself.

Lucy   That's enough of that.

Charles   She knew that this life isn't worth living. She never complained, she could always find the good in things, but deep down she knew.

Lucy   Pull yourself together.

Charles   Everybody knows, we're just taught not to think it.

Lucy   You're scaring me.

Charles   We've had it. We're doomed.

Lucy snatches the bottle and slaps him.

Lucy   Snap out of it, for God's sake. Do you have to go on and on and on about it? It's so selfish.

Charles   All right ...

Lucy   It's not all right, you ... you ... you monster ... what've ... what have you done ... ?

Pause.

Lucy puts the bottle down and goes to the door. **Charles** *follows.*

Charles   Where are you going?

Lucy   Home.

Charles   I'll come with you.

Lucy   Don't laugh at me.

Charles   I'm not.

Lucy   I'm not stupid.

Charles   I know.

Lucy   You don't. You think I'm just another scatty woman. It's so typical. I know you think I'm strange. People have always thought that. Even at school. 'Strange.' 'Quirky.'

'Loose.' I'm not. I'm perfectly normal. I'm just different, that's all.

Charles   I understand . . .

Lucy   Don't you dare say that. How could you understand? I hate it when people say that. People look straight through me. Like I'm invisible or a . . . a ghost or something. It drives me up the wall.

Charles *takes a step backwards and* **Lucy** *follows.*

Lucy   I'm surrounded by Evil.

Pause.

She leaves him and paces and fidgets. **Charles** *retrieves the bottle and drinks.*

Charles   I don't want you to leave because the last woman to leave me was dead within weeks.

Lucy   That's different. I don't love you.

Charles   Neither did she.

Lucy   But I like you. And . . . and . . .

Silence.

They embrace. They press their foreheads together and stay like that for a while.

Charles   Shh. It's all right.

Lucy   I'm scared.

Charles   What are you scared of?

Lucy   Everything.

Charles   Come on. I'll take you home.

Lucy   What colour are ghosts?

Charles   I don't know.

Lucy   Blue?

Charles   Shh.

Scene Eight

Church.

Charles, *wearing an old coat, sits with the* **Vicar**.

Charles It's like there's this force controlling me or watching over me and making things happen. The things I'm afraid of, and the things I most want, they all happen but I don't . . . I don't know why they happen. And, and why me anyway?

Vicar 'O Lord, thou has searched me, and known me. Thou knowest my downsitting, and mine uprising, thou understandest my thoughts from afar.'

Charles I don't believe in God.

Vicar Why not?

Charles Because he doesn't understand, does he? If he did, none of this would have happened.

Pause.

Vicar Do you believe in destiny?

Charles I don't know what that means.

Vicar Many people believe that events are controlled by fate which is predestined by God.

Charles Or the Devil?

Vicar Well, no.

Charles Well, what are you saying?

Vicar I'm saying perhaps it's the reason you've come to me.

Charles I came to you because I wanted to.

Vicar All right . . .

Charles I chose to, understand?

Vicar Yes, yes I see.

Pause.

Charles What about my wife? Why did that happen?

Vicar   God has called her to the kingdom of Heaven.

Charles   I know. Why?

Vicar   I don't know why.

Charles   Because it's, it's 'nice' there?

Vicar   These questions can only be answered with faith.

Charles   I don't have any faith.

Vicar   In anything?

Charles   No.

Vicar   You have no faith in humanity?

Charles   No.

Vicar   Faith in love and justice and restitution which has been with us since the birth of civilisation.

Charles   I have faith in love, yeah.

Vicar   Now we're getting somewhere.

Charles   But I don't have anyone to love.

Pause.

Vicar   Perhaps you are ready to be filled.

Charles   Filled?

Vicar   With God's love.

Charles   I don't want God's love. God's love's no good to me. Don't you understand? I've hurt people. I've done things I can't undo.

Vicar   We all hurt people.

Charles   No, I mean, really hurt people . . .

Vicar   And do you think that makes you unworthy of God's love?

Charles   Unworthy?

Vicar   Do you think that makes you unworthy of providence?

Pause.

Charles   I want to confess.

Vicar   To what?

Charles   Do it properly. 'Repent and ye shall be forgiven...'

Vicar   It's not that easy.

Charles   Why not?

Vicar   We do not believe in easy redemption. Your restitution is in your hands. You have to do it yourself.

Charles   I've tried doing it myself. It didn't work.

Vicar   Then I say, 'Bring forth fruits worthy of repentance.'

Charles   Listen to me...

Vicar   'Bring forth fruits *worthy* of repentance...'

Charles   Look at me...

Vicar   And talk to God...

Charles *grabs the* **Vicar** *roughly.*

Charles   I don't want to talk to God, I want to talk to you! I'm bad! All my life I've been bad! 'The brethren you deserve are manifest,' you said. What do I deserve? Eh...?

He lets the **Vicar** *go.*

I'm lost. Don't you understand? I don't know who I am.

Pause.

The **Vicar** *goes.*

Scene Nine

Cemetery.

Charles, *drunk, stares at his wife's grave.*

Charles   Remember the time I tried to leave? We had a ruck in the middle of the night and I got up and got dressed but you'd hidden my shoes ... to stop me leaving. But I went anyway ...

in my socks. And you followed me . . . in your dressing-gown . . . and I was walking up Trinity Road and I turned around and you were all hurt and miserable and crying . . . tears streaming down your face . . . little bubbles coming out your nose . . . And you were saying, 'I just want you to come home. I just want you to come home. Don't you understand?'

Pause.

And, and I did understand.

Pause.

I just didn't know why.

Pause.

And then, despite myself, I held out my arms and you snuggled into my arms . . . and suddenly I felt warm . . . I felt part of the world again . . . it seemed like I was doing the right thing for once.

Pause.

And it was the wrong thing. And I'm sorry.

After a moment, a **Police Constable** *and a* **Woman Police Constable** *come over.* **Charles** *stands and stares at the* **WPC**.

PC   Good evening, sir.

Charles   All right?

PC   Would you like to show me some identification?

Charles   Officer, you look just like my wife.

PC   Are you going to show me some identification?

Charles   It's uncanny.

PC   Would you come with us please, sir.

Charles   This is her grave. She's dead. Completely dead.

The **WPC** *takes the bottle. The* **PC** *takes* **Charles**'*s arm.*

WPC   Would you like to go to the hospital? Is that where you're meant to be?

Charles   No. I've had a few drinks, that's all. I'll be all right in a minute ...

He tries to walk away. They take hold of **Charles** *and pin his arms behind. He struggles.*

What are you doing?

PC   Are you going to co-operate?

Charles   I have a right to be here.

WPC   Yes, come along, don't make a fuss now.

Charles   I'm praying.

PC   I'm arresting you for threatening behaviour and drunk and disorderly conduct, understand?

Charles   I'm in mourning, the vicar knows I'm here ... I touched his cassock, that's all, I grabbed hold of his cassock.

They pull his coat down around his arms, revealing his bloodstained shirt.

Charles   Hey, I'm not a dosser ...

PC   What's all this?

Charles   What?

PC   This blood.

Pause.

Charles *takes out ID, gives it to the* **WPC** *who studies it and hands it to the* **PC** *who also studies it.*

Charles   Look, my name is Charles Strong. I own a bar on Garratt Lane. I've been working all night ...

PC   Charles Strong, I'm arresting you for assault.

Charles   No, I was drunk ... I had an accident ...

PC   Why were you drunk?

Charles   I was a bit mixed up. Business is bad ... one thing leads to ...

PC   So you decided to attack somebody.

Charles   No.

PC   Did this person attack you?

Charles   No. But . . . earlier . . .

PC   Well, why did you attack him? Eh? You could have killed him.

Charles   My wife, you see . . .

PC   He attacked your wife, did he?

Charles   No, obviously . . .

PC   Obviously . . . is it obvious?

Charles   Listen to me, help me, please . . . My wife was hit by a bus . . . I had a few problems . . . I was . . . I was . . . I was . . . I was lonely . . .

Pause.

And now all this . . . Eh?

Pause.

PC   Are you finished?

Charles   It's difficult to explain.

WPC   Come along then. We'll have a nice cup of tea and you can tell us all about it.

Charles   You're just like her. I mean it. I think you're lovely. Isn't she lovely?

They lead him away.

Blackout.

Love and Understanding

For Sean and Charlotte Flaherty and Elvin Lucic

Love and Understanding was first performed at the Bush Theatre, London, on 30 April 1997, with the following cast:

Neal	Nicholas Tennant
Richie	Paul Bettany
Rachel	Celia Robertson

Directed by Mike Bradwell
Designed by Es Devlin
Lighting by Kevin Sleep
Sound by Simon Whitehorn
Original music composed by Joe Penhall and Caleb Fawcett

Act One

Scene One

Neal and Rachel's flat. Early morning.

Neal and Richie standing in the kitchen. Richie drinking a pint of milk, a suitcase at his feet. A plane is heard overhead.

Neal   We're under the flightpath. One every two minutes.

Richie   Very nice. All yours?

Neal   Will be one day.

Richie   I'm impressed.

Neal   It actually works out a lot cheaper than renting.

Richie   Well, that's the clincher isn't it?

Neal   It's got a good bathroom.

Richie   A bathroom and everything? Wow. Have you got a shower?

Neal   Got a very nice shower.

Richie   A very nice shower? Well, that's very nice isn't it?

He looks around, takes a few steps.

Very clean.

Pause.

Neal   How's Nicky?

Richie   Who?

Neal   Nicky. Your girlfriend.

Pause.

Richie   Oh. We split up.

Neal   Again?

Richie   It's for real this time.

Neal   That's what you said last time.

Richie   It's for real this time.

Neal   Well . . . why?

Richie   I hit her.

Neal   You hit her?

Richie   That's when it started to get ugly.

Neal   Jesus . . .

Richie   That's what she said.

Neal   My God. That's terrible.

Pause.

Then what happened?

Richie   Then she hit me.

Neal   I don't believe it.

Richie   That's what I said.

Neal   You must have really provoked her.

Richie   I suppose I must have.

Pause.

Neal   How hard did you hit her?

Richie   Not very hard. Hard enough to give her a black eye but that's only because she has very delicate skin.

Pause.

The point is Nicky is absolutely the wrong person to hit. She hates violence. She even hates shouting.

Neal   Well, I know . . .

Richie   I mean it really pissed her off. That kind of thing really freaks her out.

Neal   It freaks me out.

Richie   It freaks me out. I've never been so freaked in my life.

Pause.

Neal   But you were so in love.

Richie   I loved her to bits. It was love at first.

Neal   I remember you telling me.

Richie   It was the real thing.

Neal   What went wrong?

Richie   Well that's just it. Who knows? One minute things were fine and the next minute . . . wham.

Neal   It's ridiculous.

Richie   It's absurd.

Pause.

Neal   So where is she now?

Richie   I haven't the faintest idea. Somewhere in South America.

Neal   Oh my God. When's she coming home?

Richie   She could be home tomorrow or in two years' time. She's like that. She's a very impulsive woman.

Pause.

Neal   Well, you like impulsive women.

Richie   Impulsive women are great.

Neal   Depending on the impulse.

Richie   Oh, it depends entirely on the impulse.

Pause.

How's Rachel?

Neal   Fine.

Richie   Happy?

Neal   How d'you mean?

Richie   Is she happy? You know, as opposed to sad.

Neal   I think she's happy. She spent most of this week sleeping.

Richie   Perhaps she was sleepy.

Neal   Actually she's not all that well at the moment. She's just finished six months on a children's ward so she's full of bugs and sniffles.

Richie   Poor thing. Can't you do anything for her?

Neal   Well . . . it goes with the territory.

Richie   But you're a doctor. You're both doctors. It doesn't seem very fair.

Neal   Well it isn't. Absolutely. Still . . .

Pause.

Richie   Are you ready to tie the knot yet?

Neal   No, nothing like that.

Richie   Why not?

Neal   We're happy as we are.

Richie   I'd marry Nicky tomorrow if . . . she didn't hate me . . .

Neal   Well . . . to be honest I don't think Rachel's really the marrying type. She likes her independence.

Richie   Really? She never struck me as the independent type.

Neal   She's not the marrying type, that's all I know.

Richie   Really? I'm surprised.

Pause.

Have you asked her?

.

Neal   Good God no.

Richie   Why not?

Neal   I just don't think she's ready.

Richie   Well the day you get spliced I'm your best man, all right?

Neal   Well, you never know . . .

Richie   Well absolutely. You do never know. Until you ask her.

Neal   Oh of course . . .

Richie   I mean it. I'd get a big bang out of that.

Neal   Of course . . .

Richie *straightens* **Neal***'s tie. Pause.*

Neal   So, where else have you been?

Richie   In Boston. Writing for *The Globe*.

Neal   *The Boston Globe?*

Richie   *Fenway Park Globe.* The Boston Redsox were having a good year and they needed every hack they could lay their hands on. They hadn't won a series since 1920 when they sold Babe Ruth to the Yankees. They call it The Curse. Not long after I arrived they started losing again.

Neal   The last time I saw you you were chasing ambulances and interviewing models from Croydon who used to work in a bakery.

Richie   Funny isn't it?

Neal   Incredible . . . You got any copies?

Richie   How do you mean?

Neal   The stories for *The Globe*.

Richie   I never show my work before it's published. It lets the air out of the tyres.

Pause.

Neal It's not published?

Richie No. Should it be?

Neal Well . . . yes.

Richie Listen. I've just flown six thousand miles. Any danger of a cup of tea?

Neal Coffee.

Richie Is it fresh? I only drink fresh coffee now. Ever since Ecuador.

Neal *prepares coffee.* **Richie** *takes out a packet of cigarettes and lights one, coughs, sips milk.*

Neal Oh. I'd rather you didn't do that in here . . .

Richie Why not?

Neal My clothes will smell of smoke. It's not very pleasant for my patients.

Richie So?

Neal Well . . . do you mind going outside?

Richie You really want me to go outside?

Neal If that's OK . . .

Richie It's a bit chilly . . .

Neal I don't think so . . . We're in the middle of a heatwave.

Richie You call this a heatwave?

Neal Well, I don't smoke and nor does Rachel. It really wouldn't be fair.

Richie I'll lose my train of thought. I might lose my entire inclination. Do you really think that's fair, Neal?

Neal *puts an ashtray down.*

Richie I'll get lonely.

Neal   How would you like your coffee?

Richie   Answer my question. Is it, or isn't it fair?

Neal   How do you have your coffee?

Richie   It isn't fair. It's unfair, isn't it? Cream with about six sugars.

Neal *takes the milk from* **Richie**, *prepares coffee.* **Richie** *opens his case and hands a bottle of scotch to* **Neal**.

Richie   Put a drop of that in will you?

Neal *pours, hands* **Richie** *the coffee.* **Richie** *takes the scotch and adds more.*

Neal   Have you seen your dad yet?

Pause.

Richie?

Richie   No. Why?

Neal   I just thought you could go and stay with him.

Richie   Oh I see . . . well . . . I'd rather stay here.

Neal   You have to see him sooner or later.

Richie   I was in a civil war zone a few days ago. How much more do you think my nerves could take?

Richie *pours more whisky into his coffee. Sips.*

Neal   Did you ring your mum to say you were back?

Richie   Of course I did.

Neal   What did she say?

Richie   She said, 'Oh, that's nice.' Anyway, I didn't come all this way to see them, I came all this way to see you and Rachel. No . . . I'd much rather stay here.

Pause.

Neal   You have a very strange relationship with your parents, don't you Richie?

Richie I have a very strange relationship with everybody, Neal. If you don't know that by now you soon will.

Pause.

Neal Well ... how long were you planning on staying?

Richie How long can I stay?

Neal I'll have to talk to Rachel.

Richie I'll talk to her.

Neal I'll talk to her, Rich.

Richie OK. But don't take any shit.

Neal How do you mean? .

Richie Don't let her manipulate you.

Neal Manipulate me? What on earth makes you think she'll do that?

Richie Well, I expect she's quite stern about this sort of thing.

Neal What do you mean, 'stern'?

Richie Well, I'm sure she has her rules.

Neal We just have to agree. Nothing to do with being stern.

Richie Oh, I like stern women. Stern women are great.

Neal *produces a blanket and pillow and puts them on the sofa.*

Neal I should get to work.

Richie I wouldn't mind a kip now. Shake off some of that jet-lag.

Neal Well ... feel free to use the sofa.

Richie Haven't you got a bed?

Neal I just told you. Rachel's asleep.

Richie Can't you wake her up? I'm shagged.

Neal She's been working very hard.

Richie   Neal . . . I'm winding you up. I'll be fine.

Richie *goes to the sofa, takes the blanket and wraps it around himself. He sits on the sofa with his feet up and drinks from the whisky bottle.*

Richie   Safe as milk.

Drinks.

Sound as a pound.

Neal   I think it's a little early to be . . .

Richie   I'm thirsty. You have no idea how those jumbos dehydrate you.

Neal *picks up his case and jacket and goes to the door.* **Richie** *suddenly winces.*

Richie   Fuck.

Neal   Are you all right?

Richie   Just a bit of a headache. Just . . . severe stabbing pains in my head. I've had them for months. Probably all the flying . . .

Neal   You should get out in the fresh air, clear your lungs, take your mind off things.

Richie   Are you trying to get me out of the house?

Neal   No of course not . . .

Pause.

Of course not . . . I just don't want any . . .

Richie   Any what, Neal? Wild parties? I came here because I thought you'd understand.

Neal   I do.

Richie   Maybe you could fix me up with something. Pain-killers. I am really in quite a lot of pain.

Richie *drinks.*

Neal   Well . . . if it's serious you should come to the hospital.

Have a scan.

Richie   Come to the hospital? Now?

Neal   When you've rested.

Richie   I'd love to come to the hospital. I've been waiting for you to invite me.

Neal   When you've rested.

Richie   I'm rested now.

Neal   Actually Richie, I've got a very busy morning.

Richie   I don't mind.

Neal   No. I'm really snowed under at the moment.

Richie   I don't mind.

Scene Two

Hospital. Morning.

Neal *sitting at a desk looking at scans.* **Richie**, *shirtless, sitting in a chair.*

Richie   I've always liked Rachel. Nice, uncomplicated ... clean. I bet she wears Marks and Spencer's underwear, am I right?

Neal   Actually, sometimes she doesn't wear any underwear.

Richie   No. No knickers? It's always the quiet ones.

Neal *produces a* Gray's Anatomy *and tries to read.*

Richie   When my relationship with Nicky went West I vowed that the next relationship I had would be with somebody rather bourgeois and conventional. Dull even. A woman who doesn't crave alcohol or drugs, isn't particularly promiscuous, not remotely interested in danger and machismo ... finds daytime TV entertaining and informative. No spiritual life whatsoever ... you know the sort. They're less flighty and sometimes, I suspect, more sincere.

Neal   Really?

Richie   Really. Where do I get a woman like that?

Neal   You just keep your hands to yourself . . .

Richie   I bet you two have fun playing doctors and nurses.
Or is doctors and doctors better? You could have a ball.
Rubber gloves. Stirrups. Outrageous.

Neal *sighs and goes back to his writing.*

Richie   I love the smell of hospitals. The cleaning fluids, the
raw alcohol, the ethanol, the pervasive air of a thousand
highly expensive intravenous drugs doing their benevolent task.
The nurses mincing about in their crisp, clean, starched
uniforms. I adore nurses . . . You know, places like this really
bring out the Anglo-Saxon in me. Have you got any milk?

Richie *opens the fridge.*

Neal   Stay out of that will you?

Richie   I'm looking for milk.

Neal   The only milk you'll find in there is milk of magnesia.

Richie *takes a vial from the fridge and examines it.*

Richie   You know, you could make a fortune out of this.

Neal   Richie please. You're making me nervous . . .

Richie *shuts the fridge and sits down. Pause.*

Neal   I can't see anything wrong with you. You're fine.

Richie *rests his head on the desk.*

Neal   Richie?

Richie   How about a shot of morphine? That'll perk me up.

Neal   Morphine? No . . .

Richie   Oh come on . . .

Neal   What do you want morphine for?

Richie   You mean you've never tried it? But you're a

doctor.

Neal　Are you some kind of junkie now?

Richie　A what? A 'junkie'?

Richie *laughs.*

Well, strictly speaking, I'm a speed freak.

Pause.

No but seriously ... it's a form of self-medication.

Pause.

I get ... depressed.

Neal　I'm not surprised.

Richie　Do you think it's funny?

Neal　No. Do you really get depressed? Real depression?

Richie　Well, overwhelming melancholy, certainly. Give me
a shot of morphine and I'll leave you alone.

Pause.

Neal　No. I'm sorry.

Richie　Come on. Don't be such a spoilsport.

Neal　Look ... at the end of the day all these drugs do is
induce a state of euphoria no greater or less than you'd get
from eating a good steak, having a roll in the hay with your
girlfriend or going to bed early with a good book for that
matter. It's a waste of time.

Richie　I don't have a girlfriend any more.

Pause.

Neal　The thing is Richie, you've come at a bit of a bad
time.

Richie　Tell me your problems then. Come on. Talk to me.
I'm listening.

Pause.

Neal I've got too much responsibility. I'm in charge of intensive care and I shouldn't be. I'm working every day and every night. I never see Rachel because she's working every day and every night. We haven't talked properly in three weeks. We communicate by Post-It notes. Answerphone messages, for God's sake.

Richie I hate those things.

Neal So do I. But what else can we do?

Richie I hate those ones with the tunes. You know those tacky fucking tunes?

Neal So do I. So I leave a note saying, Let's go out to dinner. Let's set aside a time for each other. Then she leaves a note saying, Yes, good idea. Only I don't get the note, because it's taken me a few days to find it and she's tidied it up, in a hurry to get to work. I don't know this, so after a few days I leave a message on the answerphone saying, Do you want to go out to dinner or not? And she leaves one saying, Of course, I already said I did. So I leave another note saying, You didn't actually but anyway, when? Then she leaves a note saying, I damn well did and I don't really like the tone of your message. Now there's something in my tone that she doesn't like . . . or something in her tone that I don't like . . . and on it goes. On and on and on. I don't know what to do. I'm at my wit's end. I mean it really is a dilemma.

Pause.

Richie Have you tried paging her?

Neal I mean it Rich. Things have been a bit funny with us lately.

Richie Funny ha ha or funny strange?

Neal Are you listening to me?

Pause.

Richie Are you still sleeping together?

Neal   How do you mean?

Richie   I mean what about bedtime? Talk to her at bedtime.

Neal   We're asleep by bedtime. I stagger in, shagged, fall asleep. She staggers in shagged, falls asleep, one of us wakes up and the other's gone to work ... there's just no ... there just doesn't seem to be any ...

Richie   Shagging?

Neal   Chance would be a fine thing ...

Richie   None at all?

Neal   Not lately, no ...

Richie   How lately?

Neal   Does it matter?

Richie   Well ... yes ...

Neal   I don't really want to go into it ...

Richie   Well of course you don't. No, of course not. I mean it's none of my business, obviously.

Pause.

I just find it astounding.

Pause.

I find it astonishing ... no sex ...

Neal   Richie ...

Richie   I'm staggered. I don't know what to say ...

Neal   Richie!

Richie   You really are in a state aren't you?

Neal   I just have a few things to sort out that's all. A few things on my mind.

Richie   It's not me is it? I'm not getting on your nerves am I? Because you know me. If I can help in any way you only have to say.

Can I borrow some money?

Neal   Look, I'm trying to tell you . . . I'm just saying . . . we need some time to ourselves.

Richie   And I'm just saying, relax. I'm here now. You and me are going to have a good time.

Richie *punches* **Neal***'s arm playfully.* **Neal** *just looks at him.*

Richie   So can I borrow some money or what?

Neal   How much do you want?

Richie   How much have you got?

Neal *takes out his wallet.*

Neal   I've got a fifty or a tenner.

Richie   Well a tenner's not going to get me very far is it?

Neal   It's all I have.

He hands **Richie** *the tenner.*

Richie   You must have more.

Neal   I don't.

Richie   Give me the fifty and I'll buy you a drink tonight.

Neal   I'm busy tonight.

Richie   Have a night off. One night off Neal. One night with your lovely girlfriend and your old pal. Marvellous.

Pause.

Neal   Actually, I'm taking Rachel out to dinner tonight.

Richie   Oh. So you're not working tonight.

Neal   No.

Richie   Oh. I see. That was all a lie, was it?

Neal   I just want to get her on her own for a few hours and . . . you know . . .

Richie   Fuck her brains out. Absolutely . . .

Neal   Make contact. It's important to me Rich.

Pause.

Richie   Anywhere in mind?

Neal   There's a nice French restaurant in the Fulham Road. By the police station.

Richie   It's a dump. I reviewed it once. The lamb's like dog food.

Neal   Well we'll have a curry then . . .

Richie   No, I can't have a curry now. I need English food.

Neal   You're not coming.

Richie   What's wrong with the pub? That'll loosen her up.

Neal   Do you understand?

Richie   Absolutely. I understand. I'm not completely insensitive.

Scene Three

Pub. Evening.

Richie, **Neal** *and* **Rachel** *sitting at a garden table.*

Richie   After Patzcuaro, we travelled around for a bit and went to Oaxaca, which is like a trendy student town, a sort of mixture of Acapulco and Bristol, really. Lots of wrought iron and vegetarian tortilla houses. Then we got a boat across the lake to San Pedro. Volcano town. A great blue fire-breathing plutonic rock placed in a bright green wilderness by God himself. Beautiful. I mean, really spectacular, Neal. We were in paradise. A nice hotel room with a balcony overlooking the water, pissed every night on tequila, everything in it's rightful place. We were very content Neal. Astonishingly happy . . .

Neal   We went to Richmond once. Went rowing in a rowing boat. On the river. You can hire them for a fiver. Lots of people do it . . .

Richie   Sometime around Christmas a man called Carlos moved into the next room. We got to know him on New Year's Eve when Nicky invited him in for a drink. My God, what a character . . . 'Yo hablo buenas historias!' he said. 'I speak the good story!' And by fuck did he have some stories . . .

Neal   My God, is that the time? Is anybody hungry?

Richie   I could murder another scotch.

Neal   I'm hungry. Are you hungry?

Rachel   Yes. Let's eat.

Richie   But we've only just got here. Have another drink. Work up an appetite.

Neal   No I think we'll get going now. I booked the table for eight.

Richie   Have another drink.

Neal   It's half past now.

Richie   You'll be fashionably late.

Rachel   I don't want another drink.

Neal   I don't want another drink either.

Richie   I'll tell you what. I'll get the round in while you make up your minds.

Richie *goes. Pause.*

Neal   Well. This is nice, isn't it?

Rachel   Oh, I don't mind.

Neal   I do. We're meant to be going out to dinner.

Rachel   Well, tell him.

Neal   I've told him. I made it absolutely clear.

Rachel   What did he say?

Neal   He doesn't care.

Pause.

Rachel   Well. I don't suppose it matters.

Neal   It bloody well does.

Rachel   Neal, don't snap at me.

Neal   I'm sorry.

Rachel   Well, what's upsetting you?

Neal   Him.

Rachel   Why?

Neal   I can't explain it. I'm just on a short fuse at the moment.

Rachel   Look. We'll have a nice drink, he can finish all his silly stories and then we can find him a hotel. All right?

Pause.

Neal   I've been meaning to talk to you about that.

Rachel   Why?

Neal   . . . I think he wants to stay for a few days.

Rachel   Well he can't.

Neal   I know. That's what I said.

Rachel   Well he can, but we're both working. I don't know what he's going to do with himself.

Neal   I know. That's what I said.

Rachel   And what did he say?

Neal   He doesn't care.

Pause.

Rachel   I'll talk to him.

Neal   You can try.

Rachel   I will.

Neal But don't let him manipulate you.

Rachel What do you mean?

Neal You know what he's like.

Rachel Oh, he's just a bit of a chancer. He'll get the message.

Richie *returns with white powder around his nose. He places the drinks and sits rubbing his nose and sniffing, grinding his teeth and so forth.* **Neal** *looks at him and indicates,* **Richie** *just stares.*

Richie . . . So meanwhile, the main coke dealer in town was a former CIA agent riddled with nine types of cancer.

Neal Richie . . .

Neal *indicates again.*

Richie Oh . . . thanks . . .

Richie *wipes his nose.*

He called himself Jack but his real name was Simon. I don't know, that's the CIA for you. They pride themselves simultaneously on their lively intellect and their macho Celtic roots . . .

Neal The CIA?

Richie Something like that, yes. Does it matter?

Neal Well . . . yes.

Richie All right. He was a piano tuner from Scunthorpe who'd just won the lottery. He was a plumber from Nebraska . . . do you want to hear this story or not?

Neal . . . No . . .

Richie Personally, I couldn't bear the cunt but Nicky developed a strong affection for him.

Neal Richie, please . . .

Richie I spent a lot of time drunk. They spent a lot of time togther. There was a chemistry between them and I was . . .

nervous but at the same time . . . strangely excited.

Rachel   You don't have to tell us this. It's none of our business . . .

Neal   Absolutely. None of our business. Drink up . . .

Richie   She was the first person in a decade who'd listened to his bullshit without looking at her watch.

Neal   Mm-hm. You're blaming the break-up of your relationship on the CIA?

Neal *laughs and stands.*

Is it just me, or is that the funniest fucking thing you've ever heard in your entire life?

Neal *starts to go.*

Richie   Are you done?

Neal   Sorry?

Richie   Have you finished?

Neal   I was only saying . . .

Richie   What? What exactly are you saying Neal?

Neal *sits. Pause.*

Richie   It wasn't sexual. No doubt about that. I checked.

Neal   How did you check?

Richie   I asked her.

Neal   You asked her? Priceless . . .

Richie   Why do you think I'm here?

Neal   You really asked her that?

Rachel   Shut up Neal . . .

Richie   Yes Neal, I asked her. And it haunts me to this day that such a delightful relationship could be ruined by something so tragically ridiculous but . . . c'est la vie.

Pause.

Neal   When are you going to stop telling these absurd stories? It's like an evening with Graham Greene. I don't think even you can tell when you're lying any more.

Richie   Are you calling me a liar?

Neal   Yes. I wasn't being subtle.

Richie   What do you mean, 'a liar'?

Silence.

Neal   I'll call the restaurant. Tell them we're on our way.

Neal *goes. Silence.*

Rachel   So. Have you found somewhere to stay?

Richie   How do you mean?

Rachel   Have you found a hotel?

Richie   Well . . . I'm staying with you, aren't I?

Rachel   Oh. Really?

Richie   Well . . . I mean if that's all right.

Pause.

Didn't Neal talk to you about it?

Rachel   Oh, he mentioned something . . .

Richie   He said he was going to talk to you about it. I mean . . . he said you were going through a bit of a rough patch and . . . I mean I understand if it's a problem.

Rachel   Well, we're just very busy at the moment . . .

Richie   Absolutely. I mean, he said you were pretty . . . stern about this sort of thing. I mean, he did warn me . . .

Rachel   'Stern'? What do you mean, 'warned' you?

Richie   He just said, you know, you were . . . a bit jumpy at the moment.

Rachel 'Jumpy'?

Richie Well he said things were, you know, a bit funny between you two at the moment. You know . . . you're both working hard. You never see each other etcetera . . . I mean . . . he was quite frank about it. And I understand.

Rachel Frank about what?

Richie He said you weren't . . . communicating any more. That's all. He just said that there wasn't any . . . communication at the moment. If you know what I mean. I mean . . . you know Neal . . . he likes to get things off his chest. He could've been a bit more discreet I suppose but . . . what could I do?

Silence.

Rachel Have I missed something?

Richie Rachel, I wouldn't worry about it. You know what he's like. I've come from the other side of the world and Neal's decided to be boring about it. You know. Things change. People change. It's no big deal.

Long pause.

Rachel Neal isn't boring.

Richie He is. He's always been boring.

Rachel He isn't boring. He's just . . . quieter than you.

Richie A little shy and retiring. Absolutely.

Rachel Unpretentious.

Richie Unpretentious and a little unadventurous sometimes . . .

Rachel Perceptive.

Richie Well absolutely. He thinks about things . . .

Rachel He does. He's thoughtful . . .

Richie Earnest even. Humourless. And a little narrow-minded on occasions but only because he's so principled . . .

Rachel   He's just not like you.

Richie   No, absolutely. Absolutely. Enough said.

Pause.

Actually, he hasn't always been boring. When we were kids he was almost preternaturally fascinated with notions of playing 'doctors and nurses'.

Rachel   Really? Who with?

Richie   Oh, some little floozy. Actually his next-door neighbour. You know what kids are like . . . It's a bit seedy really. Apparently they stripped completely naked one day and . . . she showed him everything.

Rachel   Neal?

Richie   They were on a climbing-frame at the time . . . I mean, he went into explicit detail about it. Frankly gynaecological.

Pause.

Rachel   Then what happened?

Richie   Then he showed her everything. He's been almost uncontrollably titillated by the potential of role-playing ever since.

Rachel   Ridiculous.

Richie   So you see, he's really far more complex and charismatic than you think.

Pause.

Obviously I'd prefer it if you didn't mention it to him. He gets a bit jumpy when he thinks I've betrayed his confidence.

Neal *returns.*

Neal   They're filling up. We really have to make a move.

Richie   I haven't finished my drink.

Rachel   I'm not hungry now.

Neal   Well I'm starving.

Rachel   Well I'm not.

Richie   Nor am I. I'm still thirsty.

Neal   What do you mean you're not hungry?

Rachel   I mean, I'm not hungry. I mean, I think I'd like another drink.

Neal   What do you mean?

Rachel   I mean I'd like another drink. I'm in the mood to drink. Drink and talk. You know. Communicate.

Pause.

Neal   Oh. Well . . .

He sits.

Richie   The most memorable drinking I ever did was in New York. Irish bar called Malachy's on 72nd and Columbus. The screwdrivers were like raw diazepam . . .

Neal   Have you ever heard of Wenicke-Korakoff's Syndrome?

Richie   No. Should I have?

Neal   Alcoholics get it. One symptom is confabulation, otherwise known as inane chatter, often fabricated to present a legitimate, rather than untenable account of the recent past following memory loss. Another is depletion of social skills.

Richie   Could we have that in English?

Neal   It means you can't shut up.

Richie   Well I never knew that before. How splendidly edifying.

Silence. They drink.

Rachel   I want to go to New York. I'd love to get smashed on screwdrivers in an Irish bar in Manhattan.

Richie   You wouldn't like it. It's all hairy-arsed commuters

from Buffalo blowing their wages on baseball cards and
hookers.

Rachel   No I think I'd like it. You know, one day. When
things aren't so funny between us. When I'm a little less
jumpy about things perhaps.

Neal   . . . They have those places here now. In the Fulham
Road.

Richie   Really?

Neal   Yes.

Richie   How jolly.

Rachel   We should give it a try some time. When I'm a
little less jumpy about things. Once we've got through the
rough patch.

Neal *looks at* **Rachel,** *then at* **Richie,** *then at* **Rachel** *again.*
Pause.

Neal   Have I missed something?

Richie   Do they still have that place by the river with the
wagon wheels and the Wurlitzer? Very transatlantic. Very 'go-
go'.

Rachel   The Putney Star and Garter.

Richie   That's the one.

Neal   . . . I have lunch there when I'm at Queen Mary's.
Has a rather nice view of the river . . .

Richie   Perhaps we could have a spot of lunch there
sometime?

Rachel   I'd like that.

Richie   You could take a day off. Really let your hair down.

Neal   You can't take a day off now.

Rachel   At least entertain the notion, Neal.

Richie   Yeah. Entertain the notion, Neal . . .

Rachel   How long are you staying?

Richie   How long can I stay?

Rachel   How long would you like to stay?

Richie   Well . . . long enough to have lunch at the Putney Star and Garter . . . I mean, I wouldn't miss it for the world . . .

Neal   Look . . . listen . . . look . . . listen . . .

Rachel   What's wrong?

Pause.

Neal   Never mind.

Pause. They drink.

Richie   Isn't this marvellous? It's just so wonderful to be home. It really is nice. Who's for a short? Rachel?

Scene Four

Hospital. Morning.

Neal *sitting, holding phone.* **Richie** *looking in the fridge.*

Neal   What's going on? I told you to put him through to my office . . .
Well I'm here now. Thank you . . .
I'm listening . . .
Jesus Christ . . .
Well it's not my fault . . . Who else knows?
I hope you didn't give them my name . . .
Why?

Pause.

Hello?

He hangs up.

Richie   Problems?

Neal   A heart by-pass patient on a ventilator died last week during a power failure.

Richie   What happened to the back-up generator?

Neal   It didn't come on and the only person who knew how to switch it on was sick.

Richie   Ridiculous.

Neal   Richie . . .

Richie   The press is going to have a field-day.

Neal   I know . . .

Richie   They should get their emergency procedure sorted out.

Neal   I am the emergency procedure . . . Look, what are you doing here? Stay away from that . . .

Richie *shuts the fridge*

Richie   This happened when I was working for the *Hammersmith Recorder*. We thought it was Christmas.

Richie *retrieves the bottle of scotch and pours. The phone rings.* **Neal** *picks it up.*

Neal   Yes?
No press . . .
I am not qualified to make a statement to the press . . .
Find one of the consultants.

Pause.

Are they really in management meetings or are you just saying that?

Pause.

I'm not being churlish . . .

Pause.

I have a right to be angry . . .
My nerves are shot . . .
I just want to be left alone . . .
I just want to do my job . . .
Will somebody please help me please?

Hello?

He hangs up. Silence.

Richie   You shouldn't get so wrapped up in it. Who cares?

Neal   I have to be wrapped up in it. I have to care. I do care. More and more I don't want to. But there you go . . .

Richie   I absolutely understand . . . If you don't care enough you're a bad doctor and if you care too much you'll go insane and be no use to anyone etcetera. It's a dilemma. And the answer's very very simple.

Neal   Well you'd better tell me then.

Richie   You're not cut out to be a doctor. Maybe you should try something a little less cut-throat. Like show business.

Silence.

Neal   This is my job. My thing. I like it.

Richie   Why?

Neal   Because I can make a difference.

Richie   To who?

Pause.

Neal   I'm going to go berserk in a minute.

Richie   What is it?

Pause.

Is it lack of confidence?

The phone rings. **Richie** *picks it up.*

Neal   I'll take it.

Richie   (*into phone*)   Yes?

Neal *reaches for the phone,* **Richie** *pulls it away.*

Neal   Give it to me.

Richie (*into phone*)   What do you want to know about it?

Neal   My God. Who is it?

Richie (*to* **Neal**)   Press office.
(*Into phone.*) Now shut up and listen to me. Better still, take this down, you do have shorthand don't you? There was a power failure, full stop. The back-up generator was faulty and we're still investigating the cause of that fault, full stop.

Neal   Richie please . . .

Richie (*into phone*)   Fortunately the day-to-day running of the hospital was not unduly affected and of the few patients on ventilators none came to any harm, full stop new paragraph . . .

Neal   I'm begging you . . .

Richie (*into phone*)   Unfortunately, comma, in a part of the hospital which was not affected, comma, one patient recovering from a life-threatening illness passed away during the night. Full stop close quotes.

Neal   Fuck . . .

Richie (*into phone*)   He just died in the night.

Pause.

It's a coincidence.

Richie *hangs up abruptly.* **Neal** *sits with his head in his hands.*

Richie   Are you all right?

Neal   It's unethical.

Richie   It's standard practice.

Neal   It's immoral.

Richie   We had no choice. There's no point in you sticking your neck out.

Neal   A man died. The least we can do is tell the truth.

Richie   Don't be ridiculous.

Neal   What about the family? I can't lie to his family.

Richie   Will you just dry up?

Neal   We are complicit . . . we are complicit now in a moral felony.

Richie   A moral what?

He laughs.

Neal   Will you listen to me?

Richie   Are you hungry?

Neal   Why are you like this?

Richie   Why are you like this? Moan moan moan . . . honestly. You've had a nice suburban upbringing. Loving parents. Educated at one of the finest comprehensives in Wolverhampton. Good job, nice flat, sexy girlfriend. You're practically a blueprint for mindless contentment, but you're still not happy, are you?

Neal   . . . I'm perfectly happy!

Richie *retrieves the bottle of scotch, pours, they drink.*

Richie   Neal, everything's going to be all right. Everybody has these doubts.

Neal   I see a psychiatrist friend once a month. He says I suffer from anxiety. As a favour, he doesn't invoice me, but I pay him anyway because it's against my principles.

Richie   You really suffer from anxiety? That surprises me.

Neal   It's nothing.

Richie   You'll burn yourself out.

Neal   I don't want to talk about it.

Pause.

You have your problems, I have mine.

Richie   I've never had to resort to psychiatric help.

Neal   Maybe you should. Now leave me alone.

Richie *exits.*

Scene Five

Bedroom. Night.

Rachel *and* **Neal** *lounging on the bed. Moonlight from a window.*

Rachel   Isn't the moon beautiful? And the sunset. Wasn't the sunset lovely tonight? Golden. It didn't look like England. Didn't look like London. The common, rinsed in sunlight . . . Gorgeous.

Neal   He met the Dean of the medical school today. In the cafeteria. Kept calling him James and laughing.

Rachel   Don't worry about it.

Neal   He's a clown. A misfit.

Rachel   He's just a bit lost, that's all.

Neal   Do you know why he spends his life travelling around the world? Because nobody can bear him at home.

Rachel   He did you a favour.

Neal   He lied.

Rachel   He was being economical with the truth.

Neal   One of my patients died.

Rachel   They die all the time and it wasn't your fault. If he hadn't done what he did you would have swung for it.

Neal   I know. But I can't help feeling that something terrible is going to happen. Something inexplicable and insidious and . . . unexpected. I mean where's it going to end? What next?

Rachel   You're very stressed at the moment. It's just anxiety.

Neal   Is it? Is it really?

Rachel   Yes.

She kisses him chastely.

He told me a funny story about you. He said that as a child you had a thing about playing 'doctors and nurses'.

Neal   How do you mean?

Rachel   He said there was this little girl who you became intimately familiar with on a climbing-frame.

Neal   He did, did he?

Rachel   I thought it was quite sweet.

Neal   It's nonsense. It's a lie.

Rachel   It's a rather charming one.

Neal   I hate it when he does that. He's so . . . mendacious.

Rachel   Well, I dare say it's fairly harmless.

Neal   It's stupid. It's just stupid . . .

Rachel   I wouldn't lose any sleep over it.

Neal   No. No of course not. That would be playing right into his hands.

Silence.

Rachel   Do you remember when I lived in Kilburn?

Neal   Vaguely.

Rachel   Oh you do. You remember. Things were fun in those days. Everything was fun. Just going out for a takeaway was fun. Spectacularly engrossing. We did a lot of sitting about on the floor with candles I seem to remember. We'd lie in bed for hours and hours and light candles and talk long into the night.

Neal   Mm.

Rachel   I mean we really talked. Long, long into the night. Very intense long chats.

Neal   What about?

Rachel   Oh, all sorts of things. Books, films, where we wanted to go, what we wanted to do with our lives. We'd just talk. Laugh. Giggle. Tell each other stories. You know, communicate.

She kisses him.

Let's go away somewhere.

Neal   Where do you want to go?

Rachel   I don't know. Prague. Thailand. Leeds.

Neal   I don't want to go anywhere. I want him to go.

Rachel   What about me?

Neal   You know holidays make me nervous. It's the leaving that's the worst part . . .

Rachel   And the coming home . . .

Neal   Airports make me nervous . . .

Rachel   And all that time in between . . .

Neal   I can't stop thinking about work.

Rachel   It could be worse. Look at Richie. He's haunted.

Neal   No. He's just confused.

Rachel   I think it's interesting. A 'dark side'.

Neal   I'm haunted.

Rachel   No. You're just a worrier.

Neal   What do I worry about?

Rachel   Everything. Every thought you have has an intrinsically lugubrious, sensitive quality. It's just the type of person you are. I like it.

Neal   Really?

Rachel   Absolutely.

Pause.

Neal   That's just what I like about you. The quality of your thoughts is entirely different. Generous and unassuming. You're an extremely positive person but not in a relentless, thrusting way.

Rachel   I like the way you worry about things. Some people never worry about anything and that's just boring.

Pause.

Neal   I like these conversations. I feel better already.

Rachel   My darling. I'll look after you.

Neal   I'll look after you.

Rachel   I don't need looking after.

Neal   What do you need?

Rachel   I don't need anything. A ticket to Thailand would be nice.

Pause.

Neal   See, now this is what worries me.

Rachel   Why?

Neal   Because it exemplifies precisely what I was talking about. I should be happy that you're so adventurous and independent but I'd prefer it if you needed more attention.

Rachel   Maybe I do. Maybe we both do.

Pause.

Neal   You know, it's become my aim in life to become more like you. I'd rather I became more like you as we grew old than you became like me.

Rachel   Me too. Definitely.

Neal   Maybe that's how marriage works. You become more like each other. Given the right proximity and exposure, people rub off on each other. And I want you to rub off on me.

Rachel I want you to rub off on me too.

Pause.

Neal I mean, I'd love to be married to you. I'd get a big bang out of that.

Rachel Me too. You know. One day . . .

Pause.

Neal We're never bored with each other. We never argue. No weirdness or complexity has so far manifested and maybe never will. Maybe we're immune.
I think we are.
We are. We're immune.

Pause.

Have we just proposed to each other?

Silence. **Richie** *is standing in the doorway, watching.* **Neal** *watches* **Richie**. **Neal** *pulls the sheet over* **Rachel**. **Rachel** *turns and sees* **Richie**.

Rachel Hi.

Richie Hi-ya.

Pause.

I was looking for the bathroom.

Rachel It's next door. I'll show you.

Neal It's next door. You can't miss it.

Richie *goes.*

Neal Did you see that?

Rachel What?

Neal The way he just stood there, staring.

Rachel I didn't see.

Neal He was standing there staring. For ages. Without

saying anything.

Rachel   He was probably embarrassed.

Neal   He wasn't embarrassed. He was enjoying himself.

Rachel   I don't think so.

Neal   He was staring right at you. Gazing at your naked arse.

Rachel   Why would he do that?

Neal   Why do you think?

Rachel   Don't be ridiculous.

Neal   I'm not being ridiculous. You're being . . . He was . . .

Rachel   What? Just don't worry about it.

Neal   I'm not worried about it . . .

Rachel   Well just forget about it . . .

Neal   All right, it's forgotten.

Rachel   This is our time now. You and me. Alone. Together . . .

Neal   I know. Absolutely . . .

Pause.

Rachel   What shall we do now?

Neal   He knows where the bathroom is. I showed him.

Rachel   Maybe he forgot . . .

Neal   No. You don't forget a thing like that.

Rachel   Oh Neal . . .

Neal   You don't believe me do you?

Rachel   Don't be silly. I just think . . .

Neal   I'm not being silly. You're being . . .

Rachel   What?

Neal I hate to say it but . . .

Rachel Well don't say it then.

Pause.

Neal I just think you're being a bit . . . naive.

Rachel Naive?

Neal I think you are.

Rachel Neal, for goodness sake. He probably didn't know what to say.

Neal He was watching us. Watching you.

Rachel So what?

Neal So what?

Pause.

So what?

Pause.

So, I don't like it, that's what.

He rolls over.

Blackout.

Scene Six

Neal *and* **Rachel**'s *flat. Early morning.*

Richie *lying face down on the floor, clutching a whisky bottle.* **Neal** *standing, tying his tie.*

Neal What are you doing today?

Pause. He prods **Richie** *with his foot.*

Wake up Richie.

He slaps **Richie**'s *face.*

What have you done?

He looks on the floor and picks up a syringe and vial.

You stupid prick.

He slaps **Richie**'s *face quickly.* **Rachel** *enters with a towel around her, hair wet.*

Rachel   What's all this row about?

Neal   He's knocked himself out with ketamine.

Rachel   Christ. I'll get my bag.

Neal *finds* **Richie**'s *pulse.*

Neal   Ring the hospital and tell them to send a resuscitation unit and an airway. They might need an IV so tell them to get one ready.

Rachel *goes to the phone and dials.* **Richie** *blinks and looks around.* **Rachel** *puts the phone down.*

Rachel   Thank God.

Neal   Where did you get this from? He's caned ... This is a serious general anaesthetic. I use it in the operating theatre. It's the closest thing you can do to killing someone and if you don't know how to do it you do kill them.

Richie   And you can buy it off grannies on any Moscow street corner. Relax.

Neal   You might as well do smack.

Richie   Oh I do smack all the time. The whole trip, man. Sometimes I wear an upside-down crucifix I bought in Berlin and paint my fingernails black for parties.

Neal   If I was caught using this in my home I'd go to prison.

Richie   I'd visit you.

Neal   They could've been stolen from my doctor's bag. Or my supply fridge. From right under my nose ...

Rachel   You're not helping, Neal . . .

Richie   Are you accusing me? Me? Of all people . . . ?

Neal   Yes.

Richie   Then you've got the balls of King Kong. I'm flabbergasted.

Pause.

I'm fucking astonished.

Pause.

All right. I pinched it. Shoot me.

Neal   Don't you understand? One of these days they'll cart you into my hospital on a stretcher and I'll have to save your life.

Richie   Well I hope you know what you're doing.

Neal   Don't you think I have enough to contend with?

Richie *sits up.*

Neal   How much have you got left?

Richie   Nothing.

Neal   How much Richie?

Richie   Five milligrams.

Neal   It's not funny, I've got problems.

Richie   Have you?

Neal   Either it's me or it's you. I honestly can't tell any more.

Richie *produces the ketamine. Hands it over.*

Neal   Wouldn't you say that you've gone far enough or are there depths you still haven't sunk to yet?

Richie   I'd say that I've seen God and I want to see him again.

Neal   You probably will.

Rachel   Well, it's done now. What's done is done.

Neal   What do you think would happen if every time they wheeled in somebody with a crushed skull and punctured lungs they got you and you said, 'It's done now. What's done is done'? Eh? Think about it.

Rachel   Look, you're just getting a little . . .

Neal   A little what? Anxious?

Rachel   Yes.

Neal   Fine.

Pause.

Anxious, fine.

Pause.

Over-anxious or just anxious?

Rachel   You don't have to get uptight with me.

Neal   I'm sorry. I'm sorry but . . .

Rachel   But what?

Pause.

Just don't don't do it Neal. It's not nice.

Neal   I'm sorry . . .

Rachel   OK?

Rachel *exits to the bedroom.*

Richie   You've done it now. She's upset. I can tell.

Pause.

It's the silent treatment for you for a while. I bet she's good at the silent treatment, that one. I expect you'll have to go in there and make it up to her now. Go and cheer her up. Go and give her a good thorough cheering up. A good, long, hard cheering up.

Neal   When are you going to leave us alone?

Richie   Sorry?

Neal   I mean I've had enough and I want you out of here now.

Richie   Well you'll have to lend me the money.

Neal *produces money and gives it to* **Richie**.

Richie   Are you sure you don't want to talk to Rachel about this?

Neal   She wants you out. She told me.

Richie   Are you sure?

Neal   As soon as you've found a hotel.

Richie   That could take some time.

Neal   That's not my problem. It's your problem. Understand?

Pause.

And I'd appreciate it if at some point in the future you stop telling your libidinous, vaguely deranged childhood stories about me.

Richie   I don't know what you're talking about.

Neal   That childish story about me playing 'doctors and nurses'. You were telling that at school. You just haven't changed have you?

Richie   Sometimes I vary it.

Neal   What?

Richie   Sometimes it's 'firemen'.

Neal   You're sick.

Richie   I did you a favour. At least now she thinks you're interesting, instead of spending the rest of her life only seeing you as the mincing, leftie, goody-goody jobsworth you really are. I wish I had a friend who'd do that for me.

Neal   You don't have any friends.

Richie   There's no need to get personal.

Rachel *returns wearing a towelling robe and fills the kettle.*

Richie   Are you going to work now?

Neal   We're not leaving you here by yourself.

Rachel   He can stay if he likes. I'm taking the day off.

Neal   Why?

Rachel   I'm not feeling well.

Neal   What's wrong with you?

Rachel   I don't know. I just don't want to go to work.

Richie   Nothing wrong with that.

Pause.

Rachel   I'm just run down.

Neal   Let me feel your glands.

He goes to feel her glands, she pushes him away.

Rachel   Oh, get off me . . .

Rachel *goes back to the bedroom and slams the door.*

Richie   Hysterical . . .

Neal   Now what have I done?

Richie   I love it when she scolds you. I like a good scolding . . .

Neal   What did I do?

Silence.

Richie   Neal, I really don't want to cause any problems.

Scene Seven

River. Afternoon.

Richie *and* **Rachel** *walking.* **Rachel** *holds a bunch of cornflowers.*

Richie   I fancy a swim.

Rachel   You can't swim in the river. You'll get meningitis.

Richie   Who cares?

Rachel   You know, we shouldn't have done that. I'm feeling a bit pissed.

Richie *belches.*

Richie   What was that place called? I don't like that place.

Rachel   Which one?

Richie   The first one. The Moon one. On the Green.

Rachel   It's called The Moon on the Green.

Richie   And did we?

They chuckle. They stop and soak up the sun.

Rachel   This is what your day off should be about. What's wrong with the occasional afternoon in the pub? What's wrong with the occasional sickie? What's wrong with the occasional . . . lie?

Richie   It's contra to the Hippocratic oath.

Rachel   I spend my days off studying mental patients in Springfield. Then there's the crack-ups at the Maudsley. I might join them soon if I don't get a holiday.

Richie   No. Not you.

Rachel   I just wish it was like it was before. Before we graduated, before you went away, before any of us knew anything. I want Neal to come away with me. Ditch the mortgage and the job and vanish. No work, no responsibilities, just us and the backpacks.

Richie   Where?

Rachel   Get an around-the-world ticket, go wherever we feel like.

Richie   And give up everything you've worked for?

Rachel   Oh, what's the point? Every day at the crack of dawn I float off down the High Street in the freezing cold to get on a crammed tube to go and treat the angina and asthma of chain-smokers, cancer referrals, local schizophrenics who nobody has the nerve to diagnose . . . there's no cure for any of it.

Richie   You're right. Sounds like a drag.

Rachel   But you've been places, you've met interesting people. You had an exciting career.

Richie   I wasn't very good at it.

Rachel   I don't believe that. Why all the stories then?

Richie   What does Neal think about all this?

Rachel   I may go without him.

Richie   Really?

Rachel   What else can I do? You're right. He can be a very boring person.

Richie   Don't say that.

Rachel   I don't mean to be nasty but . . .

Richie   No go on. I'm listening . . . It's unusual to find somebody so well-balanced with such a low opinion of people.

Rachel   I'm not that well-balanced. I'm quite flighty when I want to be.

Richie   I like flighty women. Flighty women are great.

Pause.

Rachel   Do you think I'm naive?

Richie   How do you mean?

Rachel   Naive. I'm naive, aren't I?

Richie   No.

Rachel   I think about it sometimes. In the wee small hours. In the 'dark night of the soul' . . .

Pause.

Richie   In the dark night of the soul you think that you're naive?

Rachel   I do.

Richie   Really? So do I.

Rachel   Do you?

Richie   In the dark night of the soul I think that I'm naive. All the time.

Rachel   Sometimes I think it's naive to expect to be . . . you know . . . happy.

Richie   So do I.

Rachel   But it's not naivety. It's just being . . . optimistic. Hopeful.

Richie   Quietly hopeful in the face of . . . overwhelming odds.

Rachel   Expectant . . .

Richie   Quietly expectant. Absolutely . . .

Rachel   Idealistic . . .

Richie   Quixotic even . . .

Rachel   What does that mean?

Richie   It means that . . . you're not naive. In fact it means the exact opposite of naive. I mean, you know, you have a certain innocence . . . but there's nothing wrong with that. I mean you're innocent but at the same time . . . extremely shrewd . . . I like it.

Silence.

Rachel   We should go back I suppose

Richie   Do you want another drink?

Rachel   You're terrible.

Richie   I know. But I've got an excuse.

Rachel   What?

Richie   I can't help it.

Rachel   That's what's terrible.

Richie   Hey. You'll like this. A horse walks into a bar and orders a beer. What does the barman say to the horse?

Rachel   Richie . . .

Richie   Come on, what does the barman say?

Silence.

Do you want me to go?

Pause.

Rachel   Do you want me to be honest?

Pause.

Richie   Not particularly.

Rachel   I think it's for the best.

Pause.

Richie   I'm going to Wales next. I've already decided. Don't try and talk me out of it . . .

Rachel   Wales is lovely. Neal and I used to go to the Pembrokeshire coast. Tenby.

Richie (*accent*)   Tenby? Tidy.

Rachel (*accent*)   Not so bad . . . Wales.

Richie   Boats, seagulls, fish and chips, cliffs. I like cliffs. It'll be brilliant. I'll rent a room. They're dirt cheap in winter, can't give them away.

Rachel   It's not winter.

Richie   I know.

Rachel   You'll be bored out of your mind.

Richie   I know.

Silence.

I had a dream last night. We were by the sea.

Rachel   We?

Richie   Not in England . . . Thailand perhaps . . . It was warm and the sky was purple and we were eating sea-urchins. It was like a beach party. A clambake, like in the Elvis movie, *Clambake.* We all had to find a bit of seafood and cook it. You and me were a team, and we couldn't find any, so we went up to this fellow and pinched his sea-urchins. Then we cooked them and we were eating them, just us, sitting on the shore in the dark, watching the stars, just absorbing the brilliance and beauty and inky wonder of it all. I had a pounding headache and as if by magic, you turned the sea-urchins into ice cream. And then I ate the ice cream and my headache went. What do you think it means?

Rachel   Nothing probably. The good ones are usually meaningless.

Richie   No, seriously. You did Freud and Jung and all that Viennese argy-bargy. Why sea-urchins?

Rachel   Well . . . it's obviously bollocks, isn't it?

Richie   I think it means something.

Rachel   No, that's what it means. Freud would say you had a thing about testicles and Jung would say you saw yourself as a testicle. Don't ask me about the ice cream though.

Pause.

Maybe it means you always want something you can't have. Something that's metaphysically-speaking not on the menu.

Richie   Nicky?

Rachel   You're always looking for somebody or something to make the unpalatable palatable. Maybe only Nicky can do that for you.

Pause.

Richie   It's the not knowing that does my head in. Not knowing where she is, whether she's all right ... Who she's with ... I feel excluded ... She hasn't even rung. Why hasn't she rung?

Rachel   She doesn't know where you are.

Richie   She could find out.

Rachel   How?

Richie   She could guess.

Pause.

Rachel *pats his arm.*

Rachel   Thanks for the flowers. Neal bought me flowers once. I told him I didn't like flowers and he never bought me them again.

Richie   Well, do you?

Rachel   Yes. They're lovely.

Pause. They look at each other. He tries to kiss her – she avoids. He tries again.

Rachel   Richie ...

Richie   I've been thinking.

Rachel   What are you thinking?

Richie   I think about you all the time. I've tried to put you out of my mind. I thought it was just lust ... but it's more than that.

Rachel   Don't be silly ...

Richie   We understand each other.

Rachel   Do we ... ?

Richie   When I'm with you, I'm watching fireworks. When I'm with you I am a firework. Electricity pulses through my veins. Moonbeams dazzle my eyes and I'm blinded. Delighted. Enchanted . . . When I'm not with you I walk about lost, staring, talking to myself, my shirt is on back-to-front, my flies undone, my trousers falling down, hollow, completely hollow. I want to preach the gospel according to Us. Yell it from the rooftops. From a multi-storey car park . . . I'm not making myself plain, am I . . . ? I think you're lovely. You are the word lovely on two lovely legs. We'll be a knockout together. We'll be Butch Cassidy and the Sundance Kid. We'll be the Cisco Kid and Pancho. We'll be the King and Queen of Happiness. It's entirely possible. I'm not afraid of looking ridiculous. I'm not afraid of anything. I mean business.

Long pause.

Rachel   Sorry . . . ? I didn't catch all of that . . .

Richie   Come and live with me in Wales.

Rachel   With you? You?

Richie   Yes. Me.

Rachel   What about Neal?

Richie   Oh, fuck Neal. Look at you. The way you look away. The way you go quiet . . .

Rachel   This is embarrassing . . .

Richie   The way you get embarrassed . . .

He kisses her.

Rachel   What are you doing you . . . you idiot. Oh, you fool . . .

He holds her, squeezes her ardently. She breaks away.

Will you stop doing that? I love Neal. We've got a mortgage. It's serious.

Richie   You said you were bored with Neal.

Rachel   I am . . . I'm not . . .

Richie. Make up your mind. What do you want?

Rachel   I don't know what I want.

Pause.

Neither do you. You're just drunk.

Richie   So are you.

She goes.

Blackout.

Act Two

Scene One

French restaurant. Evening.

Neal, Rachel *and* **Richie** *at a table, drinking wine.*

Neal *(drunk)* How much time was spent poring over ethics when we were at medical school? Eh? How many fruitless hours, weeks, months in the students' union bar bickering over, I don't know, euthanasia or something. It was the same in community medicine. Polygamy this, termination that . . . Taxing the moral reserves of . . . students? It's pointless. The most unfeeling ones just join health authorities and become bloody managers.

Richie *yawns.*

Neal Nobody cares. Nobody understands. Nobody wants to understand.

Pause.

You see what I mean?

Rachel Sorry? I wasn't listening.

Neal Medical ethics I'm talking about.

Rachel Oh, I never listened during medical ethics.

Richie Do you think that snails have the same aphrodisiac qualities as oysters?

Rachel I thought you had frogs' legs.

Richie It tasted like chicken. How was the duck?

Rachel The chocolate sauce was gorgeous.

Neal I'm a very bad doctor. I am. It's as simple as that.

Richie I've got one. A horse walks into a bar and orders a beer. What does the barman say to the horse?

Pause.

'Why the long face?'

Silence.

I need to piss.

He leaves the table.

Neal Do you think he knows he's an alcoholic?

Rachel Yes I do.

Pause.

Neal You don't think he's ...

Rachel What?

Neal In the toilet ... injecting.

Rachel I don't know. How should I know?

Pause.

Neal I'm sorry. This must be very strange for you. Things really have got a little out of hand.

Rachel Things have got very out of hand.

Neal That's Richie for you. There's a lot of things you don't know about him.

Rachel Such as?

Neal All sorts of things.

Rachel What?

Neal Well ... He's mad isn't he? I'm sure there's a few things I don't know either.

Pause.

I wanted us to be alone tonight. I needed to talk to you.

Rachel What about?

Neal Anything. I just needed to talk. Ask you if you're all right. Tell you I love you.

Rachel I love you too.

Neal *pours a glass of wine and drinks.*

Neal *(drunker)* See, I have this theory about love . . . Our minds are like the doors to a lift in a tall building. And our hearts are behind those doors. And when we fall in love, we throw open our doors, and let all our feelings out, and all the other person's feelings in and . . . Our souls hold hands and romp naked together . . . free . . .

Pause.

No . . . we're the lifts and our hearts are . . . No . . . there's all these buttons, see . . . and we press them . . .

Pause.

And then we either go up or we go down. Shall we order cheese?

Silence.

How are you feeling?

Rachel I'm just tired.

Neal You're always tired . . .

Rachel What does that mean?

Neal It doesn't mean anything. I'm concerned. Perhaps it's narcolepsy.

Pause.

It doesn't mean anything. I just wish you'd tell me what's on your mind.

Pause.

You never moan about anything.

Rachel He . . . made a pass at me this morning. Cheeky bugger.

Neal What?

Rachel We went for a walk by the river and he lunged.

Neal He lunged?

Rachel It was nothing. He squeezed my breast.

Neal My God. Are you sure?

Rachel As sure as I can be. It was definitely my breast.

Neal My God. Are you sure he wasn't just . . .

Rachel Just what?

Neal Giving you a hug or something?

Rachel I'm fairly certain, Neal. He didn't mean it. He was drunk.

Neal That shouldn't make any difference. He's always drunk.

Rachel I dealt with it. It's no big deal.

Neal It is a big deal. That's very extreme behaviour Rachel. I'll kill him.

Neal *pours more wine and drinks thirstily.* **Rachel** *takes his hand.*

Rachel Don't say any more, Neal. And don't you dare mention it to him.

Neal I bloody well will. There's a principle at stake.

Rachel Don't be so pedantic.

Neal Pedantic?

Rachel You are. You're pedantic.

Neal No. No I'm not. Particular maybe, but that's not pedantry. There's a distinct difference . . . Is there or isn't there a difference . . . ?

Richie *returns. Pause.*

Richie Anyone for pud?

Neal I think you've had yours. Or rather mine.

Rachel I've had quite enough for one evening.

Neal Shall we ask for the bill?

Rachel Mm.

Neal *tries to catch the waiter's eye, unsuccessfully.* **Richie** *snaps his fingers.*

Richie Garçon!

Pause.

(*To* **Rachel**.) Your turn.

Rachel Oh, this is ridiculous.

She gets up.

Richie Flutter your eyelashes at him.

She goes to find the waiter. Pause.

Neal Listen, old chap . . .

Neal *sips his wine.*

Richie What's wrong, old chap?

Neal This is going to sound . . . absurd . . . but I think you owe Rachel an apology.

Richie Why?

Neal I just think things have been getting a little bit out of hand.

Richie In what way?

Neal The . . . you know . . . the flirting.

Richie Flirting?

Pause.

Neal Oh come off it Richie. You've been flirting with her ever since you arrived.

Richie Flirting? Me?

Neal And the rest.

Richie What?

Neal   I know what happened. Between you two. By the river.

Pause.

Richie   Mate, I have no idea what you're talking about.

Neal   I think you do.

Richie   I don't. What's happened?

Pause.

Neal   This is going to sound silly . . . but Rachel said something happened by the river. You gave her a hug or something and . . .

Richie   A hug?

Neal   Mm.

Richie   Well I probably did. Just to cheer her up, you know . . .

Pause.

Neal   I see. OK.

Richie   Why?

Neal   I don't know. I think . . . maybe she took it the wrong way.

Richie   She took it the wrong way you say?

Neal   She says you squeezed her breast.

Richie *looks round-eyed.*

Richie   Whaaat?

Neal   That's what she said. And I hate that I have to . . . tell tales but . . .

Richie   She said I squeezed her breast?

Neal *nods. Pause.*

Richie   Hard?

Neal   I've no idea.

Pause.

Richie   Which breast?

Neal   Listen, you might have, you know, pinched her bum or something . . . in a friendly way, you know, in a, you know, a cheeky way . . .

Richie   Are you sure she meant me?

Neal   She was fairly specific.

Richie   Then I'm shocked. I'm hurt. Really.

Neal   Don't tell me this is . . . a complete surprise?

Richie   Yes.

Neal   Oh.

Pause.

Really?

Richie   The bitch.

Neal   Look, she didn't even want me to mention it . . .

Richie   I'll bet she didn't. No wonder she didn't . . .

Neal   Look, something must have happened.

Richie   She's a very uptight girl, Neal. I thought even you knew that.

Neal   What do you mean?

Richie   Oh come on. All this 'wanderlust'. All this 'My life is so dull and regimented . . .' She's a lovely girl Neal, I've always liked her and respected her and what's more I think her sensitivity is good for you . . . but she's needy. She's clingy. Insecure. I bet she's Catholic. Is she Catholic Neal? Because I hate to invoke stereotypes but . . . sometimes you have to.

Neal   . . . No. She isn't.

Silence.

Why would she make it up, Rich?

Richie   Why?

Neal   Yes.

Pause.

Richie   Because she's a liar.

Neal   You're a liar.

Richie   I'd never lie to you.

Neal   You always lie to me.

Richie   I'd never lie about a thing like this.

Neal   Neither would she.

Richie   Well neither would I. Can't you see what she's trying to do? It's the oldest trick in the book.

Neal   Now what are you on about?

Richie   She's jealous.

Neal   Of what?

Richie   Of what?

Neal   Yes.

Pause.

Richie   Well if you don't know, I'm not going to tell you . . .

Neal   Tell me. I'm interested.

Richie   Because we're such good friends, obviously . . .

Neal   Look . . . Just tell me the truth for once.

Richie   I've told you the truth.

Neal   Swear on your mother's life.

Richie   And my father's. Gladly.

Pause.

Is that it? Because, you know, if there's something on your mind, you can always talk to me.

Rachel *returns to the table, sits.*

Rachel   I put it on my card. You didn't want coffee did you?

Richie   I'll find a cab.

Richie *goes.*

Pause.

Neal   Look. This is the last I'm going to say on the subject . . .

Rachel   Oh please . . .

Neal   But I'm in a dilemma . . .

Rachel   What's the dilemma? It was nothing. Insignificant.

Neal   He denies all knowledge of it. Completely denies it.

Rachel   Well are you surprised?

Neal   Yes. It's like he has amnesia.

Rachel   Maybe he does.

Pause.

Neal   You think he just . . . doesn't remember?

Pause.

No. You don't forget a thing like this. Are you sure about all this?

Rachel   What are you implying Neal?

Neal   I'm not implying anything. I just want to get to the bottom of it.

Rachel   Well you're starting to sound . . . suspicious of me.

Neal   I'm not. What's there to be suspicious of? Suspicious?

Pause.

I'm just saying . . . why didn't you tell me before? Eh? What else haven't you told me?

Rachel   Oh just forget about it will you?

Neal   All right. It's forgotten. I won't say another word.

Silence.

I really think we should talk about this . . .

Pause.

He's my best friend. He's my oldest friend.

Rachel   Oh I wish I'd never mentioned it now . . .

She sips her wine. Pause.

Neal   Why?

Rachel   Sweet Jesus Neal. Why are you so jumpy about everything?

Neal   Jumpy?

Rachel   Jumpy, yes. You're a very jumpy person.

Neal   Jumpy? I used to be sensitive . . . Now I'm just jumpy.

Rachel   I used to think I knew you. Really knew you . . . And then you start acting like this and . . . Sometimes I don't think I know you at all.

Silence.

Neal   I worked a hundred hours this week. One hundred hours.

Rachel   So did I.

Pause.

Neal   For three years I've been languishing in that diabolical place, pushing shit up hill, postponing one crisis after another, or stuck behind a desk, studying, or writing reports. I could be at the Chelsea and Westminster if I kissed the right arses. It's all tennis elbow and people falling over at barbecues there.

Rachel You can't afford to let it get to you.

Neal Why not?

Rachel Because it's getting to me.

Neal *pours some more wine and drinks.*

Neal I'm nearly thirty and my skin's never seen the sun and I suffer from anxiety and all I'm thinking is, Somebody else is having all the fun. I'm thinking people like him are having all the fun. Even when he's not having fun he does it better than me. I've wasted my entire life!

Silence.

I'll go and see where that cab's got to.

He goes. **Rachel** *finishes off the wine. She stares.* **Richie** *returns and sits.*

Richie It'll be about ten minutes.

Rachel What?

Richie The cab. I phoned for one in the end. Less arsing about.

Rachel What did you say to Neal about this morning?

Richie This morning?

Rachel By the river.

Richie Absolutely nothing. Why?

Rachel It doesn't matter.

Pause.

Richie Well . . . I told him I bought you a bunch of flowers to cheer you up and I think it . . . cheesed him off a bit.

Rachel Why would it 'cheese' him off?

Richie He thinks I was moving in on his territory.

Rachel You were.

Richie I know but he doesn't know that. Flowers could

mean anything. He doesn't even buy you flowers, how the hell would he know?

Pause.

Rachel   He said you completely denied it, Richie.

Richie   I didn't get a chance to deny it. You know what he's like.

Pause.

Look, I told him I gave you a hug. He told me you'd taken it the wrong way. He said you always did.

Rachel   Always did what?

Richie   Took it the wrong way. With men.

Rachel   What?

Richie   It's pathetic.

Rachel   Right, that's it . . .

Richie   He's just a bit insecure. You're an extremely sexy woman. I don't know if you're aware of it . . .

Rachel   Will you please just . . . ?

Pause.

Extremely sexy woman . . . indeed . . .

Richie   Look, it's human nature. People always take it out on the ones they love.

Pause.

And . . . even if they don't really love them. People are cruel.

Pause.

And there's no explanation for any of it.

Richie *pours a glass of wine for* **Rachel** *and one for himself. He drinks.*

Richie   Think about it. Why do you love Neal so much? Why do you yearn for him when he's not around? Why are you so hungry just to talk to him, to hold him, to have him hold you when you're all worn out and just want some tenderness at the end of a long, hard day. Why do you love him so?

Rachel   Beats me.

Richie   Because you love him. Because you just do. And it's glorious. And nothing else matters. And that's the way it should be or heaven help us all. That's the way it should be or you're in serious motherfucking trouble.

Rachel   I think I take your point.

Silence. **Neal** *returns.*

Neal   I found a cab.

Richie   There's one coming. Little firm I know, on the cheap.

Neal   What, a minicab?

Rachel   Oh Neal don't be such a prick.

Silence. **Neal** *goes.*

Rachel   I know what you're trying to do, Richie.

Richie   What am I trying to do?

Rachel   I've seen this act before. I think it's a sign of serious psychological unbalance.

Richie   Yeah? And what's this a sign of?

He propels **Rachel** *onto the table.*

Rachel   Are you listening to me . . . ? I mean it . . .

Richie   Then why don't you do something about it, doctor?

He holds her down and kisses her.

Rachel   Don't . . .

Richie   Shut up . . .

Rachel   Not in here . . .

Richie   Why the hell not?

She pushes him away. Pause. They embrace and kiss.

Scene Two

Neal *and* **Rachel***'s flat. Evening.*

Richie *and* **Rachel** *sitting up in bed.* **Rachel** *stares. Lit candles dotted about the room.*

Rachel   What's wrong?

Richie   Opening night nerves.

Pause.

Too much to drink.

Pause.

I'm shy.

She strokes him under the covers.

Richie   Rachel . . .

She stops.

Give it a rest, eh?

Rachel   I was enjoying myself.

Richie   It's perfectly normal. Frank Sinatra said it means you just haven't got to know the lady properly yet.

Pause.

I'm nervous.

Rachel   Did you mean what you said by the river yesterday?

Richie   When?

Rachel   You know.

Richie   Oh that. Of course I did.

Rachel   You kept it pretty quiet.

Richie There's a lot of things you don't know about me Rachel.

Rachel I know. Neal told me you couldn't even do shorthand.

Richie What?

Rachel He said they sent you on a course with a bunch of secretaries and you still couldn't do it. Didn't have the application.

Richie What does he know about it? Lots of very experienced journalists don't have shorthand. It's not essential. It's very useful but not essential.

Pause.

I was a hack . . . big deal . . . I was hot for a while and now I'm not.

Pause.

I'm not a bad typist.

Rachel . . . Nor am I.

Richie Really? What do you write?

Rachel It's not that kind of typing. And I don't suppose it's essential. But it's very useful.

Long pause.

Richie Have you got a typewriter?

Rachel I've got a very nice typewriter.

Richie A very nice typewriter? Well that's very nice isn't it? What sort is it?

Rachel It's electric. Absolutely electric. Sensitive to the gentlest, most delicate touch. It's outrageous. I mean, when I'm hot, the results are glorious.

Pause.

Richie Are you fast?

Rachel   Oh, will you stop asking stupid questions?

Silence.

I've never felt so guilty in my life.

Richie   Have you cheated on him before?

Rachel   Of course not.

Richie   Has he cheated on you?

Rachel   No.

Richie   I never cheated on Nicky.

Rachel   I'm impressed.

Pause.

Richie   I yearn for her. I yearn for her so much I feel ill. Everything aches. Nothing works properly. There isn't a moment I don't think about her.

Rachel   Really?

Richie   Really.

Rachel   I see. Well . . .

Pause.

That's me told.

Richie   It was just a fuck.

Rachel   I know it was just a fuck but . . .

Richie   I mean it wasn't the fuck of the century, it wasn't the shag of a lifetime, I admit . . .

Rachel   It wasn't just a fuck. Not really, was it?

Richie   It wasn't even a fuck. I mean strictly speaking Rachel . . .

Rachel   You've made your point.

Silence. **Rachel** *gets out of bed and dresses.*

Richie   What have I done now?

Rachel It's not funny.

Richie Sorry?

Rachel It's not funny any more.

Richie I think it's hysterical.

Rachel I know.

Richie I mean . . . you have to laugh . . .

Rachel Do you? Why?

Pause.

Richie I'm not laughing at you.

Rachel Aren't you?

Richie I'm laughing with you.

Rachel I'm not laughing.

Pause.

Richie You have to laugh, though . . .

Rachel Why are you doing this? What is wrong with you? Why are you like this?

Pause.

Richie I'm lonely.

Richie *dresses.*

Rachel You're a very strange person Richie.

Richie I know.

Silence. **Rachel** *sits on the bed.*

Rachel Tell me what you're thinking.

Richie What do you think I'm thinking?

Rachel I don't know Richie. Nobody knows . . .

Richie 'Fuck' is what I'm thinking.

Pause.

Rachel   You'll find somebody. One day. You just have to be
... extremely patient.

Pause.

I am fond of you. But you're like a lightning rod. You're just
too much sometimes.

Richie   Sometimes ...

She gives him a hug. **Neal** *is standing in the doorway.* **Richie** *sees
him and stares.*

Richie   This isn't what it looks like.

Pause.

Neal   Why aren't you at work?

Rachel   I took the day off.

Neal   Another day off? Dear oh dear. I thought you might
have. In fact I had an instinct. I had a sixth sense.

Pause.

We must be psychic. It must be because we're so close.

Pause.

Anyway. I thought I'd surprise you.

Rachel   You did.

Neal   Yes, it seems like I did.

Rachel   Why aren't you at work?

Neal   I've resigned. Unexpected isn't it? Are you shocked?

Rachel   Just a little.

Neal   That I'm home or that I've resigned?

Rachel   Why did you resign?

Neal   Why not? Everybody's doing it. It's a culture of
resignation. Go with the flow, I say.

Rachel   Why?

Neal   Because I'm not cut out for it. Because I didn't want to lose any more patients. Because I didn't want to lose you.

Pause.

Richie   We've been talking.

Neal   Yes. I thought you might have been. I envy you the opportunity. The thing is, the only thing that puzzles me is, why in here? Why are you in my bedroom again?

Pause.

You know what I think? I think you've overstepped the mark a bit. I think you take liberties. I think this time around you've really taken a liberty, coming into my bedroom. And it is my bedroom now.

Rachel   Neal . . .

Neal   Well he does. You do. You really . . .

Pause.

You've really shot yourself in the foot this time. You've blown it clean off. Nobody can help you now. It's gone. Woosh!

Richie   You're pissed.

Neal   I've been drinking, it's true. In the pub. Under a table. Lovely. Sharpening my diagnostic skills. I see everything much clearer when I'm piss-drunk. And my diagnosis is: you're a terminal case. It's irreversible. You could always ask her for a second opinion. She's obviously a little more boned up on the subject . . .

Rachel   That's enough . . .

Neal   She's put in a bit of overtime on that one.

Silence.

Get out. Not you. Him.

Richie *goes.*

Neal   Am I imagining this? Tell me it's just my anxiety. Please . . .

Rachel   Neal . . .

Neal   Was it good?

Rachel   It wasn't anything.

Neal   Was it a laugh? Did you laugh? Did you giggle? Did you scream? Did you gasp and say 'fuck' at the point of no return? Did you cry out his name as he held you down? Did you kiss his eyes and whisper to him? Did you see something in his eyes? Did he see something in yours?

Silence.

Why?

Scene Three

Bar. Night.

Richie *drinking shots.*

Richie (*drunk*)   A horse walks into a bar and orders a beer. And the barman says . . . Why are you looking so fucking miserable for? Eh?

He laughs.

I'm the grandson of a preacherman. The son of a son of a preacherman. No . . . hold on . . . My mother's father was an Anglican vicar. Never was there a kinder, more sensitive man. Had a love of sheepdogs and wrote stories for Children's Hour during the war. My father's father, on the other hand, was an impotent sadistic cocksucker who beat his sons every day with a strap in an attempt to toughen them up for the army. The term 'character flaw' springs to mind.

He drinks a shot. He gazes vacantly.

This complex and enigmatic combination of sensitivity and viciousness was handed down through generations of emotional fucking cripples, doing for their relationships and later doing for mine.

He raises a glass. He toasts and drinks.

You disgust me. What do you know about anything? My problem is that I know too much. I'm too intelligent for this world. And what's more it's my considered and exquisitely elegant analysis that I'm just too fucking sensitive . . . (*To the bar in general.*) You're all a bunch of shits . . .

He drinks a shot.

Are you listening to me? Listen to me . . . listen to me . . .

He scatters shot glasses.

Scene Four

Hospital.

Richie *lying in a bed unconscious, tubes coming out of his nose and mouth.* **Neal** *and* **Rachel** *sitting.*

Neal   Where are you staying?

Rachel   In a hotel. It's not far. I thought we could meet for a drink sometime.

Neal   Why?

Silence.

Rachel   I phoned his mum.

Neal   Thank you. I couldn't face it.

Rachel   She said she wasn't surprised. Did you phone his dad?

Neal   I couldn't face it.

Rachel   You sound miserable.

Neal   Actually I'm feeling quite perky.

Rachel   Perky for you I suppose.

Neal   Yes. Comparatively perky I suppose.

Pause.

What is it about somebody else's misery that diminishes your own?

Rachel It's a subconscious competition for pity. With Richie we realise there is no competition.

Neal Sometimes he makes me feel quite cheerful about my life.

Rachel I miss you.

Pause.

Do you miss me?

Silence.

Neal It's occurred to me that maybe Richie genuinely tries to be good but he's just no good at it.

Rachel He's just lonely.

Neal Lonely?

Pause.

I'm lonely. Everybody's lonely.

Rachel Are you?

Neal No ... I'm just saying ...

Rachel What are you saying?

Pause.

Neal Maybe I am too uptight about things. I admit it, I am like an old woman sometimes.

Richie *stirs briefly.*

Rachel Look. He moved.

Neal He does that from time to time. It doesn't mean anything.

Pause.

Do you want to read to him?

Rachel   I think he'd prefer it if you read.

Neal   I only have *Crime*.

Rachel   It's not important, it's just the aural stimulation that's important.

Neal   Yes but *Crime* Rachel. Do you think that's wise?

Rachel   *Crime*'s fine.

Neal *reads.*

Neal   ' "We don't have many crooks here in Central City, ma'am," I said. "Anyway, people are people, even when they're a little misguided. You don't hurt them, they won't hurt you. They'll listen to reason." She shook her head, wide-eyed with awe . . .'

Lights down.

Lights up. **Rachel** *standing.* **Neal** *sitting.* **Richie** *unconscious.*

Rachel   I did all the books.

Neal   Sorry?

Rachel   I separated our books.

Neal   Oh. Thank you.

Rachel   I sorted yours out for you too. Textbooks on the bottom, real books on the top. It goes Arthritis to Dermatology, then Endocrinology to Paediatrics . . . then cowboy books.

Neal   What have you done with my cowboy books?

Rachel   They're on the top. With *Crime*. And I've taken the wok.

Neal   You've taken the wok?

Rachel   Is that all right?

Neal   What did you take the wok for? It's my wok.

Rachel   I didn't think you'd use it.

Neal   That's not the point. It's mine.

Rachel   You've got the big frying pan.

Neal   I need the big wok. It's not the same.

Rachel   What's the difference?

Neal   Well . . . if you don't know the difference between a wok and a frying pan then I'm not telling you.

Rachel   All right . . .

Neal   Well there's a principle at stake.

Rachel   I gave you that wok for your birthday.

Neal   So?

Rachel   So . . . don't be so mingy.

Neal   Mingy?

Rachel   Mingy. Yes. You're being mingy and mean-spirited about the whole business.

Neal   Well if you say so then I must be.

Rachel   Neal . . .

Neal   I'm mingy. I'm mean-spirited and mingy and jumpy and uptight. Fine. Fine. Who cares?

Pause.

I hope you didn't take my shower curtain.

Rachel   What?

Neal   The shower curtain. I like that shower curtain. It matches the tiles.

Pause.

Not the green ones. The other ones. With the pattern. With . . . with the little, slightly rococo sea-shell stencil . . .

Rachel   Oh I've had enough of this.

She starts to go.

Neal   Don't walk away from me when I'm talking to you.

Rachel   I thought we could do this together. I thought you might like to help me. I thought if we did this together and we talked about it and we . . . talked about a few other things it might be a bit easier. I thought I could come over and we could go through our things and talk about it properly and separate our things and then when this is all over . . . when I find somewhere to go . . . you could come over for dinner or something. I thought I'd cook you dinner. I thought it would be nice. I thought I was making a gesture. I thought it might help me to say I'm sorry. Because I am sorry. I am . . . so sorry Neal . . . and I'm trying not to make a scene and I'm trying to be sensitive about this and I'm trying . . . not to be so sensitive about this and just get on with it . . . I'm trying to be practical . . . I'm trying not to get all emotional about it . . . That's why I took the stupid fucking wok!

Silence.

Rachel   Nicky phoned for you.

Neal   Nicky?

Rachel   Yesterday. While I was doing the bathroom stuff.

Neal   Did you find my shaving brush? Only I can't find it. I thought he might have taken it but then I thought that that was just daft.

Pause.

Sorry. Go on.

Rachel   She wanted your address so she could send on some of Richie's things. I told her what's happened and asked her to think about coming home. She said she wouldn't come home even if he were dying.

Neal   He is dying.

Rachel *produces a scrap of paper and gives it to* **Neal**.

Rachel   She left the number of the hotel where she's staying.

Will you give it to him?

Neal Do you think she still loves him?

Rachel Maybe. Maybe not.

Neal Do you think she ever loved him?

Rachel I'm sure she adored him once.

Silence. **Richie** *stirs. He opens his eyes, stirs. Books fall to the floor.*

Neal Richie? My God.

Richie Who are you?

Neal You don't recognise me?

Richie No. You're some kind of shrink or something.

Rachel Richie, look at me.

Richie What the fuck is going on here?

He looks around.

Rachel You're in hospital. You've been very poorly.

He looks at her.

Richie Can you get me something to eat? I'm starved.

Rachel I'll get the doctor.

She exits. He looks at **Neal***.*

Richie I adore nurses.

Neal I thought you weren't going to make it.

Richie Well you're a morbid bastard aren't you?

Neal Can't you remember anything?

Pause.

Richie Something about . . . the river?

Pause. He smiles.

I expect this means I'll never be best man.

Pause.

My head is throbbing.

Neal   Hurts, does it?

Richie   It's throbbing.

Neal   Tell me if this hurts.

Neal *probes* **Richie**'s *head forcefully.*

Richie   Ow! What did you do that for?

Neal   And this?

He does it again.

Richie   Will you stop doing that? Are you insane?

Pause.

You're a fucking doctor.

Neal *slaps and chokes* **Richie**. *He stops and they stare at each other. Silence.*

Lights down.

Scene Five

Neal *and* **Rachel**'s *flat. Afternoon.*

Neal *standing, drinking scotch, drunk. A large box is in the middle of the floor.* **Richie** *sitting, staring at the box.* **Neal** *lights a cigarette and offers one to* **Richie**.

Neal   Want one?

Richie   Thanks but I couldn't.

Neal   You haven't smoked in, what is it, a week now?

Richie   More or less, yes.

Neal   Splendid. Or is it two weeks?

Richie   I don't remember.

Neal   Not since your overdose. Very wise.

Pause.

I like smoking. I think it's marvellous. I can't imagine what stopped me before. I can't believe I actually refrained from shamelessly indulging myself merely as a matter of principle.

Neal *pours another glass of scotch and drinks.*

Richie   Thanks for picking me up from the hospital.

Neal   Nobody else would.

Richie   And thanks for visiting me.

Neal   You'd do the same for me.

Richie   I would. Well, of course I would.

Neal   Of course . . .

Richie   I'm being sincere Neal.

Neal   I don't recommend that. It never worked for me.

Richie   I've changed. I feel almost absurdly positive about everything now. It's quite incredible.

Pause.

While I was in hospital I had an epiphany.

Neal   An epiphany, eh?

Richie   It was like I went outside of my body.

Neal   An out-of-body experience?

Richie   Absolutely.

Neal   Happens all the time.

Richie   It was more than that.

Neal   It's all to do with the brain.

Richie   I floated above my body and I looked down and I saw myself lying there, and I saw people gathered around, being very concerned, and . . . I felt very strange. I felt like I wanted to cry. I mean, it wasn't the fact that I was in hospital. It was the fact that other people were concerned about me. It was . . . the concern that got to me.

Pause.

Neal   Ridiculous . . .

Richie   It really surprised me.

Neal   It surprises me. Who on earth were these people?

Richie   Well, you, presumably. And Rachel.

Neal   I see.

Richie   I mean, really, it really meant something.

Neal   Really?

Richie   Yes. And I thought about you and your life, I mean really thought about it, and it occurred to me that whatever I've seen in my life, however terrible or . . . pathetic, you've seen worse.

Neal   What have you seen?

Richie   Eh?

Neal   What have you seen that's so terrible? You're an old drama queen.

Richie   Precisely. What have I seen? You've seen the insides of a human being. Got right in there to the ugly, bloody, stinking core and you still smell like a biscuit factory. Still get up in the morning and shave and do the job. At least you did until I got here.

Pause.

And there and then, I resolved to be a good, honest man. Redeem my entire sorry life. Settle down. Give up drinking. Work even.

Neal   Work? I wouldn't recommend that.

Richie   Why not?

Neal   You'll get screwed.

Richie   Why should I get screwed?

Neal   Look at me.

Richie   I agree, but . . .

Neal   You agree that you'd get screwed or you agree that I've been screwed?

Richie   I . . . both . . .

Neal   Rachel's probably being screwed right at this very minute. Which is her prerogative. But you see I think you've screwed yourself.

Richie   Don't take the piss.

Neal   On the contrary. I will take the piss. I think I have every right to take the piss. Because if you think about it Richie, it's probably my turn to take the piss now.

Pause.

Richie   You know what your problem is? You've become cynical.

Neal   You know what kind of people call other people cynics?

Richie   What?

Neal   Idiots. Cynics are realists . . . surrounded by idiots.

Richie   I'm trying to say I'm sorry.

Neal   'Sorry.' Mm. You know, I'm not sure I actually really know what that word means. And I'm fucking certain that you don't.

Long pause.

Richie   Well . . . I'll be off then.

Neal   Are you really going to Wales?

Richie   Yes.

Neal   What are you going to do?

Richie   I'm going to buy a little cottage and bury myself in life-affirming toil. What the fuck do you think I'm going to do?

Neal   And wait for Nicky? Did I tell you she rang?

Pause.

Richie   No. You didn't.

Neal   She told Rachel that she wouldn't come home even if you were on your deathbed. The funny thing was, at the time, you were on your deathbed.

Richie   When was this?

Neal   When you were on your deathbed.

Richie   Did she leave a message? A phone number?

Neal   No. Well, you could ask Rachel, only I don't have a number for her either.

Richie   Well, where is she?

Neal   I don't know. Who cares?

Richie   'Who cares?'

Neal   Who cares?

Neal *drinks.* **Richie** *goes to the box and opens it hesitantly. He produces a sombrero and puts it on. He produces a letter, opens it, reads.*

Richie   She's sent all my things. She sent some of hers too. It isn't because she's joining me, she says it's because she can't bear to be reminded of the time we spent together. I think it's a good sign.

He produces a poncho, sniffs it.

I can still smell her perfume. Look . . . one of her hairs.

He takes off lint and a stray hair. He puts the poncho on. Pause. He blows his nose on the poncho. He takes the bottle from **Neal**, *drinks.*

Neal   Have you bought your ticket yet?

Richie   Not yet.

Neal   Do you know how much a ticket to Wales is?

Richie   No idea.

Neal   Have you got any money?

Richie   A little . . .

Neal   Have you got anywhere to stay?

Richie   I thought I'd just busk it.

Neal   Do you know anybody in Wales?

Richie   You know I don't.

Neal   Not a soul? Ah.

Neal *takes out his wallet, offers money.*

Richie   I couldn't. It's time I stood on my own two feet again.

Neal   Take it.

Richie *finds his suitcase and packs clothes from the box into the case.*

Richie   I've taken enough from you.

Neal   Oh I know that. No, I'm not denying that. But I want you out of my hair.

Richie   If you insist.

Richie *takes the money.*

I'm going to miss you.

Pause. He packs.

Neal   I'll come with you. Make sure you get your train.

Richie   I said I'll miss you.

He shuts his case and stands holding it.

I'll probably be back in a year or two. You know me. You won't get rid of me that easily.

Neal   I tell you what. I'll call you a cab. It's pissing down.

Richie   Thanks. Thanks for everything. You're a real friend.

He goes to embrace **Neal**. **Neal** *turns away, picks up the phone and dials.*

Scene Six

Pub. Evening.

Rachel *is sitting at a garden table, smoking.* **Neal** *approaches the table with drinks, a pint for him, a vodka and orange for her. He sits.*

Rachel   I've got a new flat. Well, it's just a bedsit really. New Cross.

Neal   New Cross? Nice.

Rachel   It's near the practice. Sometimes I wander into Goldsmiths for a cup of coffee. It's nice to just sit there amongst the students. Look at all the noticeboards. There's always something going on.

Neal   You're looking well.

Rachel   So are you.

Neal   Are you? Are you well?

Rachel *yawns.*

Rachel   I'm tired.

Neal   Are you really? I couldn't tell. What have you been doing?

Rachel   Just sleeping.

Neal   Well what have you been doing to make you sleep?

Rachel   I went out last night with . . .

She yawns.

Neal   Who? With who?

She yawns.

Rachel Just a friend. One of the partners.

Neal You look terrible.

Rachel Thank you.

Neal Well, you know . . .

Rachel I know. You worry.

They sip their drinks. She yawns.

I've just been working too hard.

Neal It's time you did what you want to do.

Rachel I want to make money.

Neal They treat you like a slave.

Rachel I know.

Neal Well do something about it. You've always wanted to change your life. Now's your chance.

Pause.

Rachel Do you still think you made the right decision?

Neal Absolutely. I think so. I'm almost sure I did and if I didn't . . .

Rachel I meant us.

Pause.

Neal I don't know what I think. I won't know for a while.

Rachel When will you know?

Neal Months probably. Anyway, I like it like this. I think about it a lot. I worry I made the wrong decision and that one day I'll wake up and realise and it'll be too late . . . I do . . . but I also like this. I like meeting you now just for a drink by the river. For the first time in my life I feel free. Do you realise that? I've never been free. I've never been single and unemployed before. These are exciting times for me.

Pause.

Rachel We've had drinks by the river before.

Neal Have we? I don't think so.

Rachel When I lived in Kilburn.

Neal That wasn't by the river, it was by the canal.

Rachel Well, anyway . . .

Neal There is a difference . . .

Silence.

Rachel I was thinking of going away for the bank holiday. I've got some time off. Come with me if you like.

Neal Where do you want to go?

Rachel Anywhere. Who cares?

Pause.

Neal Have you thought about going abroad?

Rachel Oh, I can't be bothered.

Neal Not for the weekend. For a while. See the world. Do what you've always wanted to.

Rachel I can't be bothered. No . . . Not any more.

Pause.

I'd be lonely.

Neal You know what your problem is?

Rachel What?

Neal You're a hopeless romantic.

Rachel What's wrong with that?

Neal It's hopeless.

Silence.

Rachel Do you think we made a good couple?

Neal   You know I do.

Rachel   But it was more than that wasn't it?

Neal   In what respect?

Rachel   We were more than just 'a couple', weren't we? It was more than that, wasn't it?

Neal   I suppose it was.

Rachel   We were such good friends. Such good friends.

Neal   Absolutely.

Rachel   Soul-mates.

Neal   Good lovers. I mean . . .

Rachel   Kindred spirits.

Neal   And good lovers. Comparatively . . .

Rachel   And good lovers. Absolutely.

Silence.

Neal   Richie and I were good friends once. I learnt a lot from him.

Rachel   What did you learn?

Neal   I learnt what it's like to want to kill somebody. The thing is, I always expected him to change. I never expected you to change. And then you did and he didn't.

Pause.

Rachel   Did I?

Neal   I don't know. But I'm saying I didn't expect . . .

Rachel   What did you expect? What did you want from me in all those years? Marriage? Stability? Children?

Neal   I wanted you. I just wanted . . . you.

Pause. He drinks.

The stage slowly darkens as twilight sets in.

Neal I had a dream about you last night. We were on a roof and it was very dark, night-time, brilliant stars in the sky. It was a roof party. A barbecue on a midsummer night. And you could see right across London, all the places we'd lived together. The river and the Embankment and the water glittering in the dark. And I wasn't really talking to you but you came over in a black dress and started talking to me. You were laughing insistently at something or other and I started laughing, humouring you, in my dream, and then I saw it. This thing on your breast, like a brooch, over your heart. A cluster. As I got closer I saw it was a nest of maggots. And as we were laughing the maggots grew and hatched more maggots. And I thought of Richie. And that's when I finally knew it was over. I would never be in love with you again. We'd walk away from each other quite calmly and you'd never even notice you had this thing clinging to you. Nobody would. Only I would.

Pause.

And then I realised it wasn't maggots at all. It was rice pudding. Or bubble-and-squeak. That's what you'd been laughing about. Bubble-and-squeak all down your dress. And I went to kiss you. And I woke up.

Pause.

What do you think it means?

Pause.

Rachel Do you want another drink?

Silence.

Blackout.

The Bullet

For Emily McLaughlin

The Bullet was first performed at the Donmar Warehouse, London, on 2 April 1998, with the following cast:

Charles	Miles Anderson
Billie	Barbara Flynn
Robbie	Neil Stuke
Mike	Andrew Tiernan
Carla	Emily Woof

Directed by Dominic Cooke
Designed by Christopher Oram
Lighting by Howard Harrison
Sound by Fergus O'Hare

Characters

Charles, *fifties*
Billie, *around fifty*
Robbie, *late twenties*
Mike, *same*
Carla, *mid twenties*

The action takes place over twenty-four hours.

Act One

Night.

Living room of a house in a suburb south of London. Open-plan with adjoining kitchen area. A large window, armchair, sofa, dining table and chairs, TV, piano, drinks cabinet, staircase. **Charles** *is asleep in an armchair holding an empty tumbler. Beside him is a whisky decanter.* **Robbie** *and* **Carla** *stand with suitcases. They set them down and* **Robbie** *goes over to* **Charles**.

Robbie Out like a light.

He picks up decanter and looks at it.

Piss drunk.

Carla Is he all right?

Carla *comes over and regards* **Charles**.

He looks like you when you sleep.

Robbie In what way?

Carla You sleep with your mouth open.

Charles *snorts.*

Carla And you snore.

Robbie You never told me that. All the time?

Carla Occasionally.

Robbie Well why didn't you tell me?

Carla Sorry.

Robbie I hate the thought of being a snorer. And you putting up with it and never even telling me. What else do I do?

Carla Nothing. Anyway it's only when you're drunk.

Robbie How often am I drunk?

Carla   I'm kidding.

Robbie   I'm never as drunk as that. What other habits have I got that you don't tell me about?

Carla   You never fart in bed.

Robbie   Should I?

Carla   It just seems odd. Too good to be true. Maybe I just haven't known you long enough. Does he always drink a lot?

Robbie   Now you're working out the future. Am I going to turn into a loquacious foul-smelling old fucker or wind up teetotal and sanctimonious because 'I've seen what it does to you'? He likes a drink. He's got good reason to at the moment.

Carla   Do you think we should wake him up?

Robbie   I'll go and find Mum.

Carla   Won't she be asleep?

Robbie   She'll be reading.

Carla   Are you sure they're expecting us?

Robbie   This is a welcome committee by their standards.

Charles *stirs and mutters in his sleep.*

Carla   I'll come with you.

Robbie   He won't wake up.

Carla   He doesn't know who I am. He'll get the fright of his life.

Robbie   He won't eat you.

Carla   I'll get embarrassed.

Robbie   I'm warning you, he's going to adore you.

Robbie *kisses* **Carla** *and goes upstairs.* **Carla** *looks around. She picks up an empty whisky decanter from the floor and puts it on the cabinet.* **Charles** *wakes up with a snort. He stares at* **Carla**.

Carla   Hello.

Charles   Hello.

Pause.

Carla   I'm Carla. Robbie's . . . I'm with Robbie.

Pause.

We just got here. Robbie's upstairs.

Charles   I didn't know Robbie had a girlfriend.

Carla   We met in Singapore. We were living there.

Pause.

We met over there.

Pause.

I'm English.

Carla *smiles awkwardly and looks around.*

I'm sorry if I woke you up. Robbie said . . .

Charles   I was hoping it was Mike.

Carla   Oh. Well . . .

Pause.

He's missed you. I think he's really been looking forward to coming home.

Charles   Sit down, there's a good girl. Can't have you standing around all night after a long journey like that.

Carla *sits on the sofa. Pause.*

Charles   I was just . . . I was dreaming about Mike when you came in. I must have thought you were Mike. Or maybe I thought Robbie was. I don't know. The mind plays tricks this time of night. The mind plays tricks most of the time.

Carla   It certainly does.

Charles   Oh you know about that do you?

Carla   No well . . . yes I suppose.

Faint laugh.

Absolutely.

Charles   Yes . . .

Carla   Mm.

Silence.

What was your dream about?

Charles   He could've been anything he wanted to be, Mike. Only thing is, I don't think he wanted to be anything. He was happy just breathing. Everything made him happy. My God. Listen to me. I'm half asleep.

Carla   It's nice that you think about him so much.

Charles   Lately I think about him more than usual. Listen to that wind.

Carla   It's bitterly cold. It's quite a shock.

Charles   Yes yes. Absolutely. You're probably jet-lagged as well.

Carla   I just feel a bit . . . disorientated.

Charles   Well of course.

Silence.

Yes. You'd be surprised what you start thinking about at times like this. All sorts of odd thoughts.

Pause.

I suppose Robbie told you.

Carla   Yes. I'm sorry.

Charles   He must like you.

Carla   Well . . .

Carla *glances in the direction of the stairs.* **Charles** *notices and does the same. They exchange smiles.*

Carla My dad was made redundant a few years ago.

Charles Really? I'm sorry to hear it.

Carla Yes.

Charles What did he do?

Carla He used to be a teacher.

Charles What does he do now?

Carla He makes pots. He's a potter.

Charles I'm sorry to hear it.

Carla In some ways it was the best thing that ever happened to him.

Charles Yes. That's why I'm sorry.

They exchange smiles.

Nothing wrong with that. One of my best friends was a teacher. He was a manic depressive.

Carla Oh no.

Charles Well. I don't know why they bother, really . . . I'm kidding. When you see him . . . you know . . . tell him I know how he feels. Tell him . . . he's not alone.

Carla That's very sweet. I will.

Charles I used to be a spaceman.

She eyes him a little nervously.

For ten years. All over the place. London, Croydon, Leatherhead. *South London Guardian, South London Press, The Comet.* I got around. That's the first time I was made redundant. Haven't you ever met a spaceman before? Advertising space. The local rag. What did you think I meant? The Man in the Moon? I feel like the Man in the Moon right now. It wasn't me really. Advertising space. Lying per square inch.

Carla Of course.

Charles   I've got a big mouth. That's how I became a reporter. Talked my way into it, became a sub, then chief sub . . .

Carla   It must be hard for you.

Charles   Hard? For me? Well . . .

Silence.

Where is that boy? Doesn't even say hello to his dad.

Carla   I know absolutely. What a prat.

She goes to the stairs.

Robbie!

Charles   Listen to me, rattling on, spilling my guts.

Carla   No, go on it's interesting. Robbie's told me a lot about you.

Charles   No it's boring.

Carla   No go on. It's interesting . . .

Charles   Well . . . Robbie'll tell you. I knew about things I shouldn't have known about.

Carla   Mm.

Charles   And I let things get personal. They told me to shut up and I didn't.

Carla   What things?

Charles   Oh . . . just a silly editorial I wrote. They never even used it. Boring council things. Rubber-stamps this, multinationals that. You don't want to know.

Carla   I do. Really.

Charles   . . . No you don't . . .

Carla   I do. Really . . .

Carla *glances at the stairs.* *Silence.* **Charles** *glances at the stairs.*

Charles (*despite himself*)   See, the thing is, say some

multinational puts up a few million to develop a piece of
council land. Land which by rights they should be using to
build accommodation. Obviously the council is supposed to
say no. But of course in the present climate . . . post-recession,
mid-boom etcetera etcetera, they can't resist. They put it to
the planning committee and then you find out that, surprise
surprise, the bankers on the committee have all been
organising finance for the development, the builders on the
committee want the contract, the housing associations haven't
the funds to put in a bid – the press officers arrange a lovely
photo opportunity – and six months down the line the
borough is plunged into a development nightmare.
Everybody's happy. The publishers are happy – nice story
about creating local jobs, the fat cats are happy, no more
nasty council houses in their back yards, the unions are
ecstatic . . . but I was never happy. Because it's undemocratic.
It's unprincipled. And apart from anything else, it's a fucking
nuisance. The noise, the traffic, streets full of lorries, skips
etcetera. It's untidy. I mean, personally I couldn't give two
fucks what they do with the homeless, but what I don't like,
what really gives me the pip, is it's fucking cheating. It's
wrong!

Carla I see . . . Robbie!

Charles Have you noticed how many developments have
sprung up in London in the past year?

Carla I haven't been here . . .

Charles Too many greedy people seizing their moment. It's
beginning to look like Croydon.

Robbie *comes down the stairs.*

Carla Hi ya.

Robbie How are you Dad? It's good to see you.

Charles I'm fine, how are you?

Robbie I'm very well.

Charles Have a scotch.

Robbie   Actually a glass of wine would be nice.

Charles   A glass of wine? I'm offering you a scotch.

Robbie   I know it's just that, well, this is going to sound silly but where we've just been you can't get wine for love nor money. I'm gagging for it.

Charles   Is that so?

Carla   Ridiculous but true.

Charles   Red or white?

Robbie   White.

Charles   Haven't got any.

Robbie   Red?

Charles   Fresh out. Have a scotch. Get a couple of glasses Robbie, there's a good lad.

Robbie *goes to the kitchen and searches the cupboards.* **Robbie** *returns with glasses.* **Charles** *indicates the decanter in the cabinet.* **Robbie** *fetches it and* **Charles** *pours.* **Robbie** *drinks and walks around the room as he talks.*

Charles   How's work?

Robbie   I'm waiting for a transfer. They were going to base me in Bangkok when offshore shares went through the roof but it fell through when everything else crashed. I mean the price of software in Jakarta is just horrendous and as for Kuala Lumpur . . .

Charles   How long's this been going on?

Robbie   How do you mean?

Charles   All this globe-trotting. Isn't it time you got a proper job?

Robbie   . . . I've got a proper job. I just move around a lot.

Charles   And it's a steady income is it?

Robbie   It's as steady as the market is. When the market's good they all want installations. I went to Borneo last year. Kalimantan. But as I say . . . you know . . .

Charles *pours himself another drink.*

Robbie   Have you got anything lined up?

Charles   Don't be daft. What would I have lined up?

Robbie   It's not like you to hang around.

Charles   I haven't gone yet. I was just telling Karen . . .

Carla   Carla . . .

Charles   Carla. I'm embroiled in a vendetta.

Robbie   What do you mean?

Charles   Sit down. I'm not going to break my neck looking up at you all night.

Robbie   You haven't been had up for slander again have you?

Charles   I wasn't had up for slander. My God.

Robbie   That's what Mum said.

Charles   It was libel. Do you want to hear this or not?

Robbie   Sorry, go on.

Pause.

Charles   There was a takeover.

Robbie   Yeah. Mum said.

Charles   New staff. New offices. New software.

Robbie   Mum said. On the phone.

Charles   New software to teach us how to use the old software . . .

Robbie   Ridiculous.

Charles   . . . The point is these people were powerful, wealthy, squeaky clean. New brooms. And the old brooms aren't prepared to toe the line. The old brooms know what they're doing and don't appreciate interference.

Robbie   Mm-hm . . .

Charles   But the new brooms have friends. In the council. In business.

Robbie   Friends? Well that's terrible.

Charles   Half of them are fucking Freemasons for God's sake.

Robbie   Freemasons? On the council?

Charles   Yes. Bi-i-ig fucking deal. I'm the first to admit it's no big deal. People have known about it for years.

Robbie   But that's terrible. You should write to the Prime Minister about this.

Charles   Well it's not the point. The point is I've been wronged.

Robbie   Has anyone else been laid off?

Charles   A dozen of us sent to the knackers. Senior staff. The 'troublemakers'. The lefties. They'd rather pay peanuts to some twenty-five-year-old with no opinions and a degree in Quark. Are you with me?

Robbie   No. I'm lost.

Charles   It's a conspiracy. A deliberate campaign to remove whoever they want to remove.

Robbie   Well that's terrible . . . terrible.

Robbie *stands and goes to his case. He takes out a small parcel.*

I brought you a present. I got it in Singapore.

He hands **Charles** *the parcel.*

Open it.

Charles   Oh well. You didn't have to.

Robbie   I wanted to.

Charles *unwraps the parcel and pulls out a dictaphone, pocket-sized.*

Robbie   It's a dictaphone.

Charles   I can see that. Yes, very nice. Very neat.

Charles *examines it reluctantly.*

Robbie   You never know when it could come in handy. I just thought . . .

Charles   You never know, absolutely.

Robbie   You could use it at . . . work . . . or . . . I've got one. I wouldn't be without it. We can record letters to each other. When I'm off on my travels. Send each other tapes.

Robbie *reaches over and switches it on.*

Charles   Well I'm lost for words.

Robbie   Say something.

Charles   I don't know what to say.

Charles *just stares at it.* **Robbie** *reaches over and rewinds it.*

Charles's voice   Well I'm lost for words.

Charles   I see . . . very good.

Charles *presses 'Record'.*

Robbie   I know you don't like writing letters.

Charles   Oh, that bad is it?

Robbie   I just thought it would help us . . . communicate.

Charles *rewinds.*

Robbie's voice   I just thought it would help us . . . communicate.

Charles *rewinds.*

Charles's voice   Well I'm lost for words.

Charles *switches it off.*

Charles   Very nice . . . thanks.

Charles *puts it down and pours another drink. He drinks. Silence.*

Robbie   Well, we're off to bed.

Charles   Oh.

Robbie   We're a bit tired.

Charles   Oh. I see . . .

Robbie   How long have you been up?

Charles   You want me to go to bed?

Robbie   Only if you're tired.

Charles   But I'm not.

Carla *stands.*

Carla   Robbie . . .

Robbie   Well aren't you tired?

Carla   Not especially.

Charles   No no. I'll go. I know the score.

Robbie   Come on, Dad. I didn't mean . . .

Charles   No I'm cream-crackered. It's been a long day.

Charles *gets up.*

Your mum's made up the beds. Put a little lamp in there for you. And a little bedside table for you to put your bits and bobs on Karen.

Carla   Carla. That's sweet of her.

Charles   You used to share that little room with Mike. She's put a table in there and everything. A little bucket if you get up in the night.

Robbie   Classy.

Charles   Well is that a problem?

Robbie   No it's fine. Thanks.

Silence.

Charles   I'll leave you to it.

Charles *goes.*

Robbie   What did I do?

Carla   It was a bit insensitive.

Robbie   He just hates gadgets. It's like when they ring me and get the answerphone. It doesn't matter that we're eight thousand miles apart and haven't spoken in months, they refuse to leave a message. They think I'm hiding or something.

Carla   I think it upset him.

Robbie   He was already upset. He'd be more upset if I just tip-toed around treading on eggs.

Carla   I'm not saying tread on eggs . . .

Robbie   I was already tip-toeing around treading on eggs. I thought I'd break the ice.

Carla   Maybe you should have bought him booze in Duty Free.

Robbie   Then I'd have to drink it with him and then I'd be drunkenly tip-toeing around treading on eggs breaking unbreakable ice.

Carla   It's not that bad.

Robbie   I hate it when he's like this.

Carla   It's only for a few nights. I'm sure he'll be fine in the morning.

Carla *sits.*

There's nothing we can do about it now.

Robbie   That's right. It's too late now. We're trapped.

Carla   Can we forget about it now please?

Robbie   OK, OK, it's forgotten. I won't say another word.

Pause.

Did you hear that? The Freemasons? It's ridiculous.

Carla   He was just a bit drunk. You say that sort of thing when you're drunk.

Robbie   I've never said anything that ridiculous.

Carla   Yes you do.

Robbie   I don't get paranoid about it.

Carla   Don't exaggerate, he's just a bit freaked out.

Robbie   I'm a bit freaked out now.

Carla   Not as freaked out as him I shouldn't think.

Robbie   No. I suppose not.

Silence.

Carla   How's your mum?

Robbie   She's coping. Well, it's her job, if you know what I mean.

Carla   I thought you were never coming down.

Robbie   I had to wake her up. It was strange. I sat on the bed and watched her sleeping for a while. Have you ever watched your parents sleep? I mean sleeping properly in their bed. Because when you're a kid they don't sleep, do they? They just don't. They stay awake all night . . . guarding the house.

Carla   Do you think they're all right?

Robbie   They look so vulnerable and . . . disappointed when they sleep.

Pause.

Carla   It's a brand new culture of redundancy. During the recession people got used to the notion of redundancy – they really believed there were no jobs. Nowadays when an organisation wants to do it they have to be much more sneaky. They invoke technological advance or elegant notions of early retirement and quality of life. Psychologically what aggravates it for somebody of your dad's age is that he's of a generation who a) believe that employment is everything and b) paradoxically was weaned on the notion that as long as you have your health, you should be happy – which of course is anathema to contemporary capitalism. I mean, it's quite Darwinian and really a lot more complex and subtle than you imagine.

Pause.

Robbie   I thought you'd say that.

Carla   It's perfectly understandable. The chances are there are a few Freemasons skulking in the undergrowth. The issue isn't whether he's right or wrong. The point is that he needs validation.

Robbie   So you think we should just agree with everything he says?

Carla   Tell him what he wants to hear.

Robbie   No. I don't think we should encourage him.

Carla   Just don't be too harsh on him. He doesn't mean any harm.

He stares into space. She holds his hand.

Anyway. I thought you wanted to sleep. I could do with a good long hard sleep. As long as we don't make too much noise . . .

She cuddles up.

It's not the same without noise but . . .

She caresses him.

Let's have a bath.

Robbie   The Freemasons . . . ?

Carla   Then you can give me a nice massage. A nice . . .

She winks at him.

. . . good, long, thorough 'massage'.

Robbie   A massage . . . ?

She winks again.

Oh, I see what you mean . . .

They kiss.

Carla   Shall we go upstairs?

Robbie   No. We can 'massage' down here.

Carla   Don't be silly.

Robbie   Then we'll have a bath 'cos we'll be all hot and sweaty and steamed up.

Carla   No.

Robbie   That's the way it usually works.

Carla   No. Not here.

Carla *stands.* **Robbie** *stands and suddenly lifts her off her feet, swings her around and dumps her back on the sofa. They giggle. They kiss briefly. He reaches under her skirt.*

Carla   Don't take my knickers off. Someone will come in.

He takes her knickers off.

No, we're going upstairs.

Robbie   I don't want to.

Carla   Don't be silly. Why not?

Robbie   I used to share that room with Mike.

Pause.

Carla   Come on. Let's run you a bath.

Robbie   Just a quick one?

Carla   No.

They tussle a moment, giggling. **Charles** *appears at the top of the stairs, unnoticed.*

Robbie   Come on. Just one little massage on the sofa.

Carla *sighs.*

Carla   Go on then. Assume the position.

Robbie *stretches out face down on the sofa.* **Carla** *straddles him and runs her hands over his back, massaging him.*

Carla   Your muscles are so tense.

She works her way down and up briefly and stops.

Finished. Is there any other muscle you'd like me to massage?

Robbie *turns over.* **Carla** *slowly unzips his trousers. She blows on her hands and rubs them together. She reaches a hand into his trousers delicately.* **Charles** *coughs loudly and* **Carla** *instantly withdraws her hand.*

Robbie   Was that you?

They look around wildly. Pause.

That's fucking clever. Do it again.

Pause. **Carla** *hesitates so* **Robbie** *touches himself in the same fashion.* **Charles** *coughs and comes down the stairs. They look at* **Charles**. **Robbie** *zips up his trousers hurriedly.* **Carla** *picks up her knickers and hides them.*

Charles   I just came down to tell you the water's hot.

Carla   Lovely. Thank you.

Charles   Fresh towels in the bathroom. Your mum's seen to that.

Robbie   Thanks Dad.

Charles   I just thought I'd tell you in case you'd forgotten where everything was. You don't want to be wandering about all night looking for things.

Robbie   Thanks Dad.

Charles   He will. I've seen him staggering around. Dozy bugger. He fell down the stairs once. Do you remember that? (*Laughs.*) All the way down to the bottom. Mum thought he was dead. Piss drunk is what he was. Don't you remember?

Robbie   That wasn't me.

Charles   Plastered.

Robbie   That was Mike.

Charles   Then he puked everywhere. I'm serious. (*Laughs.*) Gallons of the most putrid yellow crud everywhere.

Robbie   Yes. It was certainly pretty funny, Dad.

Pause.

Charles   Do you want that bath or don't you?

Robbie   No, we're going to bed.

Charles   All right. You get some sleep. You're going to need it by the looks of things.

Silence.

Well. I'll say good night.

Carla   Good night.

Robbie   Good night Dad.

Pause.

Charles   See you in the morning.

Robbie   OK.

Silence.

Is everything OK?

Charles   I'm all right. Just ... you know ... The funny thing is see, I don't feel redundant. Everybody says to me, You're redundant now. But I don't feel it. I don't know where to put myself. It's like growing old. Everybody tells you you're getting old but I don't feel old. I feel the same as I've always felt. I feel fifteen. Tell me something Carla, how old do you feel?

Carla   I don't know. About twenty-five I suppose.

Charles   Really?

Carla   I do. Yes.

Charles   Oh.

Silence.

Shove up son, there's a good lad.

Charles *sits between* **Robbie** *and* **Carla**. *It's a tight squeeze.*
Charles *looks at* **Robbie**. *Then at* **Carla**. **Robbie** *and* **Carla**
look at each other.

Charles   How old do you feel?

Robbie   Right now about a hundred.

Carla   I think I felt fifteen for a long time.

Charles   Really?

Carla   And then I was twenty-one for a long time.

Charles   You look twenty-one.

Carla   Well . . .

Charles   You're only a baby. You're just kids. You know,
having you two around tonight has really put the lead back in
my pencil. It's really cheered me up. I feel . . . almost positive
about things now . . . It's had quite an effect. Really . . .

Robbie *yawns, looks at his watch, stands.*

Charles   Well. I'll say good night again.

Carla   Night night.

Charles *gets up and goes.* **Robbie** *sits.*

Robbie   We should have got a hotel. Not even told them
where we were.

Carla   I thought you preferred this.

Robbie   No. You said you'd prefer this.

Carla   Because I thought you'd want to be with your family.

Robbie   I distinctly said I'd prefer a hotel.

Carla   But I just assumed . . .

Robbie   You shouldn't have assumed. I distinctly said, you assumed.

Carla   Now you're just being pedantic.

Robbie   Pedantic?

Carla   I can't believe we're arguing about this.

Robbie   Nor can I.

Silence.

We'll leave in the morning. Get a hotel. It's nonsense.

Carla   But you've only just got here.

Robbie   We'll just pack our bags and go. We won't even tell them.

Carla   No. It's too sneaky.

Robbie   Sneakiness is our only hope.

Carla   What about your mum?

Robbie   She'll understand.

Carla   Robbie. Come on.

Robbie   What do you mean come on? Don't tell me to come on.

Carla   Well what's wrong?

Pause. She holds his hand.

Cheer up.

Robbie   Don't tell me to cheer up. I hate that. People only tell you to cheer up when they've run out of sympathy. What they really mean is 'stop whining'. What they really mean is 'Fuck you, I'm not even listening . . .'

Carla *yawns. Silence.* **Carla** *goes to the stairs. She pauses.*

Carla   Are you coming up?

Robbie I'll see you in a minute.

Carla I'll see you in a minute then.

Robbie Well don't I get a kiss?

She comes back, kisses him on the forehead and goes up the stairs. He sits in the semi-darkness alone. Lights down.

Lights up. **Charles** *sits where* **Robbie** *was sitting. He is wrapping electrician's tape around his waist, taping the dictaphone to himself. He pulls his pyjamas up over the tape, rests his arms on the arm-rests and stares straight ahead.* **Mike** *appears at the window.* **Charles** *stares and closes the curtains. He pours a drink. He drinks.* **Billie** *comes in wearing a dressing gown.*

Billie What are you doing down here? You must try and get some sleep.

Pause.

I've washed the sheets.

Charles They talk about me as though I'm invisible. As though I'm not even here.

Billie Robbie worries about you. They've come a long way.

Charles They fall asleep like babies. I expect it's all that massage. Nothing gets you to sleep like a nice massage.

Billie Massage? You've never had a massage in your life.

Charles I've never had a good night's sleep either. I've got nothing to tire me out.

Billie *goes to the sofa and sits beside* **Charles**. *She holds his hand. He drains his glass and goes to the cabinet.*

Billie Don't have another Charles.

He pours another and drinks.

Charles It's not what's happened to me, it's the way it's happened. Ten years and not so much as an apologetic phone call. An invitation for lunch to discuss it. Fucking elevenses to say goodbye would do. Not a dicky bird.

Billie   It's what you make of what's happened, Charles. You know that. It's about getting up in the morning and . . . facing the day.

He drinks.

Charles   Excommunication. I've been swatted away like a fly.

Billie   You had a letter. They offered to meet you and you said no.

Charles   I haven't had a letter.

Pause.

A letter was posted addressed wrongly so I returned it.

Billie   Well, that's them told . . .

Charles   They spelled my name wrong. They got 'Charles' right. It's the surname I'm talking about. How was I to know it was for me?

Pause.

If they want me out they should put it in writing, addressed correctly, stating their intent clearly. Then I know where I stand.

Billie   They have stated their intention.

Charles   I'm not talking about procedure. I'm talking about respect. And self-respect. It's hardly professional. It's one thing to get the boot but to be booted out by amateurs takes the biscuit.

She goes to the table, rifles through a stack of papers and produces a letter as he speaks.

Billie   What's this?

Charles   I forgot to post it.

Billie *opens the letter and reads.* **Charles** *takes the letter back and reads.*

Charles   'Expectations'? What about my expectations? I just accepted a promotion, Chief sub. I could have taken early retirement and got a proper payout. It's a fucking cheek.

Billie It says, 'the present position, doesn't meet . . .'

Charles It says, 'in'. 'In.' In the present position 'I' don't meet the criteria. The chief sub is the criteria. I'm the chief of all the other subs. I am the criteria by which they're measured. I am the criteria. I'm Mister Criteria. They've slipped up. That 'in' is going to cost them . . .

Billie So you've got them on a technicality. Now what?

Charles It implies incompetence. It's got nothing to do with 'downsizing'. They are desperate to get rid of me.

Billie It's just a little ambiguous, that's all. It's just semantics. All they're going to do is re-word the letter.

Charles Now you're lecturing me on semantics. My job is semantics. I am Mister Semantics. They can't re-word the letter. It's too late now. I've got it in writing.

Billie Oh Charles this is getting us nowhere. Come to bed. You must sleep.

Charles I don't sleep any more.

Charles *drinks and reads the letter again.*

I'm over the hill. It's too late to start again and too early to stop. I've got nowhere else to go. I'm finished.

Pause.

I didn't even want the job in the first place. Chief sub? Chief shit-shoveller. Clearing up everybody else's droppings. You know the first job I ever did? Middlesex Hospital opening. It was officially opened by the Queen Mum. It was common knowledge the government had overspent by about fifty million on dodgy contractors. It was a scandal. Anyway I turned up late and I couldn't find the press junket. Wound up lost on the fire escape. I emerged in a corridor not three feet from HRH. They got rid of me pretty sharpish, let me tell you. I wrote a story about it. Said she needed a face-lift and

by the way she was endorsing corruption. Damn nearly got
the bullet. They said it was seditious. Treasonable. The truth
is, they couldn't afford to back it up in court. Small fry. If I'd
been on a national paper they'd have made me editor. If I'd
been freelance . . . I could've owned my own paper. A daily
paper. A broadsheet. A tabloid would have done me. When I
was in space I knew every major advertiser in the country. I
knew the best reporters. I knew everybody. Heavyweights. I
could have started my own weekly standing on my head. Free
advertising for the first two issues, crank up the rate, float it
on the stockmarket, I'd have my bum in butter by now.

Billie   Why didn't you?

Charles   Why? I'll tell you why . . . I'll tell you.

Pause.

I had a family to raise.

Billie   I was working.

Charles   I didn't want you working.

Billie   I could go back to work now.

Charles   I don't want you working.

Billie   But it's made you so bitter.

Charles   Bitter? I am not bitter! My sainted auntie! Bitter?

Silence.

Billie   Well there's nothing you can do about it now.

Charles   You're sure about that are you?

Billie   Charles. What are you thinking?

Charles   What do you think I'm thinking?

Billie   The mind boggles.

Charles   (*snorts*)   *Your* mind boggles?

Pause.

I'm going back to work. And I'm not leaving until they prove

I can no longer do the job in a court of law.

Pause.

Don't try and stop me. I've made up my mind.

Pause.

I'm serious. I'll be at my desk tomorrow morning at nine thirty precisely.

Billie   You're supposed to be clearing your desk tomorrow and forgetting about it until you know what the settlement is going to be.

Charles   There won't be a settlement. That's why it's worded like this.

Billie   Wait and see.

Charles   And if the settlement turns out to be six months' supply of sweet fuck all what do I do then?

Billie   Well what on earth are you going to do all day?

Charles   I shall sit at my desk and do what I always do.

Pause.

You don't believe me do you?

Billie   You can't prove any of it. They'll make mincemeat of you.

Charles *opens his dressing gown to reveal the dictaphone.*

Charles   Oh I'll prove it. By the time I'm through . . .

Billie   Where did you get that?

Charles   Robbie bought it. It's a present.

Silence.

What did you get?

Billie   I don't know whether to laugh or cry. They're not going to tell you anything. They'll just call the lawyers.

Charles   And I'll prove to their lawyers that this is personal and without legal foundation.

Billie   Can we talk about this in the morning?

Charles   No. We'll talk about it now.

Pause.

Everywhere I look there's reminders. I walk about the High
Street wondering what to do and it's all there. The newspaper
office. Old friends. I see people. I hear them talk. I can't talk
to them. I can't face it. I see . . . you don't know what I see.

Pause.

I think I've seen Mike. At night. When I go out to look at the
garden. I see him walk past. He stops. He just looks at me.
Looks at the house. He looks like he could do with a bath. A
bath before it all goes. We'll have to sell. Then how will he
find us?

Billie   You've got Robbie here now. Make the most of it.

Charles   Robbie doesn't understand me the way Mike did.
Mike . . . turned his back on the world. I know how he felt.
At last I know. Tonight, sitting here in the gloom, I
understand him.

Charles *pours a drink.*

They're both as bad as each other. Disappearing. Never
phoning. Do you think . . . it's us?

Pause.

Feel that. My chest. It's like a pigeon caught inside my rib-
cage. Flapping about, sucking up all the air, draining me. It's
the same every night. It's fear. I've never been afraid of
anything in my life.

Billie   It's the scotch. And your blood pressure. I want you
to see a doctor.

Charles   I don't need a doctor. I need things to be how
they were.

Billie   Things will never be how they were.

Charles You know, the last time I felt another person's hands on me was when I had my fucking vasectomy. You don't touch me the way you used to. I haven't felt your skin in months. When was the last time we played spoons? You wrap up like Scott of the Antarctic at bedtime.

Billie That's enough. You know that's not true.

Pause.

Charles Let's get out of here. Let's go for a walk.

Billie It's four o'clock in the morning.

Charles We'll walk to One Tree Hill. The two of us stealing through the sleeping suburbs. Stealing a few moments just for the two of us. Before the rest of the world wakes up. You and me. Alone.

Billie We're always alone.

Charles It's not the same.

Billie I can't go out like this.

Charles You've got knickers on.

Billie What has got into you?

Charles Kiss me. Kiss me . . .

Silence. **Charles** *grabs* **Billie** *around the waist and kisses her. He puts a hand up her nightdress.* **Robbie** *appears on the stairs and stands still, unseen, watching.*

Charles Come on. I'll give you a massage.

He takes her elbow and tries to walk her to the stairs.

Billie Will you stop this. Stop. Stop.

He lets her go. They stand staring at each other.

Charles What have I done?

She starts to go.

Don't you walk away from me when I'm talking to you.

Billie *stops.*

Charles   All right then. Be like that.

Billie   I'll say good night.

Charles   Hey . . . hey!

She stops. Pause.

Well don't I get a kiss?

She kisses him on the forehead. **Charles** *goes to the piano, plays a few bars of 'Don't Get Around Much Any More' and stops, staring into space.* **Billie** *doesn't move.* **Robbie** *goes. Lights down.*

Lights up. Early morning. **Mike** *is in the kitchen, going through the cupboards for food. He opens the fridge and finds a banana and a pint of milk. He goes back out and stands eating, drinking the milk, looking around.* **Robbie** *is on the stairs now wearing a dressing gown.* **Mike** *notices him and stops.* **Robbie** *and* **Mike** *stand facing each other, motionless. They stare at each other. Silence.*

Robbie   What are you doing here?

Mike   What are you doing here?

Robbie   I've been away.

Mike   Where have you been?

Robbie   Far East.

Mike   Nice.

Robbie   It was. Where have you been?

Mike   You like it out there? Good lifestyle?

Robbie   Very much.

Mike   Heated swimming pools. Beautiful scenery. Sweaty equatorial heat every day of the year including Christmas, gin and tonic after work in neon-lit cocktail bars, parties at the ambassador's residence . . . sounds jolly.

Robbie   It was.

Mike   So what are you doing here?

Pause.

Robbie   I came to see Dad.

Mike   You came all that way to see Dad?

Robbie   He's lost his job.

Mike   Again?

Robbie   He's in bits.

Mike   Oh. I see.

Pause.

Robbie   Where have you been living?

Mike   Shepherd's Bush. Well, more Acton really. Willesden. Actually Harlesden. Put it this way, if I had a hat I'd hang it in Hammersmith, but we'll call it Shepherd's Bush.

Pause.

It's not a squat.

Pause.

Anyway I was just passing and I saw the light on and I thought I'd pop in.

Robbie   It's five o'clock in the morning.

Mike   I was hungry.

Robbie *sighs and sits down.*

Mike   I've still got my key. Sometimes I come by and ... you know ... watch the place. I never come in. I just watch.

Pause.

What do you want me to say? 'I missed you.' It's a coincidence.

Robbie   I think they think you're dead. They don't know what happened to you. Nobody knows what happened to you.

Silence.

Mike   Could you get me something to eat?

Robbie *goes to the kitchen and puts toast in the toaster.*

Robbie   I've been getting quite sentimental . . . going through all our old stuff. Meccano. Airfix models. Scalextric. It's all there.

Mike   They only bought you Meccano because they wanted you to be an engineer.

Robbie   There's a lot of things they wanted us to be.

Mike   That's my point.

Pause.

Robbie   Remember that Christmas when we both got Slinkies. Two so we wouldn't fight. Yours got tangled up.

Mike   I never had a Slinky.

Robbie   You did. I tried to fix it. Then Dad threw it away.

Pause.

The beds haven't changed. Kiddies' beds.

Mike   Because we were kiddies. Bunk beds. You were always on top.

Robbie   Bunk beds? No, they were just normal beds.

Mike   Oh yeah. I'm thinking of somewhere else.

Robbie *hands* **Mike** *a plate of toast.* **Mike** *eats hungrily and noisily.*

Robbie   Do you want a bath?

Mike   No. What would I want a bath for?

Robbie   So you can get clean.

Mike   What do you mean? I'm perfectly clean.

Robbie   Mike you stink. I'm sorry but it's horrible.

Mike   What are you implying?

Robbie Have a bath and I'll cook you an omelette.

Mike No, I can't stay.

Robbie What do you mean? You have to see Mum. You have to stay.

Mike *just looks at him and hands the plate back. He goes to the door.*

Robbie Mike. Mike . . .

Mike *stops.*

Robbie Just stay for dinner. Mum's cooking a roast. You remember when we were kids. Roast beef on Sundays. Roastie potatoes. Crispy brown onions. Then we'd go to the pictures. The matinee. *The Man With the Golden Gun.* I've been to the island where they filmed that. Ko Phi-Phi. How could you not remember? Mars Bars and Jelly Tots. Sherbet Fountains. Every Sunday when we got our pocket money. We were spoilt.

Mike *just looks at him.*

Robbie Then we'd come home and go up to our bedroom and talk about it for hours. Re-enact bits. The smells of the kitchen wafting up the stairs. All cosy and warm waiting for dinner. On Friday nights Mum would cook a fondue and wear her kaftan and those ridiculous silver mules with the heels and . . . Dad would . . . you know listen to jazz and play the piano . . . I mean, it's ridiculous but . . . that's what it's all about, isn't it?

Mike This was in the seventies, yeah?

Robbie Yeah. It was . . . it was a very special time.

Mike I don't remember.

Mike *takes out a cigarette. Lights it and offers one to* **Robbie**.

Robbie I don't smoke.

Mike Why not?

Robbie I don't know, I just never took it up.

Mike   You will.

Robbie   Will I?

Mike   Yeah. And they'll drive you to drink.

Robbie   Glad to see you haven't lost any of that sparkling cynicism. You're as bad as Dad.

Mike   What do you mean?

Robbie   You're so similar it's ridiculous.

Mike   Piss off.

Robbie   You are, always have been. I don't think you realise.

Silence.

I'm sorry.

Mike   How is he?

Robbie   He's not exactly taking it on the chin. He told me it was some kind of conspiracy.

They giggle.

Mike   When I was little he used to tell me he was the British and European middleweight boxing champion and three times Father of the Year.

Robbie   Did he ever tell you he was there when Ronnie Biggs escaped from Wandsworth prison?

Mike   Dressed as a woman.

Robbie   They're always dressed as women aren't they?

Mike   That's his sense of humour. Stupid but harmless.

Robbie   I actually believed it until I was about fifteen.

Mike   So did I.

Mike *lights his cigarette and smokes.*

Robbie   I wouldn't do that in here. They'll go mental.

Mike They already are mental. Are they asleep?

Robbie Of course they're asleep.

Mike You weren't asleep.

Robbie I couldn't.

Mike Well why?

Pause.

Did you have nightmares?

Pause.

Robbie I have dreams about Dad. About . . . murdering him. Ever since I was small. I dream about hitting him. Really beating the crap out of him. Sometimes even drowning him or . . . stabbing him. But mostly I dream that he's dying already. And I have to save him. I find him in the bath and he's drowned. And I try to wake him up and I can't. And I yell and scream as hard as I can but it's no use. He's stiff as a board. It's horrendous.

Pause.

Mike You have those dreams too?

Pause.

Robbie Do you think Mum gets them?

Pause.

Do you think it's normal?

Mike I've no idea.

Robbie Why do you think we get them?

Billie *appears on the stairs and stares at* **Mike** *and* **Robbie**.
Silence.

Mike Hi.

Robbie How are you, Mum?

Silence. She goes to **Mike** *and holds him. She kisses him.*

Billie   My boy. My little boy . . .

Blackout.

Lights up. Morning. **Mike** *and* **Charles** *sit facing each other across the dining table.* **Mike** *has a plate of breakfast in front of him.* **Charles** *wears a shirt and trousers with an untied tie around his neck.* **Billie** *opens the curtains and goes to the kitchen where she prepares breakfast.* **Carla** *and* **Robbie** *sit at the table quietly.*

Charles   Look at this. You eat like a tramp. Listen to the sound effects.

Billie   Leave him alone. Mike there's a cup of tea here.

Charles   He's going to choke in a minute. Look at you. You look like a tramp. All unshaven and twitchy.

Billie   Don't take any notice. Robbie, come and get your egg. Who wants soldiers?

Robbie   I'm not hungry any more.

Billie   Give it to your dad then. And take your brother his cup of tea. And find out who wants soldiers.

Robbie *goes to the kitchen and takes cups and a plate of breakfast out and sets them down in front of* **Mike** *and* **Charles**.

Robbie   Who wants soldiers?

Carla   Yes please.

Robbie   Carla wants soldiers.

Robbie *sits.* **Charles** *and* **Mike** *drink tea.*

Charles   What's this?

Billie   It's your egg.

Charles   Since when did one egg constitute breakfast? I can't be expected to go to work on one egg.

Robbie *takes his plate back to the kitchen.* **Charles** *ties his tie. They all look at each other.*

Mike   Hysterical.

Robbie *takes the plate back to* **Charles**. **Charles** *eats quickly and noisily.*

Charles   Now I've got egg on my tie. Look at this. No co-ordination. That's a sign of age, that is.

He takes out his hankie, licks it and dabs at the tie.

Oh my goodness I'm enjoying myself. This is the happiest day of my life. Look at my lovely family. The sun shining outside. Bacon sizzling in the pan. The smells. Fresh coffee on the stove. I've never been so excited in my life. I can't contain myself. Robbie, have you told your brother your stories yet?

Robbie   Which stories?

Charles   About Borneo.

Robbie   What about it? I just worked there.

Charles   Absolutely. He worked there. In fucking Borneo. The wild man of Borneo. You do make me laugh.

He laughs. Everybody else just looks at him. Silence. He wipes his eyes. He continues eating.

Billie   Never mind Borneo. I want to hear all Mike's stories.

Mike   How do you mean?

Billie   I want to know where you've been for the past five years.

Mike   I don't have any stories.

Charles   You've always got a story, ever since you were tiny. Come on, spill the beans.

Pause.

Mike   You wouldn't understand.

Charles   What wouldn't I understand?

Mike   I'd rather not talk about it.

Billie   Well you can tell me later.

Charles   When I was in space, I could walk into any pub in

Chinatown and I'd get a beer and a welcome just so they could hear my stories. And by fuck did I have some stories. I was their link with the outside world. Ronnie Scott's? Leave it out. I used to play there before we were married.

Billie   That's right. You played pool there.

Charles   I played piano thank you very much.

Billie   In the back room where the pool table was.

Charles   I remember when Jack Spot used to run Soho from a fruit shop in Frith Street until the Kray twins cut him to pieces. Straight up. Your mother was nursing him at St Mary's in Paddington when they came in to fetch him out of bed dressed as nurses.

Billie   I don't know what you're talking about.

Charles   You were famous for that little incident. You don't forget a thing like that.

Mike   No, you don't forget a thing like that. Two of England's most notorious psychopaths prancing about dressed as nurses right under your nose.

Everybody looks at **Mike**. *Pause.*

Charles   It's true. Ronnie Kray liked to dress up as a nurse.

Billie   Now you're just being silly.

Charles   Ronnie Kray was an iron hoof. Everybody knows that.

Mike   Only why did they come to fetch him out if they put him there in the first place?

Charles   To put him to work son. Feed him to the monster. Same reason any of us gets out of bed. To go to work for a bunch of crooks. I learnt something about your mum that day as well. Nerves of bloody steel. I damn nearly proposed to her on the spot.

Billie   I treated a grocer called Carter. I gave him a wax bath on his hands. That's all I remember.

Charles *takes his plate to the kitchen. They drink their tea.* **Charles** *produces a novelty 'bra and panties' pinny and offers it to* **Billie**.

Charles   Here you are, put your sexy pinny on. Give me a real thrill.

Billie *puts the pinny on without a word.*

Charles   Oh boy. Now I'm starting to go. What a combination. Now I've got you where I want you.

Charles *smacks* **Billie** *on the bum.*

Wa-hey.

Billie   Stop that.

Charles *puts his arms around* **Billie** *from behind and kisses her neck. He lifts* **Billie** *off her feet.*

Charles   Wa-hey.

Billie   Will you please stop doing that please.

Charles   Mind your backs. Lady with a baby!

Billie   Put me down.

Charles   Say please.

He jiggles her up and down. He kisses her.

Billie   You bugger.

She kisses him.

Charles   Even better, a chaste kiss on the choppers. Say please or I'll tickle you.

Billie   Come on Charles, enough is enough.

He tickles her.

You're hurting me . . . how many times do I have to tell you?

He drops her clumsily. **Billie** *smoothes her clothes.* **Charles** *sits.*

Billie   The soldiers are ready.

Robbie *fetches them and serves them to* **Carla**. **Charles** *watches*

Carla *eat.* **Mike** *stops and puts his knife and fork down to watch* **Carla**. **Carla** *puts her knife and fork down.*

Charles   Any good? Does your mum's culinary expertise measure up to the lofty standards enjoyed in the tropics?

Carla   It's lovely, thank you.

Charles   Have some more. Come on, get it down you.

Carla   No, I've had plenty thank you.

Charles   Come on. You'll waste away. Look at you. You're only little. Look at this.

He tweaks **Carla***'s arm.* **Carla** *resumes eating intermittently.*

Robbie   Dad . . .

Charles   Such a skinny little thing. She's all skin and bone.

Billie   There's no need to forcefeed her Charles. We're not making paté . . .

Carla   It's all right. Really.

Charles   Come on.

Robbie   Dad please . . .

Carla   No thanks.

Charles   Come on. It's lovely.

Carla   I said no. Thank you . . . I've quite enough to be getting on with.

Charles   Well, that's me told. (*Laughs.*) No you're all right. I'm joking.

Billie   Have you got brothers Carla?

Carla   Two.

Billie   That's nice. Younger or older?

Carla   Both younger.

Billie   You must be used to this then. Quite an expert.

Carla Oh you know it's . . .

Billie You must miss them.

Carla I do. In fact I was saying to Robbie being around your family makes me miss them even more.

Billie I'm not at all surprised.

Pause.

Mike (*to* **Carla**) Rob tells me you're going to be a doctor.

Carla I've got a year to go. I did my foreign elective in Java.

Mike I'd like to be a doctor. That way I'd always know what's wrong with me. (*To* **Robbie**.) It's no coincidence that both you and Dad have meaningful long-term relationships with medics. Women in general have always had an instinctively calming effect on me but there's something particularly reassuring about medically skilled women.

Billie It's called charm Mike. And you could use some.

Charles You've got work lined up in London I take it?

Carla We're just taking it easy for a while.

Billie You must be exhausted. You'll need a rest before your finals.

Charles Absolutely, have a rest, you've earned it. Mike's been resting for five years, haven't you son?

Mike I've had plenty of jobs.

Charles Like what?

Mike This and that.

Charles Oh this and that? That's a good job, that is. Very popular with the criminal element isn't it Bill?

Billie Does it matter Charles? Really.

Charles Yes it does matter. He's an educated man. My father never said a word to me. No advice. Didn't believe in it. He was tough. Boy was he tough. You think I'm hard on you . . . I'm a fucking marshmallow compared to him, hard as nails but . . . he did his best.

Mike   If you want me to go away again you only have to say.

Charles   I want you to be happy, son! That's what being a father means. And when you're happy, I'm happy. Is that so wrong?

Pause.

You used to be such a great little bloke. So . . . friendly and outgoing and entertaining. Charismatic. And I look at you now. Living in strange places. You don't have any money. Always tense, moody, dark . . . I don't know what happened. Why are you so resentful? Where did I go wrong?

Silence.

(*To* **Billie**.) Where's the shoe polish? I thought I saw it under the sink.

Billie   Black or brown?

Charles   Black sweetheart, black. Work shoes are black. I'm wearing a tie and flannels. Use your head.

Billie *produces polish and a brush and takes it to* **Charles**. **Charles** *holds up a pair of shoes and begins polishing them.* **Billie** *goes back to the kitchen.*

Billie   Did you have a nice time abroad Carla?

Carla   I liked Malaysia and Thailand. Java was a bit of a nightmare. The fundamentalism and the poverty . . . for doctors it's soul-destroying.

Robbie   You liked Singapore.

Carla   I quite liked Singapore. Robbie and I met at Singapore zoo.

Robbie   It's one of the best zoos in the world actually.

Mike   One of the best zoos in the world? Really?

Charles Oh yes? And why's that?

Robbie Money.

Mike No. You don't say.

Robbie A lot of investment from the multinationals. All of them, Esso, Exon, McDonald's. Microsoft had an enclosure so I got free tickets. I got a lot of things free actually. They really looked after me. They liked me because I understood their notion of dignity in adversity. I never made a fuss.

Charles *looks at* **Robbie**.

Billie Well. That's very nice for you Robbie.

Carla They all sponsor an enclosure. They take it very seriously. There's a lot of competition over who sponsors what.

Robbie I was rooting for apes.

Mike Rooting for apes?

Robbie My sponsorship preference was an ape enclosure.

Mike In case you got homesick.

Charles You can't beat London zoo in my book.

Robbie Oh, this is a different kettle of fish entirely, Dad. Huge enclosures. Lots of very illustrious people hanging about.

Carla It's an open zoo. The animals are a lot freer and happier.

Charles I'd be happy with dozens of slope-eyed multinationals paying my bed and board. Bum in butter those animals by the sound of it. Not like London zoo. They only tried to close it down. It makes me sick!

Pause.

Billie Well. I was happy there. Things are coming together for me at last. There's talk of taking a new software system to Amsterdam. Nothing's concrete but it would mean I could work a little closer to home.

Pause.

It's not definite yet. It's just to implement an idea I've been working on. Ways of streamlining efficiency, improving the flow of communication. It's all a bit boring really but it means I could come home for a while.

Silence.

Then again . . . if it doesn't happen I'll just sod off back to Singapore and make loads of money. Who cares? As long as you have your health.

Billie   Well I think it's wonderful news Robbie. You've made my day.

Charles   Have you got it in writing?

Robbie   I got a fax in Singapore.

Charles   A fax? Addressed to you?

Robbie   It was a general mandate to say that my patent was being considered.

Charles   But it's not definite.

Robbie   It's hopeful.

Charles   Don't talk to me about hopeful. Is it or isn't it definite? And I repeat, have you got it in writing?

Robbie   I said I've got a fax.

Charles   That's not writing.

Robbie   They like my work.

Charles   'Like' is worthless. Do they really like it?

Robbie   Why shouldn't they?

Charles   Why? What have you done to distinguish yourself that's so special? Have you got a contract?

Robbie   Of course I have.

Charles   Not worth a pinch of shit unless you are indispensable. You know what your trouble is son? You're naive.

Robbie Well that's me told.

Mike Were you ever indispensable Dad? And what happened to your contract?

Pause.

Charles *looks* **Mike** *directly in the eye.*

Charles You know I think you've aged, son. That'll be the booze I expect.

Charles *spits on his shoe and continues polishing.* **Carla** *puts her knife and fork down and pushes her plate away.*

Billie Have you decided what you want to do Carla?

Mike Absolutely. Have you asked her? Go on, ask her.

Carla Well . . . I don't know.

Mike No come on. Don't hide your light under a bushel.

Carla Well to be honest . . .

Mike We want you to be honest obviously.

Carla I have . . . I have mixed feelings about Singapore.

Mike Why?

Carla I don't know . . . little things . . .

Mike God is in the detail. Go on.

Carla I don't know . . .

Charles Stop saying 'I don't know'. Spit it out, we'll be here all day.

Pause.

Carla It's . . . well . . . it's just very . . . you know, materialistic. Technocratic I suppose. You know, there are more robots. I mean real robots, per capita in Singapore than anywhere else in the world.

Robbie Robots?

Carla   You know this . . . it's just that . . . computers for instance, and computer courses are everywhere. And money . . . money is the sole criteria for personal success etcetera and the use of computers to make money, and the use of robots to make the computers that . . . make the money. Little children in schools are terrifyingly computer literate. They learn that a) All problem solving can only be tackled from the point of view of computerised logic – and b) The binary logic of machinery is utterly pervasive so that they never take into account the complexities and the ambiguities of the human existence. They begin to think like . . . like robots. I found it all a bit . . . creepy, really, that's all.

Robbie   Creepy?

Carla   You've seen it yourself. You programme these things. It's insidious.

Robbie   What absolute twaddle.

Carla   It's true.

Charles   It makes sense to me.

Mike   And me.

Carla   In Java people are losing jobs they've had all their lives and finding themselves rifling through rubbish dumps for their food . . .

Robbie   You weren't saying this when you were knocking back Mango Daiquiris beside my rooftop swimming pool. You didn't say that when we flew to Ko Samui all expenses paid.

Carla   It's the principle of the thing . . .

Robbie   It's not your problem.

Carla   It is when I'm up to my neck in depressives. You know what I mean.

Robbie   Do I?

Carla   Robbie . . .

Charles   I know what she means.

Robbie Well you would.

Mike Me too. I know exactly what she means.

Robbie *looks from* **Carla** *to* **Mike** *to* **Charles** *and back to* **Carla**.

Robbie Look . . . listen . . . look . . . listen . . .

Charles Principles. Integrity. A woman after my own heart. I think it's marvellous.

Mike Marvellous.

Charles You're cheering me up no end.

Robbie Oh for fuck's sake.

Carla What's wrong?

Robbie Nothing absolutely nothing. You go ahead. I'll talk about my life and what's happening to me and to us and you can tell them about the robots and the binary logic and how you once read a George Orwell novel and how you met Mother Theresa and you were in the debating team at Guy's. It's very edifying. Really.

Pause.

Mike Did you really meet Mother Theresa?

Carla It was just one of her envoys.

Mike One of her sisters, yeah? Wow.

Robbie *and* **Carla** *stare at each other. Silence.* **Charles** *stands and straightens his tie. He puts on his jacket.*

Charles I'm off. Another day another dollar.

Billie *goes to him.*

Billie Why don't you stay at home today? Go back to bed and I'll bring you up a cup of coffee and the papers. I'll run you a bath. A nice hot bath. I'd like a nice hot bath. A nice hot steamy bath.

She kisses him.

I could give you a massage.

She massages his shoulders. **Charles** *considers.*

Charles   . . . No. I'll be late for work.

Charles *puts on his shoes.*

It's not over yet. I haven't even started yet.

Mike   Are you expecting a settlement?

Robbie *puts his head in his hands.*

Charles   Peanuts. And you know what you get when you pay peanuts.

Robbie   Well, monkeys, obviously.

Charles   And what do monkeys do? They eat, fornicate and hang by their testicles shitting on each other from a great height just like everybody else in the world!

Charles *kisses* **Billie**.

Robbie   I wish you'd wait until you've seen a lawyer.

Charles   They're all the same. They give you the funny handshake with one hand and fleece you with the other. Prancing about like little girls telling each other their secrets. My father would have given both his balls to join the Masons. They wouldn't have him. Broke his heart. My father . . . my dad . . .

He stares. Silence. **Robbie** *stands.* **Charles** *throws a playful one-two at* **Robbie** *and ruffles* **Mike**'s *hair.*

Charles   Eh? Cheeky chops. You look after your mum while I'm at work.

Charles *goes. Silence.*

Billie   Don't be too harsh on him, son. Try not to judge him. He loves you so much.

Billie *goes to* **Robbie**, *puts her hands on his shoulders and sits him down.*

He's just a little bit lost at the moment. He is a good honest principled man. Deep down.

Mike   Extremely deep down.

Billie   Sometimes you just have to be big about things.

Silence. **Billie** *picks up a remote control on the table.*

He's forgotten his keys.

Robbie   He's not driving is he?

Mike   I'll go. I want to talk to him.

Robbie   What do you want to talk to him about?

Mike   I just want to talk to him. Because he's such a complex and fascinating mass of contradictions.

Robbie   I'll drive him.

Mike   No I'll drive him. We've got a lot of catching up to do. Give me the keys.

Mike *reaches for the keys,* **Billie** *holds onto them.*

Billie   You stay away from the pub.

Robbie   I'll go, Mum.

Mike   I won't go to the pub, I promise. (*To* **Robbie**.) Lend us a fiver.

Robbie   Piss off.

Mike   Don't tell me to piss off Robbie.

Robbie   Well don't be such a wanker.

Billie   That's enough.

Mike   Don't call me a wanker Robbie. Believe me, that's the last thing you want to call me. (*To* **Carla**.) Lend us a fiver.

Robbie   I don't believe this.

Mike   I'm winding you up.

Robbie   This is stupid, it's just stupid!

Billie   I said that's enough. If you boys are going to fight you can go outside.

Mike   Mum ... why don't you sit down for a minute?

Pause.

Billie   He's got a tape recorder in his underpants.

Pause.

Mike   Why?

Robbie   Because he's paranoid.

Mike   Well I think he's right. He should do it. Better to die on your feet than live on your knees as they say.

Billie   When I was a girl, my father did something I'll never forget. It wasn't long after the war, during rationing, and somebody in the market had given me a tangerine. Of course to me it was a treasure. And I took it home to show my dad and he asked me where I got it and when I told him he stood me on the table and he said 'Jump.' I was only about four 'Jump into my arms and I'll catch you.' And he held his arms out and I jumped off the table and I flew through the air and he took two steps back and I landed flat on my face. Smack. I got quite a shiner. And he said to me, 'Now you've learnt.' Learnt? I was four years old. I didn't know what he was up to. And he said, 'Never, my girl, ever trust anybody ...' Maybe he was right. Or maybe he was being a touch paranoid. But the point is, for thirty years, the only person I've ever trusted is your father. So you just watch what you say about him.

Robbie *and* **Mike** *exchange glances.* **Billie** *hands the keys to* **Robbie. Robbie** *goes.* **Billie** *goes to the kitchen and prepares food.*

Mike   Are you all right? Really?

Mike *hugs* **Billie.**

Billie   I'm just tired sweetheart.

Mike   Why don't you go and have a lie down?

Billie   Yes. That's all I need. A nice sleep.

She takes her pinny off and goes. Silence. **Mike** *just stands there.*
Silence.

Mike   I want to go to university.

Carla   Oh, it's not all it's cracked up to be.

Mike   It is. It's important. I used to live near a university.
In Shepherd's Bush. I went in there once to find out about it.
Because I feel . . . I felt . . . there must be something I can do.

Carla   What would you like to do?

Mike   I have no idea.

Carla   There must be something you always wanted to do.
Why not?

Mike   Why not? Because I'm stupid.

Carla   Says who?

Mike   I worked it out for myself.

Carla   My parents always had this thing about me being too
bright. Every time I made a mistake they'd say, 'You're too
bright to make a mistake like that.' At school I was always
getting teased for being an egghead. Teased for getting good
marks. Teased because I didn't smoke or swear. I even got
teased for getting jokes before anybody else did. And I was
always expected to . . . rise above it but I expected to be able
to . . . talk about it. It was a no-win situation really . . .

Mike *sits beside* **Carla** *and stares at her.*

Mike   The first job I ever had I was a teaboy at QPR.
Every morning at ten and every afternoon at three I'd take
the management a little pot of tea on a little tray with . . .
biscuits and things. Problem was I couldn't keep my mind on
the job. You see . . . I had this girlfriend. I'd phone her every
day. Every single day. She had a car. She used to drive . . . so
fast. Like the wind. She'd drive me to the sea. Very fast. So
fast that I'd . . . I'd be giggling and hanging onto my seat and
she'd be giggling, hanging onto the steering wheel. And I'd be

hanging onto her. And we'd sit on the beach in the summer in our swimming costumes and I'd stare at her legs. Just stare at her legs. I'd never seen such beautiful legs. Long and thin and powerful. White and smooth. Like porcelain. Dancer's legs. I mean I remark about her legs, but only because they were remarkable. More than that was her warmth and wit. She was astonishingly intelligent and just, you know, very nice. Delightful. We were delighted with each other.

Carla *laughs a little, humouring him. Pause.*

Mike   She was my first serious girlfriend. She was . . . the love of my life. You remind me of her. A lot of girls remind me of her. You always see the dead in the living.

Silence.

Carla   I'm so sorry . . .

Mike   That's how I lost my job as teaboy. See, I was in my room one day, in my room upstairs, and her mum phoned and she said she'd . . . she was coming back from the seaside and on the way there'd been some kind of accident. Yes . . . a Dover-bound juggernaut. She was with this boy, this old boyfriend, the one she had before me and they'd been drinking. Apparently. They'd been . . . they'd been seeing each other again. I . . . I went to the hospital and I sat by her bedside in the hospital, watching as a . . . a large, dark blotch over one eye spread to the other and the lights went out. I watched as the . . . the lights went out . . . and I'd . . . I was holding her hand and saying to her to . . . you know . . . live. Because I couldn't believe this was happening. But she couldn't. Couldn't hang on . . . not even for me.

Pause.

After that I wasn't very good at . . . I wasn't much good at anything. I tried to talk to people about it. I talked to all sorts of people. Strangers. In pubs. I tried to talk to Mum. I tried to talk to Dad but . . . You know I think he thought it was my fault. I think he thought I was just being a troublemaker. Robbie was busy with his university friends and . . . I don't resent them. I just get a bit angry sometimes. To think she could go like that and nobody . . . even seemed to notice. And I just thought . . . I still think . . . it's fucking nonsense – life's too short . . .

Pause.

Sometimes . . . some days . . . I see her . . . everywhere I look.

Silence. He stares into space.

Well. It's nearly eleven. Time for a drink. Lend us a fiver?

Pause. He goes.

Blackout.

Act Two

Lights up. **Carla** *sits at the table reading a medical textbook.* **Robbie** *walks in rattling car keys.*

Robbie I think my dad's going insane.

Pause.

I said . . . are you listening to me?

Carla *puts her book down.*

Robbie All that business at breakfast. Trying to get you to eat all that breakfast and being all, you know, nice to you.

Carla So?

Robbie It's pathetic. You should have seen him in the car. Wouldn't stop talking.

Carla So?

Robbie Wrenching his head out of the window to yell at complete strangers. You should have seen him last night. One minute he was yelling, then he was trying to seduce her for Christsake.

Carla So? You do that all the time.

Robbie . . . What?

Carla Just because they're old it doesn't mean they have to stop having sex.

Robbie It's not what he does, it's the way he does it. He's hyperactive. Telling one stupid interminably long and complex story after another. It's painful.

Carla He's your dad. That's what dads do.

Robbie Your dad didn't do this when he was made redundant.

Carla You have to consider the circumstances of his life. a)

He's had a hard life. b) The family circumstances aren't ideal with you out of the country and Mike being . . . the way he is. And c) there's his personality to consider. He's getting particularly depressive and aggressive about this because that's his personality type. Type A. Whether or not a person can handle a life-changing catastrophe is more often than not down to purely accidental antecedents. Luck and circumstance. Your dad's simply manifesting his own idiosyncratic response to the situation which, unluckily, is quite extreme.

Robbie *picks up the book and looks at it. He puts it down.*

Carla   I'm sorry. What do you want me to say?

Robbie   I want you to agree with me!

Pause.

Carla   I want to go home. I want to spend some time with my family.

Robbie   Why?

Carla   I miss them.

Robbie   What's the point of escaping from my family only to go and stay with yours?

Carla   I like my family.

Robbie   Why?

Silence. They stand staring at each other.

I'll go and pack.

Carla   I want you to stay. I want you all to resolve . . . I want you to resolve things for yourself.

Robbie   Resolve things for myself. Why?

Carla   Because I can't.

Robbie   Is that a . . . what? An ultimatum?

Silence.

Carla   Why don't you tell them the truth?

Robbie   The truth about what?

Carla   You know what I'm talking about.

Robbie   Tell my parents the truth? I've never heard anything so ridiculous in my life.

Carla   I think you should tell your dad.

Robbie   He wouldn't even begin to comprehend. You've seen him. He's wound up ready to ping. He'll blast off.

Carla   It's what he wants to hear. I'm serious. You've no idea the relief depressed people derive from learning of other people's disastrous vicissitudes.

Robbie   You've seen me trying to tell him things. It's like talking to a dog.

Carla   I think it might bring you closer together.

Robbie   You know what I think? I think you like my family more than you like me, that's what I think. Have you been listening to a word I've said? Christ you depress me when you don't listen.

Carla   You depress me when you think I don't listen when actually I do listen. I'm always listening. To everybody.

Robbie   Well maybe that's your problem. You're just too nice.

Carla   That's not fair. That's a horrible thing to say.

Silence.

Robbie   Where are you going?

Carla   I'm going for a walk. I need some time to think.

She goes. Lights down.

Lights up. **Billie** *lays the table for dinner.* **Robbie** *sits watching* **Billie**. *She stops and smiles.*

Billie   I'm sorry. It's not much of a homecoming.

Robbie   Nothing I haven't seen before.

Billie Yes, quite.

Pause.

It'll all be over in a week or so. It usually is. He'll win or
he'll lose and we'll all calm down and everything will go back
to normal. I'm looking forward to getting to know Carla. She
seems sweet. I'll enjoy having another woman around.
Another girl to gossip with. We've been so excited, you've no
idea. Does she gossip? I don't suppose she does. She's very
unassuming . . .

Robbie The thing is Mum, we'll probably head off
tomorrow.

Billie Oh. So soon. It's all been decided has it?

Robbie We'll be back. Maybe next year. I mean this is
home.

Billie I understand.

Robbie I'm really at their mercy. Business is business.

Billie Well I wouldn't know about that . . .

Robbie It's not as simple as you think . . .

Billie Don't tell me things aren't as simple as I think
Robbie, please. I'm really no stranger to complexity. I am
your mother, after all.

Silence.

I keep expecting a knock on the door from the police. This is
what Mike used to do.

Robbie We're getting married.

Pause.

Obviously we'll want to be married here. Have the family
around. Have a real family wedding . . . a proper . . .
celebration.

Pause.

What do you think? Mum?

Billie   I don't know what to think.

Robbie   I love her to bits. It's the real thing. I thought you'd be happy.

Billie   I'm very happy for you. I'm delighted. Really. Genuinely thrilled.

Carla *comes in shaking off rain. She watches. Silence.*

Carla   What's happened?

Robbie *stands and pushes past her.*

Robbie   We've got packing to do. Haven't we?

Carla   Have we?

Robbie   Yes . . . we have . . . I thought we talked about this?

Pause. He sighs and goes upstairs. **Carla** *starts to go.*

Billie   I expect you're looking forward to settling down after all this upheaval. Not settling down but . . . making your own home. It's quite exciting. Have you got a date?

Carla   For what?

Billie   For the wedding.

Pause.

Carla   I think we've got a few years to go before we start thinking about –

Billie   I've put my foot in it –

Carla   No it's just –

Billie   He's probably just –

Carla   Said something to you and –

Billie   Said something completely different to you, absolutely. Just like his father. That's what they do. They gild the lily.

Carla   Well they –

Billie   They –

Carla   They lie –

Billie   They lie, how right you are.

Pause.

It makes life so complicated.

Robbie *appears at the top of the stairs.*

Robbie   Sweetheart . . . are you coming up?

Carla   In a minute darling.

Robbie *goes.*

Billie   You reach an age when shifting ground is . . . so draining. It's not exciting any more. It just . . . wears you out. Charles and I were younger than you when we got married. By the time we were your age we'd had the boys. Charles didn't become a junior reporter until he was in his thirties. Imagine that. A man with a young family and he was a junior. All his colleagues were kids – younger than you. I put the boys through nursery and went into physiotherapy part-time. I loved it. Did it for ten years and gave it up when Charles got promoted. And now this . . .

Pause.

I look at Robbie and he seems so . . . detached. So knowing. It's your generation. It's as if you instinctively grasp the pointlessness of it all. Or am I missing something here?

Carla   Robbie isn't working in Singapore. He hasn't done for months. He picked up a few weeks' work at Microsoft in Product Support Services . . . helping little old ladies format their Christmas shopping lists over the phone. Then somebody developed a software package specifically for little old ladies and . . . After that he couldn't sleep . . . Kept having nightmares . . . It took him three weeks to tell me. I just thought he was homesick.

Billie   So did I.

Carla   I was . . . waiting for him to tell you.

Billie   So was I.

Lights down.

Lights up. **Billie** *lays a fire.* **Charles** *comes in and they stand staring at each other.*

Charles   What's wrong?

Billie   Where shall I start?

Charles   Don't start. Just relax Billie. Relax. The boys are home, I'm home, everything is in its rightful place. For once . . . everything is as it should be. It's just you and me and our lovely family.

Billie   What's happened?

Charles   Nothing else matters.

Billie   Charles . . .

Charles   From now on I'm a family man.

Billie   Calm down . . .

Charles   From now on I'm Mister Fucking Family.

Billie   . . . And tell me what happened today.

They sit at the table. He produces the dictaphone and puts it on the table. He produces a document and places it on the table beside the dictaphone.

Charles   You've got to listen to this. I've never been so excited in my life.

Charles *switches on the tape recorder.*

Charles's voice   Isn't it a lovely day? Have you seen it? Have you been out yet? My goodness. The sky is so blue.

Charles *gestures and fast-forwards.*

Boss's voice   You have signed I presume.

Charles's voice   No.

Billie *looks at* **Charles** *and he gestures reassuringly.*

Boss's voice   You haven't signed the letter?

Charles's voice   I haven't received a letter. I never got it.

Boss's voice   Oh.

Charles *chuckles to himself.*

Charles's voice   Is that a problem?

Charles *laughs.*

Boss's voice   Our solicitors have drawn up a settlement.

Charles's voice   Never got it.

Charles *pushes the document towards* **Billie**. *She picks it up and reads.*

Boss's voice   This is a fair settlement. You can wait at your desk for six months and it won't change.

Charles's voice   I don't doubt it.

Boss's voice   Except that there may be no settlement in six months.

Charles *switches it off.*

Charles   Now they're using threats. Evidence.

Billie   What is it evidence of?

Charles   Well, they're going to renege on the settlement, obviously. If I put up a fight they'll pull the whole deal.

Billie   What do you want from them . . . ?

Charles *presses 'Play', gesturing throughout the next speech.*

Charles's voice   I want to work! I don't want to just stop my life . . . grind to a halt . . . I want something . . . better . . . I want what everybody else wants. I want to be treated with respect! I want my dignity! And I want an apology! I want a fucking apology!

Boss's voice   The world doesn't owe you a living Charles.

Charles's voice   It does, it does!

He switches off the tape. Silence.

Billie   And what did he say?

Charles   They're making me see a counsellor. Ridiculous but true. Actually . . . it's quite funny, it turns out they've made appointments for nearly everybody.

Billie   With a psychiatrist.

Charles   It's ridiculous. Still, I wouldn't have missed it for the world. This explains everything.

Charles *fast-forwards.*

Counsellor's voice   You talk about a conspiracy. Why?

Charles's voice   Because they want to get rid of me.

Counsellor's voice   Who's behind the conspiracy?

Charles's voice   You wouldn't understand.

Counsellor's voice   Try me.

Charles's voice   They know who they are.

Counsellor's voice   Who are they?

Charles's voice   You wouldn't understand.

Charles *fast-forwards.*

Counsellor's voice   Do you find yourself losing your temper with colleagues?

Charles *fast-forwards.*

Counsellor's voice   How are you getting on with your family? How are you getting on with your wife?

Charles *switches it off.*

Charles   Got him! They're finished. They couldn't resist getting personal. All the evidence I need.

Billie   This is madness.

Charles   Ah. That's what they want you to think.

Billie   You don't know what you're talking about.

Charles   They want you to think I'm crazy.

Billie   You are.

Charles   That's what they want you to think.

Billie   Why?

Charles   To save on early retirement!

Silence. **Charles** *stares.*

Twenty years ago there'd be strikes across the nation. When I was axed from space, you'd have thought I was mad if I didn't make a stink.

Billie *goes to the kitchen and returns with a pen. She places it on the table beside the document and dictaphone.*

Billie   I want you to settle with them. Settle. Invest. Pay off the rest of the mortgage. Rest. Have a holiday . . . We could go abroad.

Charles   Where? The Far East?

Billie   Florence. Tuscany. Live in the middle of nowhere. Start again. I'll learn Italian . . .

Charles   Learn Italian. Good plan, Billy. I'll grow carnations, shall I? Drive the school bus.

Billie   Charles, I don't care what you do, just don't do this . . . Stay and get another job. You're a . . . a brilliant man. You'll find something else. You always do. Why not? Why have you let yourself become so angry . . . ? What are you afraid of?

Charles   Everything.

Billie   Why?

Charles   Because I'm good at it. Somebody has to be angry, somebody has to be afraid.

Billie   Why?

Charles   Will you stop saying that! Why shouldn't I? Why should I start again? Why should I accept it . . . 'soldier on'? Where is it written? 'Turn the other cheek'?

Billie   It's the way of the world. Haven't you learnt that yet?

Charles   I've got a better one. Try this for size. 'Know thyself.' Because I do, Billie. And I know . . . that I can't do it any more. I won't lie down again. I'm not that type of man.

Billie   What type of man are you then?

Charles   . . . 'Go abroad'? Why must you humiliate me? Am I not humiliated enough? Can you not see this? Must I spend my entire life humiliating myself to convince you? For just one shred of understanding?

He pounds his fist on the table.

For a shred of understanding.

He snatches the document, screws it up and tosses it to the floor.

Screwed up and thrown away. All of us. The human race. Comes to us all.

Robbie *is standing at the top of the stairs.*

Robbie   What the hell is going on here?

Charles   Who rattled your cage?

Robbie   What are you shouting about?

Charles   I'm not shouting.

Robbie   It's like listening to the fucking wrestling.

Billie   Shut up Robbie. You don't know what you're talking about.

Robbie   Well don't let him talk to you like this.

Billie   I'm not letting him.

Robbie (*to* **Charles**)   What's your problem, Dad?

Charles   I haven't got a problem.

Robbie   Why are you like this?

Charles   But son I'm not like this. There is no Why. It's you. You've had a problem since the moment you got here and one of these days your boss or your brother or your girlfriend is going to tell you what it is.

Robbie *turns away, takes a few steps, sits.* **Carla** *appears, unseen, at the top of the stairs. She stands watching.*

Charles   What's the matter son?

Robbie   I'm depressed.

Charles   We're all depressed.

Robbie   See ... what you don't understand ... you'll never understand, is ... how can I put this ... there are people out there who aren't remotely depressed. People who are happy, successful, well-balanced, they lead uncomplicated lives filled with witless optimism and certainty and hope and peace and a degree of naive innocence. You know what I mean, Dad. It's really quite normal.

Charles   Who are these people?

Robbie   Me. And ... Carla. Her whole family.

Charles   Anybody else?

Robbie   They may not have your edge. Your finely attuned and astute powers of observation. Your utterly idiosyncratic but nevertheless weirdly penetrative insight, but at least they have fun.

Charles   Do you think I'm enjoying this?

Robbie   Yes I do.

Silence.

Robbie   The thing is ... Carla and I enjoy simply being together and nothing else really matters.

Charles   Oh son, when are you going to stop thinking with your dick?

They stare at each other. **Charles** *picks up his tumbler and drinks.*
Robbie *sees* **Carla** *and goes upstairs. They exit.* **Charles** *sits.*

Charles   Where's Mike?

Billie   Where do you think he is?

Charles   I've no idea. That's why I'm asking you.

Billie   Mike turns up every six months and forages for scraps
like a stray dog going through the rubbish. He lets himself in
with his key and steals money from my purse to buy booze.
He's been doing it since the day he left.

Charles   Why didn't you tell me?

Billie   Charles, if after thirty years I thought you would
listen I would tell you things.

Charles   I'm listening now. Is there anything else I should
know?

He picks up the dictaphone and records.

I'll record it for posterity. Tell me the truth.

Billie   But Charles, I can't tell you the truth because you
can't live with the truth. The truth is you don't have the right
to do this to us. The truth is you've bitten off more than you
can chew. You've waged war all your life and most of the
time you're waging war on the wrong people. For thirty years
I've watched you running around wagging your tail and
barking at everything in sight ... thirty years of supporting
you so you can throw that settlement to the floor and snarl in
our faces while everything that I hold dear collapses around us
... and what have you done for me? Have you ever thought
about what I want ... ?

Charles *switches off the dictaphone.*

Charles   I've heard it all now. I can't even lose my job
properly. Maybe I do need a shrink. You know, the ridiculous
thing is sometimes I think I must do. Do you know what ...
do you know what that feels like?

Silence. **Billie** *goes to the kitchen and stands at the sink. She opens a* *cupboard and takes out a bottle of pills. She swallows two pills with a glass of water. She puts her pinny on.*

Charles   What's for dinner?

Billie   Roast.

Charles   With . . . roastie potatoes . . . courgettes?

Billie   Sprouts.

Charles   Sprouts. Oh.

Pause.

Peas?

Billie   No.

Charles   Just sprouts. You know I hate sprouts.

Billie   You didn't ask for peas.

Charles *retrieves the document and produces a pen. He unfurls the document and writes on it, murmuring under his breath.*

Charles   I'll put it in writing. One roast dinner with English lamb; not chops, a leg thank you very much in case you plan on fucking that up as well; with two veg; that is to say with roast potatoes and legume of choice; that is to say greens but definitely no sprouts; specifically courgettes and peas . . . No pud because I don't fucking like pud . . . Signed most sincerely . . . by order . . .

He signs the note and gives it to **Billie**.

This is my house . . . this is still my house . . . If you don't like it you know what you can do.

Billie *takes off her pinny. She hangs it neatly.*

Billie   It's our house. And I'm not putting up with this.

Charles   Oh you'll put up with it. You'll put up with it until it sinks in. And I'll tell you why. Because I love you.

Pause.

Billie   It isn't enough. Am I making myself plain?

Charles   Perfectly.

Billie   Good. Good night.

Billie *goes up the stairs.* **Charles** *picks up the dictaphone, sits and plays the tape.*

Counsellor's voice   'How are you getting on with your wife? How are you getting on with your family?'

He fast-forwards.

Billie's voice   '. . . You've bitten off more than you can chew . . .'

He switches it off. He goes to the piano and plays a few bars. It becomes discordant. He pauses and tries again but it is still utterly discordant. He slams the lid down hard. He pauses, listens, lifts the lid and slams it down again. He picks up the can of lighter fuel and squirts fuel into the stove. He picks up the box of matches and strikes one, carefully lighting the stove. **Charles** *squirts more fuel onto the fire, making it flare up. He drops the can, holds his hands out for warmth. He stares into the flames. Pause. He goes to the stairs.*

Charles   Billie . . . Billie . . . Sweetheart . . .

He shakes his head absent-mindedly and tuts. He stares. The sound of wind, rain. He goes upstairs. Lights down.

Lights up. **Carla** *sits at the table with a suitcase by her side. A 'Slinky' appears on the stairs. It travels down the stairs.* **Robbie** *comes down the stairs behind it wearing pyjamas. They look at each other.* **Robbie** *sees the suitcase and stares at it.*

Robbie   Do you want me to pack?

Pause.

I'll just go and pack then shall I? We'll . . . just get on a train and go and see your family. I've never met your family. I'm looking forward to it.

Pause.

Or we could just get on a plane and go home. Back to Singapore. Our home. Check into Raffles. Have a bath and a

massage. In Ko Samui we'd massage each other every night.
Lying under those big fans, all sandy and hot and sweaty and
sticky. Tricks with fruit. That's what it's all about. Nobody has
that here. People grow old and die here never having
experienced the delights of a strategically placed frozen
banana. There is a better life to live. This is not a life.

Carla Is that it? Pushing pieces of fruit into my pussy?
That's your epiphany?

Robbie Yes. Isn't it obvious?

She stands and picks up her suitcase.

Carla Why did you tell her we were getting married?

Robbie We were . . . getting married?

Carla You heard.

Robbie I might have said something about . . . why not?

Carla Because we're not getting married.

Robbie I know that . . .

Carla Why didn't you tell her what happened in Singapore?

Robbie I told her what she wanted to hear.

Carla What do you tell Mike when he needs somebody?

Robbie Has he been talking to you about his girlfriend?
She wasn't his girlfriend. She was the town bike. He's never
had a girlfriend. He's a liar. He's as mad as a snake. He used
to walk to Wandsworth Bridge telling anybody who'd listen he
was going to throw himself off. He'd get half-way there,
completely forget what he was meant to be doing and come
back again.

Silence.

You don't believe me do you?

Carla I don't know who to believe . . .

Robbie Why do you think he told you that story?

Carla   I don't know . . . I don't care . . . I can't do this any more . . . it's too complicated . . .

Robbie   I thought you liked 'complicated'. I thought that was the deal.

Carla   Maybe I do.

Robbie   You do.

Carla   Maybe I ask for it.

Robbie   You do.

Carla   Maybe I've got 'USE ME' written on my forehead.

Robbie   You have.

Carla   You *wanker*. Why do you say these things . . . ?

Robbie   Why? I'll tell you why. I'll tell you . . .

Pause.

Because you're naive. Because a) you don't know anything, you've never experienced anything but you want to because you think it'll give you depth. b) . . . b) You think you know everything anyway. And c) . . . because you're a stupid bitch. I knew this was going to happen. I knew before we even got here.

Carla   So did I.

Silence.

We've broken the spell, haven't we?

Robbie   What spell . . . ?

Carla   This isn't you Robbie.

Robbie   Who is it then?

Lights down.

Lights up. Early morning. **Charles** *sits awake in his chair.* **Mike** *walks in, staggering drunk, shaking off rain. He stops and looks at* **Charles**. **Mike** *and* **Charles** *eyeball each other.* **Mike** *sits. Silence.*

Mike   Did you have a nice day at work?

Pause.

Dad? Seriously, I admire your . . . determination.

Charles   Let me tell you about drinking, son. My whole family were drinkers. My mum was a Scot. Maybe it was the Celtic fire that set them all off. Maybe it was her Presbyterian pedantry which drove everybody else to drink. I don't know. But my uncles, my father's brothers used to get tanked. Really tanked. And they'd come around staggering and swearing like a bunch of bloody navvies and . . . Mum would take one look at these . . . wankers she called family . . . and it would all go off. My dad would sit in the corner not knowing where to look. I'd play the piano, a beaten-up upright from Denmark Street. I'd play it to interrupt the . . . the noise. And the better I got, the quieter they got. Until they stopped me. Those men . . . the men would gather around the piano and down would go that lid on my fingers. Down would go that lid . . . They thought I was a poof. Because I was musical. I was ten years old and they . . . they broke my fingers . . . But boy . . . did they teach me something. They taught me everything I know today.

Mike   What did they teach you?

Charles   They didn't teach me anything!

Pause.

Mike   People were laughing at me in the pub. They were watching the football. All the lads. I hate football. I think footballers are stupid. I think lads are stupid. They all thought I was strange. People think I'm strange. I can tell. Do you think I'm strange?

Charles   'Strange'? No. You're my son.

Mike   Where's Mum?

Charles   I've no idea.

Mike   What do you mean?

Charles *shrugs.* **Mike** *lights a cigarette.*

Charles   Do you have to do that in here?

Mike   Under the circumstances, why not?

Charles   Because I don't like it, that's why not.

Mike *reaches over and takes* **Charles***'s tumbler. He pours more whisky and drinks.*

Mike   Where is she?

Charles   She'll be back.

Mike   When?

Charles   When she's good and ready. Let me give you a bit of advice son. If you ever marry, if you ever find the right girl, take a damn good look at the family.

Robbie *appears at the top of the stairs.*

Mike   Where's your girlfriend?

Robbie   What do you want her for?

Mike   I need to talk to her.

Robbie   What about?

Mike   . . . Nothing. I just . . . wanted to talk.

Robbie   I just came down to tell you . . . you can sleep here tonight if you want. I don't mind. I'd like the company.

Pause.

Mike   Oh . . . thanks . . .

Robbie   Don't thank me. Everybody contributed.

Mike   Where's Mum? Why did she go, Dad? Did you get a bit nasty with her?

Charles   Nasty? I'll show you nasty.

Charles *pushes* **Mike** *in the chest.*

And when I get nasty . . .

He pushes him again.

I don't piss about.

Mike *pushes* **Charles** *in the same way.*

Mike   Piss off.

Pause. **Mike** *and* **Charles** *stare at each other.*

Robbie   Mike sit down, please.

Pause.

Charles (*to* **Mike**)   I. Have. Lost. Everything.

Mike *and* **Charles** *push each other simultaneously. They grapple and it becomes a clinch.*

Mike   So. Have. I.

Robbie   For fuck's sake Mike.

Mike *and* **Charles** *hold onto each other, half-wrestling, half-embracing. They let go abruptly.* **Charles** *breathes deeply.* **Robbie** *helps him into a chair. Silence.*

Charles   Some families ... some families are like this. They just are. And some families go through life with absolutely nothing happening to them. We were like that once. I remember. You see it's moments like this ... when you stop laughing, when it suddenly becomes serious, when you can't laugh any more because now you see a pattern emerging ... when you no longer choose to let it go ... when the chickens first start coming home to roost and you find yourself no longer able to humour those chickens ... that make your life what it is. They're your destiny ... Have I been such a bad father?

Robbie   No ...

Charles   Am I such a failure?

Robbie   Dad ... listen to me ...

Charles   Robbie why can you never tell me the truth?

Robbie   Because you're my dad ...

Charles   And you're my son. What do you want, a medal?

Pause.

Oh son, it's been a long night, eh? I've got a lot on my mind. I've got a lot on my mind.

Charles *pours a drink.*

Get yourselves a glass each and have a drink with your dad. Keep things in perspective.

Pause.

Come and sit beside your old dad and keep him company. Is that so difficult? Son? Son . . .

Charles *gestures to* **Robbie** *and* **Mike**. **Mike** *goes, slamming the door behind him.* **Charles** *slumps in his chair and stares.* **Robbie** *kisses* **Charles** *on the forehead. Silence. Lights down slowly.*

Blackout.